Utopia as Method

Utopia as Method

The Imaginary Reconstitution of Society

Ruth Levitas
University of Bristol, UK

palgrave
macmillan

First published 2013 by
PALGRAVE MACMILLAN

Palgrave Macmillan in the UK is an imprint of Macmillan Publishers Limited, registered in England, company number 785998, of Houndmills, Basingstoke, Hampshire RG21 6XS.

Palgrave Macmillan in the US is a division of St Martin's Press LLC, 175 Fifth Avenue, New York, NY 10010.

Palgrave Macmillan is the global academic imprint of the above companies and has companies and representatives throughout the world.

Palgrave® and Macmillan® are registered trademarks in the United States, the United Kingdom, Europe and other countries

ISBN: 978–0–230–23196–2 hardback
ISBN: 978–0–230–23197–9 paperback

This book is printed on paper suitable for recycling and made from fully managed and sustained forest sources. Logging, pulping and manufacturing processes are expected to conform to the environmental regulations of the country of origin.

A catalogue record for this book is available from the British Library.

A catalog record for this book is available from the Library of Congress.

For Rob,
companion in the quest

Contents

Preface and Acknowledgements

In 2002, Tom Moylan, founding Director of the Ralahine Centre for Utopian Studies at the University of Limerick in the Irish Republic, invited a number of established scholars in utopian studies to reflect on how they had used utopia in their own work. Those papers were eventually published as a collection edited by Tom Moylan and Raffaella Baccolini as *Utopia, Method, Vision*.[1] My own contribution developed the idea of utopia as method in terms of the Imaginary Reconstitution of Society, or IROS. I had written about utopia as method before, in an article on social policy published the previous year,[2] but these discussions led me to reconsider H. G. Wells's claim that the imagination of utopias is the distinctive and proper method of sociology. I have spent my professional life as a sociologist, and my interest in utopia has always been regarded as at best marginal, and at worst distinctly suspect. This book is the last academic book I shall write before retirement, and it seemed the right time to ask not what sociology can tell us about utopia, but what utopia can, as Wells suggested, tell us about the trajectory and limits of sociology. The book was eventually completed with the support of a University Research Fellowship from the University of Bristol in 2009–10 and a Research Fellowship from the Leverhulme Trust in 2010–12. I am hugely grateful both to the University of Bristol, where I have worked for over thirty-three years, and to the Leverhulme Trust for enabling me to bring this project to some kind of conclusion. Whether that conclusion is a successful one is for the reader(s) to judge; this is the best account I can give at the present time of my attempts to think through the meaning of utopia as concept and as method, its implications for a publicly engaged sociology, and its potential contribution to the making of a better world.

The Ralahine Centre has been an important intellectual context for my work on utopia over the past decade, including the conference and associated publication on *Exploring the Utopian Impulse*,[3] the 2008 annual meeting of the Utopian Studies Society Europe (USSE) and an ongoing series of shorter workshops. Colleagues associated with Ralahine have been unfailingly hospitable, welcoming and intellectually generous, and I appreciate their friendship and engagement. USSE itself, inaugurated with drunken enthusiasm in a bar at New Lanark in 1988, is entering its twenty-fifth year. Now chaired by Fátima Vieira, with the support of

Lorna Davidson and Jim Arnold from New Lanark, it has been the locus of discussions with too many people to list: the 2012 conference in Tarragona alone brought together over a hundred scholars from twenty-three countries and five continents. I have made occasional trips across the pond to the Society for Utopian Studies, which holds an annual conference in North America. My work has also grown out of participation in the William Morris Society, the Schumacher Institute, and, of course, professional networks of sociology, especially the Sociology Department at Bristol. The need for change is kept in sharp focus by my membership of the large team conducting the ESRC-funded 2012 survey of Poverty and Social Exclusion in the United Kingdom.

I have given many lectures and conference papers over the decade of this book's gestation, and written several articles on related themes. None is reproduced here in full, but parts of some are incorporated into the wider argument. I am grateful to the original publishers for permission to re-use selections from the following pieces: 'Looking for the Blue: The Necessity of Utopia', *Journal of Political Ideologies*, 2007, 12(3): 289–306 (Taylor and Francis); 'Introduction: The Once and Future Orpheus', *Utopian Studies*, 2010, 21(2): 204–14; 'In Eine Bess're Welt Entruckt: Reflections on Music and Utopia', *Utopian Studies* 2010, 21(2): 215–31 (Penn State University Press); 'Back to the Future: Wells, Sociology, Utopia and Method', *Sociological Review*, 2010, 58(4): 530–47 (Wiley); 'For Utopia: The Limits of the Utopian Function under Conditions of Late Capitalism', *Contemporary Review of International Social and Political Philosophy*, 2000, 3(2/3): 25–43 (Taylor and Francis); 'Pragmatism, Utopia and Anti-Utopia', *Critical Horizons*, 2008, 9(1): 42–59 (Equinox Publishing); 'Being in Utopia', *Hedgehog Review: Critical Reflections on Contemporary Culture*, 2008, 10(1): 19–30 (Institute for Advanced Studies in Culture, University of Virginia); 'Towards a Utopian Ontology: Secularism and Postsecularism in Ernst Bloch and Roberto Unger', *Journal of Contemporary Thought*, 2010, 31: 151–69 (Forum on Contemporary Theory). I am also grateful to Jim Boyes for permission to reproduce lyrics from *Jerusalem Revisited* at the end of Chapter 3.

It seems invidious to select from the many organizers, participants, reviewers and editors, as well as students, whose responses have contributed to my thinking. But equally, there are some who should be thanked. Those whose conversations and interventions have been important include Phillippa Bennett, Nicky Britten, Nathaniel Coleman, Lynne Copson, Lorna Davidson, Vincent Geoghegan, Diana Levitas, Susan McManus, Gregor McLennan, Stella Maile, Tom Moylan, Jenneth Parker, Lucy Sargisson, Nigel Singer, Jane Speedy, Sarah Street,

Maggie Studholme, Gillian Swanson; my thanks to you all. Several others have generously read and responded to parts of the book: my warm thanks to Davina Cooper, Jane Edwards, Richard Hobbs, Sarah Payne, Randall Smith and Daniel Thistlethwaite. Jem Thomas and Tom Moylan resolutely read the whole, and I am deeply grateful to both for their careful criticism and encouragement. Thanks also to Jem and to Anne-Marie Cummins, for stalwart friendship and for crewing *Spirit of Utopia*. The skipper, Robert Hunter, my partner for over thirty years, has read repeated drafts of the manuscript; he is, in the deepest sense, the co-creator of all that I do, the mirror of my best self, my best critic and my unfailing companion in the quest. And while I have been writing, Graham and Sara have given us three grandchildren, Caleb, Seth and Hannah, constantly reminding me of the point of it all: to make it better, if we can, for those who come after.

Introduction

In 1906, H. G. Wells argued that 'the creation of Utopias – and their exhaustive criticism – is the proper and distinctive method of sociology'.[1] Wells's claim may seem counter-intuitive in terms of common understandings of utopia and of sociology. But although sociology may, as he says, have sought to distance itself from utopia, both conventional sociology and critical social theory have unavoidable utopian characteristics, increasingly recognized in recent discussions. A utopian method relevant to the twenty-first century may be somewhat different from that which Wells envisaged, but is both appropriate and necessary. It provides a critical tool for exposing the limitations of current policy discourses about economic growth and ecological sustainability. It facilitates genuinely holistic thinking about possible futures, combined with reflexivity, provisionality and democratic engagement with the principles and practices of those futures. And it requires us to think about our conceptions of human needs and human flourishing in those possible futures. The core of utopia is the desire for being otherwise, individually and collectively, subjectively and objectively. Its expressions explore and bring to debate the potential contents and contexts of human flourishing. It is thus better understood as a method than a goal – a method elaborated here as the Imaginary Reconstitution of Society, or IROS.

The reconstitution of society in imagination and in reality is a pressing need. The economic shockwaves of 2008 and the ensuing global recessions laid bare the instability of global capitalism and its inability to provide sustainable livelihoods for the world's population. The huge profits extracted from the economy in the financial sector were intermittently in the public eye, but attention was largely deflected from the bankers who provoked the crisis onto governments and citizens. Across Europe, the crisis was manipulated to drive through neo-liberal policies reducing social protection and enforcing savage cuts in real incomes, public spending and public sector jobs. The avowed intention of national, European and international bodies was to restore economic growth and business as usual. But by 2012, individual economies and the Eurozone itself were brought close to collapse. In Britain, thirty years of widening inequalities were exacerbated by policies which hit the poor hardest, with women estimated to bear eighty per cent of the burden. These policies were imposed by enormously wealthy government ministers cynically claiming that 'we are all in this together'. The crisis was used to secure the position of the rich within developed nations at the expense of the poor, but international inequality is even more extreme. In 2000 the United Nations set eight millennium goals with the intention that they be met by 2015. They included the eradication of extreme poverty and hunger, and ensuring environmental sustainability. These aims will not be met in the foreseeable future and can only be met with a qualitative change in global social and economic organization.

The ecological crisis is even deeper and more far-reaching. Carbon emissions, global warming and climate change challenge our whole way of life. Higher temperatures mean rising sea-levels, unstable weather patterns and pressure on usable land resources. Forced migration will present intensified social and political challenges. Current policy responses involve minor reductions in emissions of greenhouse gases, the pursuit of carbon neutrality, the technological fix of carbon capture, and carbon trading. Other aspects of pollution are largely ignored but include the 2011 earthquake in Japan which exposed not only nuclear fuel rods but the wider danger of relying on such technology for 'clean' energy. Resource limitation already puts upward pressure on food and energy prices – which are related, as biofuels replace food crops on scarce land resources from which subsistence farmers are evicted. Global 'development' means rises in commodity prices and increased competition for raw materials as well as a greater global demand for water – and these struggles are likely to lead to more armed conflict.

The economic and ecological crises mean that change is both essential and inevitable. It is the nature of that change that is in question. We need to think about what kind of social and economic system can deliver secure and sustainable livelihoods and ways of life for all. For those who still think that utopia is about the impossible, what really is impossible is to carry on as we are, with social and economic systems that enrich a few but destroy the environment and impoverish most of the world's population. Our very survival depends on finding another way of living.

To argue that utopian thinking may help us here raises questions about the concept of utopia and about what it might mean to talk of utopia as a method. There are different ways of thinking about the idea of utopia itself. Chapter 1 begins by reprising the argument of my earlier book *The Concept of Utopia*: utopia is the expression of the desire for a better way of being or of living, and as such is braided through human culture. It argues further that utopia in this sense is analagous to a quest for grace which is both existential and relational. But the most culturally prevalent understanding is quite different: utopia is commonly dismissed as an irrelevant fantasy or traduced as a malevolent nightmare leading to totalitarianism. This anti-utopian discourse equates utopia with a blueprint producing violence and terror, and gives rise to a politics of quiescent subordination to the dictates of capitalist markets. The opening chapter includes a critique of this anti-utopian case in its recent formulation by John Gray.

A definition of utopia in terms of desire is analytic rather than descriptive. It generates a method which is primarily hermeneutic but which repeatedly returns us from existential and aesthetic concerns to the social and structural domain. Part I is concerned mainly with this hermeneutic method. Chapters 2 and 3 excavate the utopian resonances of the colour blue and music and illustrate the unavoidable return to the social. In the case of music, this includes performance, and especially the relations between musicians in performance, as a site of ideal social relations or as a prefigurative and transformative practice. This is the third way of thinking about utopia itself: the attempt not just to imagine, but to make, the world otherwise. Within utopian studies, the focus here has primarily been on intentional communities which create alternative enclaves or heterotopias, although some clearly intend the prefiguration or instantiation of a transformed world. The idea of prefigurative practice may usefully be extended to social practices which intend or embed a different way of being. People seek to live differently in myriad individual and collective ways. There is a growing literature on mundane or everyday utopianism, where alternative or oppositional social practices create new, or at least slightly different, social institutions. Historically, in Britain alone we might consider the cooperative movement, the Settlement Movement, progressive schools or the formation of the League of Nations; more contemporary examples range from music education to Transition Towns. But while socialist and environmentalist politics are easily labelled utopian, implying a mix of radical alterity and impossibilism, it is important to recognize the utopianism of right-wing politics, both at the level of improvised institutions and especially at the level of the state and the global market. Many social practices and most political programmes embed an idea of the good society and an attempt to implement it.

The fourth way of thinking about utopia entails a more holistic outline of an alternative society, leaning towards greater systemic and institutional specificity, and thus constituting a more sociological model. A more restrictive definition confines the term to accounts of alternative social arrangements and the lives lived within them. Thus Lyman Tower Sargent construes utopia as a 'non-existent society described in considerable detail and normally located in time and space'.[2] (Sargent, like others who constrain the category in this way, also recognizes a broader category of utopianism which corresponds to that element diffused throughout culture as the bearer of longing and anticipated redemption.) These more holistic descriptions do not remain at the level of abstract principles such as equality and justice but deal with concrete instantiations of these in specific social institutions, described systemically as an integrated whole. Typically, such works embed a contrast with the present to which they stand as critique, articulating also the reasons for the ills of contemporary society. They are necessarily the product of the conditions and concerns of the generating society, so that whether they are placed elsewhere or in the future, they are always substantially about the present. Sometimes, but not always, they posit a process of transition, evolutionary or revolutionary, and identify the agents of change. Such descriptions may take the form of novels, travellers' tales, political programmes or works of political theory. Some commentators strive to restrict utopia yet further to a largely self-conscious literary genre, typically beginning with More. Although in principle such descriptive definitions in terms of content and literary form make possible a separation between utopian and non-utopian texts, in practice this is not simple. The boundaries of literary genres are porous, and literature, poetry and song are, like art and music, amenable to exploration through the hermeneutic utopian method. The writer Bruno Schulz suggested that story-telling is itself a utopian practice, narrative itself an intrinsically utopian expression.[3] Nevertheless, it is evident that relatively holistic descriptions of possible or impossible alternative societies constitute a narrower field than more diffuse cultural representations of lack and longing. Such descriptions are closer to what Wells had in mind, and closer to his own literary practice.

It is this more holistic approach which most obviously underpins the method of utopia as the Imaginary Reconstitution of Society, the construction of integrated accounts of possible (or impossible) social systems as a kind of speculative sociology. This is not the invention of a method for social analysis, for social science or for social reconstruction. It identifies processes that are already entailed in utopian speculation, in utopian scholarship and in transformative politics and indeed in social theory itself. It names methods that are already in play with the intention of clarifying and encouraging them. It makes a claim about the relationship between utopia and the discipline of sociology.

For the Imaginary Reconstitution of Society intrinsically necessitates thinking about the connections between economic, social and political processes, our ways of life, and what is necessary to human flourishing. It requires a holistic approach fundamental to the distinctive character of sociology. Thus Part II of the book explores the changing relationship between utopia and sociology from the institutionalization of the discipline (Chapters 4 and 5); the transformation of utopia itself that followed the cultural and postmodern 'turns' (Chapter 6); and the problematic revival of interest in utopia in contemporary sociology (Chapter 7). Some of the difficulties Wells identified remain pertinent, including the insistence on the scientific character of sociology. Contested ideas of possibility render some overt sympathy for utopia quite anti-utopian, while some overt suspicion of utopia is accompanied by hopeful, visionary openness to the future.

The encounter between sociology and utopia implies reconfiguring sociology itself. Sociology must affirm holism and must extend this to include 'the environment', locating our human and social existence within the 'natural' or material world. It must embrace the normativity that it has systematically sought to exclude, address the future which it has systematically sought to evade and engage with what it means and might mean to be human. Insistence on the historical determination of human nature distances such existential questions, but all images of the good society unavoidably posit what is necessary for human happiness and human flourishing.

This encounter also implies thinking differently about what constitutes knowledge. It challenges the assumption that sociology constitutes a form of knowledge while utopianism is simply a form of speculation, and seeks to legitimize utopian thought not as a new, but as a repressed, already existing, form of knowledge about possible futures. Advanced Western societies, especially those without evident strengths in producing the visible material means of life, are sometimes now described as 'knowledge societies' or 'knowledge economies' as if this constituted some third, post-industrial, stage of development after 'agricultural' and 'industrial' stages. This terminology disguises two important facts. One is that all societies involve knowledge. Indeed the forms of knowledge held by indigenous peoples have been expropriated or exterminated: they involved wide and deep knowledge about the land, its flora and fauna, weather and migration patterns, the medicinal properties of plants, as well as complex cultures and mythologies which served to sustain systems of values protecting means of livelihood and ways of life. Similarly both agricultural and industrial societies depend on knowledge. The second is that agricultural, extractive and manufacturing industries are still fundamental to Western ways of life. Advanced Western nations can misperceive themselves as 'knowledge economies' or 'knowledge societies' only by ignoring their dependence on and exploitation of systems of production largely exported to developing nations – by not thinking about the global economy as a whole. The discourse also occludes processes of exploitation within the advanced economies themselves.

The distinctive feature of knowledge in the contemporary global economy is its commodification. Increasingly, knowledge is not something possessed as part of 'the commons', but is privately owned and exploited for profit. All societies restrict access to knowledge, especially knowledge that generates power or profit, but the contemporary extent of this is unprecedented. Knowledge is also very fragmented. This is partly the result of complexity and necessary specialization but is also connected to the institutional organization of knowledge and especially the emergence of separate 'disciplines' within universities. The current emphasis on interdisciplinarity is, of course, an attempt to overcome some of these problems and return to more integrated thinking, while discursively reinforcing the primacy of disciplines. This fragmentation accompanies a short-term orientation to problem solving in which the future appears only as an extrapolation of the present: 'if present trends continue'. Favoured forms of knowledge are those which are non-evaluative and highly specialized and which can be sold as 'real' knowledge under the badge of 'science'. Other, exploratory, evaluative, holistic forms of knowledge do not receive this endorsement. The consequence is a situation better described as the stupid society than the knowledge society. The explication and defence of utopia as method challenges these assumptions.

The interpretation of descriptions of alternative worlds is always problematic. There are recurrent attempts to classify utopias in terms of form and function. Russell Jacoby makes a distinction between iconoclastic utopias which express the dream of a better life but resist its precise definition, which articulate 'a longing that cannot be uttered', and blueprint utopias which 'map out the future in inches and minutes'.[4] Miguel Abensour differentiates between heuristic utopias best understood as exploratory hypotheses and systematic utopias intended as literal plans. In both these distinctions the non-literal reading is privileged, and the literal interpretation rejected. As George Kateb says in his defence of utopia, 'any serious utopian thinker will be made uncomfortable by the very idea of blueprint, of detailed recommendations concerning all facets of life'.[5] The distinctions made by Jacoby and Abensour are also primarily descriptive, although Abensour, as we shall see, links the heuristic utopia to the particular function of the education of desire. Yet some degree of literal plausibility is necessary to either a critical or a transformative role. The French sociologist André Gorz argued that 'it is the function of utopias, in the sense the term has assumed in the work of Ernst Bloch or Paul Ricoeur, to provide us with the distance from the existing state of affairs which allows us to judge what we *are* doing in the light of what we *could* or *should* do'.[6] This reading is supported by Bloch's claim that 'utopian conscience-and-knowledge ... confutes and judges the existent if it is failing, and failing inhumanly; indeed, first and foremost it provides the *standard* to measure such facticity precisely as departure from the Right'.[7] This suggests that utopia is at least a regulative ideal, a standpoint or measure for evaluating our circumstances and actions. As such, its literal plausibility and desirability are crucial. But neither Gorz nor Bloch would be content to leave it there, for if utopia is no more than that, it is stripped of the transformative capacity that both of them intend – a transformation both of existential experience and of the objective structures of the social world that generates that experience.

Part III maps out the Imaginary Reconstitution of Society as a method, and one which has three aspects. The first of these is an analytical, *archaeological* mode; the second an *ontological* mode; and the third a constructive, *architectural* mode. The architectural mode is precisely what characterizes the literary form of utopia, and gives it its sociological character. It involves the institutional design and delineation of the good society – and, in the case of intentional communities or prefigurative practices, its partial concrete instantiation. The archaeological mode complements this, for it involves the interpellation of absent or implicit elements in political, literary or artistic utopian 'accounts'. Its similarity with archaeology lies in the excavation of fragments and shards and their recombination into a coherent whole. The point of such archaeology is to lay the underpinning model of the good society open to scrutiny and to public critique. And the ontological mode is concerned precisely with the subjects and agents of utopia, the selves interpellated within it, that utopia encourages or allows. These modes or facets of the utopian method are analytically separable from one another but are also intertwined; for the distinctive characteristics of IROS are its holism and its institutional specificity. Wherever we start in the process of imagining ourselves and our world otherwise, all three modes must eventually come into play.

In Chapter 8, which addresses the archaeological mode of IROS, we shall see how the ideas of meritocracy and growth that are supported across the range of public discourse imply modes of social organization that are far from sustainable or equitable. In Chapter 9, we revisit questions of ontology and grace, since imagining ourselves and our social relations otherwise is a necessary and unavoidable aspect of imagining a better society. Chapter 10 deploys IROS in architectural mode. In this final chapter on what needs to change, we are directly concerned with the principles and institutions of a potential alternative world – yet one which needs to be treated as a hypothesis rather than a plan.

There are several advantages of utopian thinking *as a method*. It is holistic. Unlike political philosophy and political theory, which have been more open than sociology to normative approaches, this holism is expressed at the level of concrete social institutions and processes. It allows, as both Gorz and Bloch suggest, an element of ethical and institutional separation from the present. Although the critical edge of utopianism depends upon imagined alternatives possessing a reasonable degree of internal coherence and at least theoretical possibility, it is less constrained by what now seems immediately possible. Importantly, its explicitly hypothetical character enables us to insist on utopia's provisionality, reflexivity and dialogic mode. Explicit alternative scenarios for the future are fundamental to any kind of democratic debate. This means envisioning alternatives, but also setting out the images of the good society buried in the constant barrage of political rhetoric and policies. The utopian method involves both making explicit the kinds of society implied in existing political programmes and constructing alternatives. It entails also considering the kinds of people we want to become and that different forms of society will promote or inhibit. Our institutional arrangements affect both the imagination and the reality of human flourishing through the values, skills, capabilities, experiences and relationships they encourage or suppress. To put it another way, utopia as method is concerned with the potential institutions of a just, equitable and sustainable society which begins to provide the conditions for grace.

Part I

1
From Terror to Grace

Utopia as desire

The very term utopia is fraught with difficulty. Its meanings are various and contested in both academic and lay discourse. Thomas More coined the word as the title and locus of his 1516 *Utopia* in a pun which conflates *outopos* or no place and *eutopos* or good place. Consequently utopia is widely understood as an imagined perfect society or wishfully constructed place which does not and cannot exist. Such imaginings are held to be unrealistic so that utopia has connotations of impossibility and fantastical dreaming, divorced from the hard and the joyful realities of the world and life we actually inhabit and where, as Wordsworth put it, 'we find our happiness, or not at all'.[1] New generations are inducted into the view that utopia is dangerously escapist through popular children's literature. In *Harry Potter and the Philosopher's Stone*, Harry spends two nights gazing at his lost family in the Mirror of Erised, around which runs the inscription 'Erised stra ehru oyt ube cafru oyt on wohsi' (I show not your face but your heart's desire). On the third night, Professor Dumbledore intercepts Harry and tells him that the Mirror of Erised 'shows us nothing more or less than the deepest, most desperate desire of our hearts. ... However, this mirror will give us neither knowledge or truth. Men have wasted away before it, entranced by what they have seen, or been driven mad, not knowing if what it shows is real or even possible'. The mirror will be removed and hidden, and Dumbledore counsels Harry that '[i]t does not do to dwell on dreams and forget to live'.[2] Defending utopia entails insisting that the identification and expression of the deepest desires of our hearts and minds, and those of others, is a necessary form of knowledge and of truth.

The relation between desire and utopia can be read more positively. *The Concept of Utopia* explores the ways in which social theorists and utopists have used the term, revealing quite contradictory positions.[3] Karl Marx and Friedrich Engels (and indeed Lenin) were less hostile to social dreaming and imagination of better worlds than is often supposed, but the contrast between utopian and scientific socialism is unequivocally in favour of the latter: utopia is ascribed the function of distraction from political engagement in transformative class struggle, thus unwittingly supporting and preserving the status quo. In contrast, Karl Mannheim contended that utopia was the proper description of ideas which when they pass over into conduct, tend to shatter, partly or wholly, the order of things prevailing at the time. Both Herbert Marcuse's work and Edward Thompson's reformulation of the relationship between Marxism and utopia complicate matters. I concluded that most definitions rested on one of the form, or the function, or the content of utopian expressions, and that this placed unsatisfactory limits on understanding the historical shifts in the utopian imagination. I argued for greater clarity about usage and in favour of the more open definition of utopia as the expression of desire for a better way of living and of being. This analytic rather than descriptive definition reveals the utopian aspects of forms of cultural expression rather than creating a binary separation between utopia/non-utopia. It allows that utopia may be fragmentary, fleeting, elusive. It mirrors an existential quest which is figured in literature, music, drama and art, and which, as we shall see, Dennis Potter described as looking for the blue.

If utopia is understood in this sense, its forms and functions as well as its explicit content are historically variable. Those functions may include compensation (or consolation), critique or change; but one element in the transformative process is what Abensour calls the education of desire. Where utopian literature is concerned – and this may be equally true of other artistic forms – Abensour sees the main function as estrangement or making the familiar unfamiliar. The utopian experiment disrupts the taken-for-granted nature of the present. It creates a space in which the reader may, temporarily, experience an alternative configuration of needs, wants and satisfactions. As I argued in *Concept*, the claim here is that utopia works towards an understanding of what is necessary for human fulfilment and towards a broadening, deepening and raising of aspirations in terms different from those dominating the mundane present. Or, as Thompson glosses Abensour:

> And in such an adventure, two things happen: our habitual values (the "commonsense" of bourgeois society) are thrown into disarray. And we enter into Utopia's proper and new-found space: *the education of desire*.

This is not the same as "a moral education" towards a given end: it is, rather, to open a way to aspiration, to "teach desire to desire, to desire better, to desire more, and above all to desire in a different way".[4]

This has similarities with Bloch's idea of *docta spes*, informed or educated hope. *The Concept of Utopia* was of course strongly influenced by the work of Bloch, whose three-volume *The Principle of Hope* had recently been translated into English. Bloch posited the existence of a utopian impulse, an anthropological given that underpins the human propensity to long for and imagine a life otherwise. The origins of this impulse lie in the human experience of a sense of hunger, loss and lack: a deep sense that something's missing. Crucially, Bloch argues that this lack cannot be articulated other than through imagining its fulfilment. Everything that reaches to a transformed existence is, in this sense, utopian. Bloch claims that the whole of philosophy is necessary to do justice to what is meant by utopia – but his examples go far beyond philosophy, to include myths, fairy-tales, theatre, new clothes, alchemy, architecture and music as well as the more conventional forms of the social utopia. The need always to historicize the idea of human nature should make us cautious about such a claim to universality, but such imaginings are braided through human culture. In Bloch's account, music, art and literature not only carry utopian desire but offer a glimpse of what it is that is missing. Although all cultural artefacts are shaped by the social and historical circumstances of their production and reception, Bloch argues that some have an element that cannot be reduced to these conditions. He calls this transcendent element *cultural surplus*, which produces, at the moment of encounter, the *fulfilled moment* – a prefiguration of wholeness or a better way of being.

Read in this way, utopia does not require the imaginative construction of whole other worlds. It occurs as an embedded element in a wide range of human practice and culture – in the individual and collective creative practices of art as well as in its reproduction and consumption. Utopian method here is primarily hermeneutic. We can explore culture (in its broadest sense) for its utopian aspects, its expression of longing and fulfilment. The strength of this analytical definition is that it encourages the identification of an element that different cultural forms have in common, although in so doing, it may also at times gloss over important differences between them. If we start from here, it is evident that contemporary culture is saturated with utopianism, even (or especially) where there is no figurative representation of an alternative world. Non-verbal and non-figurative forms of expression such as colour and music are sometimes seen as having a direct route to the emotions. The implication is that they have a particular capacity to evoke and express the longing at the core of utopia, often held to be beyond words. Chapters 2 and 3 illustrate the necessity and ubiquity of utopia in this existential sense.

Bloch is frequently represented in utopian studies as giving a kind of blanket endorsement to all forms of 'utopian thought'. In a way this is true. Yet Bloch can also be quite sardonic, referring to 'a beautifying mirror which often only reflects how the ruling class wishes the wishes of the weak to be'.[5] He is also adamant that wishful thinking or abstract utopia (which is a start) needs to become will-full thinking in reaching concrete utopia. For Bloch, the development from abstract to concrete utopia is a process rather than a classification, the process of *docta spes*. It is in part a move from the purely fantastic to the genuinely possible. It is also a move from the potentially fragmentary expression of desire to social holism, a move from speculation to praxis and to the social and political pursuit of a better world. Gershom Scholem suggests that for utopians such as Bloch, even to see this as a move is strictly speaking inaccurate: 'After all, that restitution of all things to their proper place which is Redemption reconstructs a whole which knows nothing of such separation between inwardness and outwardness'.[6] Bloch represents utopia as a form of anticipatory consciousness. The central idea of *not yet* carries the double sense of not *yet* (but expected, a future presence) and still *not* (a current absence and lack). The not yet operates at two levels: the subjective, individual not-yet-conscious, the essentially creative preconscious utopian impulse, that which is on the verge of coming to consciousness; and the objective, external condition of the world, the not-yet-become. The not yet is real; for Bloch, reality includes the *horizon* of future possibilities and the *novum* as it comes into being. He refers to the perception of the future in the present as *Vor-Schein*, pre-appearance or anticipatory illumination. Utopia as forward dreaming is not an esoteric byway of culture nor a distraction from class struggle, but an unavoidable and indispensable element in the production of the future, for 'the hinge in human history is its producer'.[7] The subject position of human flourishing is figured by Bloch in terms of human dignity as the upright gait, 'the individual who is no longer to be humiliated, enslaved, forsaken, scorned, estranged, annihilated, and deprived of identity'.[8] Bloch concludes *The Principle of Hope* with the aspiration for the world anticipated as outcome of this process:

> But the root of history is the working, creating human being who reshapes and overhauls the given facts. Once he has grasped himself and established what is his, without expropriation and alienation, in

real democracy, there arises in the world something which shines into the childhood of all and in which no-one has yet been: *Heimat*.[9]

Against utopia

The most common objections to utopia reflect hostility to the fundamental utopian wish to make the world otherwise. Public discourse and political culture are profoundly anti-utopian, portraying utopia as an impossible quest for perfection whose political consequences are almost necessarily totalitarian. This position is predicated on the climate of the Cold War and the later capitalist triumphalism that accompanied the fall of communist regimes after 1989. It contains two implicit equations: 'utopia equals totalitarianism equals communism equals Marxism equals socialism', and 'communism equals totalitarianism equals fascism'. The founding texts of contemporary anti-utopianism date from the 1940s. Friedrich von Hayek's 1944 *The Road to Serfdom* argues that all state intervention leads inexorably down the slippery slope to dictatorship. Karl Popper's 1945 *The Open Society and its Enemies* and his later lecture on 'Utopia and Violence' reinforced the anti-utopian position, as did works by Hannah Arendt, Jacob Talmon and Isaiah Berlin in the 1950s. Norman Cohn's 1957 *The Pursuit of the Millennium* made a specific link between medieval millenarianism and both Nazism and communism.[10] Arendt and Talmon develop the idea of totalitarianism, a term which is problematic and which obscures as much as it reveals about forms of political domination, coercion and repression. Its deployment encapsulates the view that utopia is intrinsically prone to violence. Talmon claimed that utopianism 'brought totalitarian coercion'.[11] Arendt argued that totalitarianism implied terror for its own sake, together with the intention to transform human nature. Berlin picked up the theme of human nature in the phrase 'the crooked timber of humanity'.[12] Taken from Kant, who used it in an argument that a good social order would enable the better development of the individual, in Berlin's hands it signals the irredeemability of human nature and thus the hubris of utopia. Writers like Ralf Dahrendorf, Judith Shklar and Leszek Kolakowski in different ways claim that utopia posits a static, perfect and harmonious whole, at odds with the complexity of the real world.

There have been many critiques of this anti-utopian position, including those by George Kateb, Keith Taylor and Barbara Goodwin, Russell Jacoby and Lyman Tower Sargent.[13] Jacoby argues that much, perhaps most, of twentieth-century violence, including the mass slaughter of the 1914–18 War, had little to do with utopians, so that the attribution of violence to utopia simply does not hold water. The problems of coercion, terror and violence are of course real. What is at issue is how far such problems are attributable to utopianism. Moreover, laying totalitarianism at the door of utopia is a political move that is intended to make any aspiration to social change impossible. As Jacoby puts it, anti-utopianism is always 'a political reply to the political project of realizing utopia'.[14] He also points out that utopianism does not consist solely or even primarily of detailed plans intended for implementation. Sargent, the foremost authority on utopian literature, endorses this, saying that '[v]ery few actual utopias make any pretence to perfection', and that 'many utopias welcome the possibility of change'.[15] And yet it remains the case that 'conventional and scholarly wisdom associates utopian ideas with violence and dictatorship'.[16]

One influential exponent of this kind of anti-utopianism is John Gray. His 2007 book *Black Mass: Apocalyptic Religion and the Death of Utopia* has two core arguments. One is that the project of neo-conservatism in the United States, and especially its foreign policy in the Middle East, should be understood as a utopian project. Utopian accents, he says, have shifted from Left to Right. It is true that right-wing politics are too rarely identified as utopian. Thatcher's class war from above can be so understood. So too can the expansionist and retaliatory response of the United States to 9/11. The attacks launched first on Afghanistan and then on Iraq – in an operation called 'Enduring Freedom' – clearly embodied an idea of the good society as well as an intention to impose it.[17] However, for Gray, what defines the American Right as utopian is its intention to rid the world of evil, its belief that this is possible and its use of violence to this end. But for Gray the origins of this mindset lie on the Left, in the passing youthful involvement of early neo-conservative ideologues with Trotskyism. Ultimately, then, the violence of US foreign policy is attributable to Trotsky's thinking, endorsing 'violence as a condition of progress' and insisting that 'the revolution must be global'.[18]

The central element of Gray's discussion of political history is a very particular definition of utopia itself, which embeds an intrinsic link between belief in human perfectibility and violence and terror. Drawing on Cohn's characterization of millenarianism, Gray claims this link to be rooted in Christian apocalyptics and to persist across two millennia. Utopia is defined in terms of impossibility, its specific, invariable content being harmony and the perfectibility of people: thus '[t]he pursuit of a condition of harmony defines utopian thought and discloses its basic unreality'. Harmony is impossible because human needs and desires are contradictory: 'it seems to be natural for human beings to want incompatible things'.[19] Paul Ricoeur would concede that the delusion of the compatibility of all desired ends is detectable in some utopianism, but only in what he describes as its pathological and escapist forms. This does not negate utopia's more general character as constitutive of our imaginative understandings of ourselves, the contingency of present political arrangements, and alternative possibilities.[20] For Gray, '[a] project is utopian if there are no circumstances under which it can be realized. All the dreams of a society from which coercion and power have been for ever removed – Marxist or anarchist, liberal or technocratic – are utopian in the strong sense that they can never be achieved because they break down on the enduring contradictions of human needs'.[21] Oddly, Gray also describes as utopian social arrangements that are theoretically possible or which have actually existed in the past. In these cases, the impossibility of utopia must rest in some external conditions, not in the anticipation of perfect harmony. Thus '[a] project can also be utopian without being unrealizable under any circumstances – it is enough if it can be known to be impossible under any circumstance that can be brought about or forseen';[22] this of course begs the question of the validity of the knowledge claims themselves and the political interests they serve.

The link to totalitarianism lies in utopia's imputed belief in the perfectibility of humankind. Attempted remodelling of humanity is what, for Gray, defines both Leninism and Nazism as totalitarian.[23] Utopia does not *necessarily* result in totalitarianism: other (unspecified) factors need to be present for totalitarianism to emerge. In particular, if utopia is contained within voluntary communities, it is, as he puts it 'self-limiting'. Intentional communities are 'often ridiculous but usually harmless'; their disappearance 'is enough to establish their utopian character'; they entail 'withdrawal from the world' rather than an 'attempt to remake the world by force', apparently the only two alternatives.[24] But although Gray refers to Hayek's free-market utopianism as a 'delusive vision', his argument reprises Hayek's claim in *The Road to Serfdom* that intervention by the state is a slippery slope: it is 'when state power is used to remake society that the slide to totalitarianism begins', and 'totalitarianism follows whenever the dream of a life without conflict is consistently pursued through the use of state power'.[25] For '[t]he fact that the utopian project can only be promoted by the dismantling of existing institutions leads to a programme that goes well beyond anything attempted by existing tyrannies'.[26] Why such a project should not also involve institution-building is not addressed.

In sum, then, Gray dismisses utopia in quite conventional terms: it is contrary to human nature and, in consequence, gives rise to totalitarianism, violence and terror.

Gray, like most of us, is inconsistent. Having defined utopia in terms of its claims to human perfectibility, he quotes with seeming approval a description of Adam Smith's vision as 'an imperfect utopia, or, differently put, a utopia suited for imperfect creatures' – which in Gray's terms is an oxymoron.[27] But this raises the problem of his characterization of utopia itself. J. C. Davis argued that utopia is a particular mode of thinking about the ideal society. Its defining characteristic is the proposal of institutional means for managing the inevitable gap between wants and satisfaction and the potential social conflicts that flow from this discrepancy. It is different from Arcadia and Cockaygne, which respectively close the scarcity gap by imputed reduction in real needs or provision of unlimited satisfactions. It is different from what Davis calls the perfect moral commonwealth, in which scarcity is managed by universal moral restraint, and it is distinct, above all, from millennialism.[28] Davis's typology gives insufficient attention to the necessary social construction of needs and wants, but it does underline the point that not all ideal societies or utopias do, as Gray claims, posit human perfectibility. Many of them address the question of conflicting desires and in some cases conflicting interests. Gray's conceptualization of utopias as a series of 'projects' is also problematic: it reads them as political blueprints, a position countered by utopian scholars.

The politics that flows from Gray's position is profoundly conservative: 'As in earlier outbreaks of utopianism the achievements of the past have been damaged in the pursuit of an imaginary future'.[29] Construing utopia as dangerous in this way supports the view that there is no alternative to the present and to the ravages of global capital. All forms of radical alterity are rendered illegitimate unless they can be contained within or coopted to the existing system. In the end, Gray dismisses the whole of Western culture, including the Enlightenment, liberal humanism, the idea of human progress and the idea of universal human rights as incipiently utopian; all are teleological and all imply the perfectibility of humanity. Gray seems to have come late to the rejection of the grand narrative, the idea that history has a plot. He asserts that dystopia is more appropriate to our time than utopia, yet fails to engage with the dystopian turn of the late twentieth century or the scholarly commentary on this. And ultimately, we are left with what Gray defines as realism. We will return to the relation between realism, pragmatism and utopia in Chapter 7. Meanwhile, some brief points can be noted.

The first is that Gray reverts here to the question of interests: 'Realists accept that states are bound to rank what they take to be their vital interests over more universal considerations',[30] inviting the question of whose interests are articulated in the state. Here the legitimacy of state action is implicitly endorsed, whereas in relation to any kind of 'remaking the world' it has earlier been comprehensively rejected. And here, too, there is an acceptance of the legitimacy of a collective subject, something which, again, in relation to 'utopianism', has been negated: 'humanity cannot advance or retreat, for humanity cannot act: there is no collective entity with intentions or purposes'.[31] The 'cardinal need' of realism 'is to change the prevailing view of human beings', to accept our 'innate defects', and to privilege, therefore, the myth of the Fall over the myth of the End.[32] For Gray, utopian projects are products of a 'view of the world ... that believes political action can bring about an alteration in the human condition',[33] and they are to be rejected – a counsel of despair.

Despite its evident weaknesses, Gray's argument has been very widely disseminated and is reproduced by some otherwise visionary people. Richard Holloway, former Bishop of Edinburgh, echoes Gray in his declaration that the 'intoxicating dangers of utopian thinking' presage terror: 'More misery and disillusionment has been visited on humanity by its search for the perfect society and the perfect faith than by any other cause. The fantasy of crafting the ideal society or establishing the perfect religious system is far from being an endearing form of romanticism: it all too easily turns to terror. Listening to the voice that commands us to follow its perfect blueprint for rebuilding Eden usually results not in heaven but hell on earth, whether in the home-grown or built-for-export version'.[34] Holloway echoes Gray in his suggestion that the root cause of this is utopia's failure to take account of human nature and human imperfection: 'Naïve perfectionism has been one of the most blighting aspects of utopian politics, the attempt to impose perfect systems on imperfect people'.[35] But Sistema Scotland, the Raploch music education project modelled on Venezuela's El Sistema and pioneered by Holloway, is in many ways a prefigurative and utopian project, as we shall see in Chapter 3.

Grace notes

Gray's approach ignores the extent to which 'the human condition' is historically shaped, but he does thereby draw attention to the necessity of utopia's engagement with what it means to be human. If utopia is understood as the expression of the desire for a better way of being, then it is perhaps a (sometimes) secularized version of the spiritual quest to understand who we are, why we are here and how we connect with each other. Both the fulfilled moment and *Heimat* can be understood in relation to the existential components of alienation. For Marx, alienation had four components. The first two concern the labour process and commodification of products under capitalism. Wage labour is a system in which people sell their labour power, and both the process of work and what is produced are externally controlled and literally alienated or separated from the intention, ownership or control of the worker. This has profound existential consequences which go beyond the material facts of expropriation, exploitation and dispossession. It divides us from each other and from our essential humanity. Marx describes this as alienation from others and alienation from 'species-being': in the commodification of our relationships with others they become means to our ends rather than ends in themselves; and the treatment of ourselves as commodities distorts our humanity. *Heimat* is the expression of a desire for a settled resolution of this alienated condition, while the fulfilled moment is the fleeting glimpse of what such a condition might be. It is a quest for wholeness, for being at home in the world.

Bloch's project has been described as an attempt to fill the gap into which the Gods were imagined. The longing for *Heimat* and for the fulfilled moment can also be understood as the quest for a (sometimes) secular form of grace. 'Grace' has both secular and religious meanings. Its secular forms are predominantly active: it is the root of gracefulness and graciousness; we may act with good or bad grace. In both Catholic and Protestant Christianity, grace is freely given by God to fallen humanity, independent of human action, will or desert. In Catholicism, a distinction is made between habitual grace, 'the permanent disposition to live and act in keeping with God's call', and actual graces 'which refer to God's interventions'.[36] However, grace here is not exactly an existential state. Because it belongs to the supernatural order, it is outside our experience and can be known only by faith. This unknowable aspect of grace and the presumption of its divine origin are illustrated in the trial of Joan of Arc, both in the transcript and in the plays by George Bernard Shaw and Jean Anouilh, one route through which these events and words enter twentieth-century secular culture. Joan is interrogated about whether she believes herself to be in a state of grace. She replies: 'If I am not, may God put me there; if I am, may He keep me there'.[37] Grace is the antithesis of sin, and in the first instance can only be given, not earned. Thomas Aquinas posits that 'in the state of sin before grace, sin itself is an obstacle to earning grace. But once one has grace – to begin good works – one can earn further grace as the result of those works. Such further graces are not, however, the first grace; nobody earns that for themselves'. Grace is also the defence against death. Thus 'God does provide grace to heal death'.[38]

Such a view of grace is incompatible with a secular understanding, as it depends on belief in a divine giver and thus a divine being. However, the Protestant and existentialist theologian Paul Tillich gives a very different account. Tillich was Professor of Theology at the University of Frankfurt from 1929 to 1933, when he was sacked for his anti-Nazi views and moved to the United States. Born in 1896 and an almost exact contemporary of Bloch, he tried to arrange for the translation and publication in English of *The Principle of Hope*; had he been successful, this would have been available to Anglophone readers several decades earlier. Tillich's theology employs what he calls a 'method of correlation'. It begins with the ontological questions raised by existential philosophy, and seeks answers in terms of what Tillich claims as Christian revelation, but in unconventional terms which can be read by both critics and sympathizers as compatible with atheism. His portrayal of grace bears a secular interpretation, yet one which points to the inadequacy of secular language to encapsulate the human experience and aspiration at issue here. There are, argues Tillich, no adequate substitutes for the terms sin and grace that carry appropriate gravity and intensity. The recovery of their proper meaning 'leads us down into the depth of our human existence'. Sin, says Tillich, is not an act of wrong conduct and should never be used in the plural. It is a state of separation, something we all experience: 'separation among individual lives, separation of a man from himself, and separation of all men from the Ground of Being'.[39] Separation is part of the human condition, necessarily born from the existential anxiety provoked by the unavoidable knowledge of our inevitable death. Grace is the polar opposite of sin. It entails connection, acceptance, reconciliation, wholeness. '[G]race occurs in spite of separation and estrangement. Grace is the *re*union of life with life, the *re*conciliation of the self with itself'.[40]

The reference to the ground of being echoes a central element in what Aldous Huxley, following the seventeenth-century philosopher Leibniz, calls the perennial philosophy, a common element in all religions especially in their mystical forms.[41] Huxley also discusses different forms of grace, including its occurrence in Mahayan Buddhism, and its general congruence with Buddhist ideas of enlightenment. For Tillich, grace is emphatically not a matter of belief or of moral progress. We are struck by grace: 'a wave of light breaks into our darkness'.[42] This captures the epiphanic quality of the incursion of redeemed experience into the mundane, which transforms both our relation with ourselves and our relations with others:

> In the light of this grace we perceive the power of grace in our rela-
> tion to others and to ourselves. We experience the grace of being
> able to look frankly into the eyes of another, the miraculous grace of
> reunion of life with life. We experience the grace of understanding
> each other's words. We understand not merely the literal meaning
> of the words, but also that which lies behind them, even when they
> are harsh or angry. For even then there is a longing to break through
> the walls of separation. We experience the grace of being able to
> accept the life of another, even if it be hostile and harmful to us, for,
> through grace, we know that it belongs to the same Ground to which
> we belong, and by which we have been accepted. ... For life belongs
> to life. And in the light of this grace we perceive the power of grace
> in our relation to ourselves. We experience moments in which we
> accept ourselves, because we feel that we have been accepted by that
> which is greater than we.[43]

The power of the term grace lies both in its intrinsic reference to emotional depth and in its otherness. In Chapters 2 and 3 below, where
utopia is used as a hermeneutic method in the exploration of colour and
music, grace is a recurrent theme. And that is, perhaps, because utopia
in this sense shares the quest for what Tillich describes as 'the aspect of
depth in the totality of the human spirit'. The metaphor of depth itself
points to that which is 'ultimate, infinite, unconditional' or 'the state of
being ultimately concerned'.[44] It is the 'awareness of the Unconditioned',
an ontological awareness that is 'immediate, and not mediated by infer-
ential processes'. Tillich argues for tracing 'the unconditional element
in the creativity of nature and culture' and suggests that '[t]he presup-
position of this many-sided attempt is that in every cultural creation – a
picture, a system, a law, a political movement (however secular it may
appear) – an ultimate concern is expressed, and that it is possible to
recognise the unconscious theological character of it'. The supposition
of utopia as a hermeneutic method is the parallel secular claim, that in
many (if not all) aspects of culture, we can recognize the (sometimes)
unconscious utopian aspect. Tillich says that 'in poetry, in visual art,
and in music, levels of reality are opened up which can be opened up in
no other way. ... But in order to do this, something else must be opened
up – namely, levels of the soul, levels of our interior reality'.[45]

There are close parallels between Tillich's theology of culture and George Steiner's 'wager on transcendence'. Steiner seeks to demonstrate how 'in art or music or literature there is a freedom of giving and receiving in which giver and receiver are themselves transcended, and which makes the creative experience the guarantor of our proper human stature'.[46] The arts conjure real presence or the absence of real presence, or at least absence and the edge of presence, which are the longing and anticipated fulfilment that lie at the heart of the utopian quest. They reach to 'that quick of the human spirit which we call grace'.[47] As for Bloch, the aesthetic encounter may have an incursionary quality. It is, says Steiner 'the most "ingressive", transformative summons available to human experiencing', in which '[a] mastering intrusion has shifted the light'; and he refers to 'unbidden, unexpected entrances by irrevocable guests'.[48] The basis of Steiner's claim, like Tillich's, is existential, and he suggests that the assumption of substantive meaning implies a position that is onto-theological – that is, it depends on a claim about human experience that is beyond logic or verification. For Steiner, as for Tillich and Bloch, the core issue is the facticity of death. Thus art alerts us to 'the unassuaged, unhoused instability and estrangement of our condition'. Steiner does not, however, aspire to *Heimat*, to being at home in the world. Rather, the aim of art is to make us 'alertly, answerably peregrine in the unhousedness of our human circumstance'. Nevertheless, the question that Steiner says all art asks is an unequivocally utopian question, precisely congruent with Abensour's education of desire: 'What do you feel, what do you think of the possibilities of life, of the alternative shapes of being which are explicit in your experience of me, in our encounter?'.[49] And just as the education of desire aims implicitly or explicitly at social transformation and the instauration of concrete utopia, so Steiner asserts that this interrogation intends change, not least in our encounter with human others.

It intends change. Yet in the latter part of the twentieth century, Western culture saw the sequestration of utopian energies in the domain of art and culture. This move was linked to several distinct characteristics of the period, including fear of totalitarianism, scepticism of totality, and loss of faith in the proletariat as an agent of radical change. It was predicated on the anti-utopian climate of the Cold War and on a deeper cultural pessimism. In the shadow of the Shoah, Theodor Adorno wrote that:

> Art's Utopia, the counterfactual yet-to-come, is draped in black. It goes on being a recollection of the possible with a critical edge against the

real: it is a kind of imaginary restitution of that catastrophe, which is world history; it is freedom which did not come to pass under the spell of necessity and which may well not come to pass ever at all.[50]

Even Marcuse, a utopian optimist in 1968, had by 1979 come to rely on *The Aesthetic Dimension* as the last refuge of transformative desire, whose role was to construct subjects and agents capable of social transformation: 'Art cannot change the world, but it can contribute to changing the consciousness and drives of the men and women who could change the world'.[51] But there is a question of how the aspiration for a transformed existence moves out of the realm of culture through the formation of *political* subjects and agents, and there is a risk that the tendency to label transformative practices 'art' may sequester and corral them, thus reducing their political force. In practice, utopia as a hermeneutic method returns us time and again to the social. With all cultural forms and artefacts there are questions of cultural production and reproduction. In the case of music, many commentators attribute its particular utopian power to the putatively prefigurative *social* relationships between performers as well as to the resonance of music itself. But to address the social, economic and institutional basis of human happiness, human wellbeing, or even human survival requires an approach that is more holistic, structural and sociological.

Steiner reminds us that 'we come after'. After the Shoah, which Steiner discusses with infinitely more moral seriousness than Gray, and which makes impossible the straightforward Arnoldian supposition that the humanities humanize. The preoccupation with loss and consolation in the aesthetic sphere may even distract us from the suffering surrounding us in the real world, rather than move us to change that, or recognize our own role in its reproduction. After, also, poststructuralism and deconstruction, which sever word from world and imply the treatment of languages and semiotic systems as necessarily internally referential rather than externally representative. Steiner's own mandarin and androcentric tendencies, the conservatism of some of his judgements, and his emphasis on 'high' rather than 'popular' culture should remind us that we also come after Pierre Bourdieu. We need to remember that – as Dennis Potter suggests – the aspiration to the existential experience of grace is demotic and may be met in very different ways and different places. Moreover, those very works which may be harbingers of grace may at the same time be implicated in the use of cultural capital to sustain class divisions, exploitation and domination.

Tillich is adamant that the (religious) orientation to ultimate concern must not dissolve itself into art. Utopia too must resist such dissolution. The suggestion that grace might have a transformative effect on social relations points in the direction of *Heimat*, that projected state in which grace is more accessible and more stable. Again, we can find this in contemporary writing including writing widely read by children. Philip Pullman refuses, as Bloch does, the idea of heaven, or utopia, elsewhere. For us, there is no elsewhere, and the task before us is to build the Republic of Heaven. Utopia also entails refusal, the refusal to accept that what is given is enough. It embodies the refusal to accept that living beyond the present is delusional, the refusal to take at face value current judgements of the good or claims that there is no alternative. Pullman's *His Dark Materials* has at its core the refusal of the idea of original sin (and, intertextually, the refusal of the tropes of C. S. Lewis's *Narnia* series). Indeed, for Pullman, puberty is not a fall from privileged innocence and purity; the possibility of sexual love, experience and wisdom constitute a fall into, rather than a fall from, grace.

But Tillich himself is ambivalent about attempts to instantiate the Kingdom of God on earth and sees utopia poised between terror and grace. Steiner too suggests that utopia makes transcendence pragmatic.[52] Tillich opposes the positive and negative characteristics of utopia: truth and untruth; fruitfulness and unfruitfulness; transformative power and impotence. He concludes by arguing for the transcendence of utopia. Utopia strives to negate the negative in human experience. Truth lies in utopia's expression of what is, individually and socially, necessary to human fulfilment. Untruth lies in the goal of overcoming that estrangement which – deriving as it does from human finitude – is an inescapable element of experience. Fruitfulness lies in the capacity of utopia to anticipate human fulfilment and thereby to open up real possibilities for the future. Its unfruitfulness is that it can do this only by pushing beyond what is actually possible, by failing to distinguish emergent possibility from impossibility. One might say that Tillich here posits the intrinsic impossibility of a decisive move from abstract to concrete utopia, not just in imagination but in reality. Indeed, he points out that '[t]he decision whether something is possible or impossible has as referent not present reality but something that is on the "other side" of reality, and it is because of this situation that *every utopia is a hovering, a suspension, between possibility and impossibility*'.[53] Utopia has real power to transform the given, social world, including the economic. That power derives from wholeness, 'the power ... to push out of the ground of discontent ... in all directions of being'.[54] But untruth and unfruitfulness lead also, through the inevitability of disillusion, to impotence. Disillusion is the result of failing to recognize the necessary provisionality of utopian projections:

> This disillusionment must be discussed metaphysically, not psychologically. It is a disillusionment experienced again and again, and in such a profound way that it disrupts man in the deepest levels of his being. Such disillusionment is an inevitable consequence of confusing the ambiguous preliminary with the unambiguous ultimate. However provisionally we live in the future, we actually live always in the preliminary and the ambiguous. But in the movement from present into future what utopia intended as final and therefore fixed as absolute proves contingent in the flux, and this contingency of something regarded as ultimate leads to bitter disillusionment.[55]

Such disillusion produces fanatical anti-utopianism, especially where people turn against their own past sympathies and commitment. Jacoby notes in this context the early Marxist sympathies of Popper, Talmon and Arendt. Disillusion also produces terror, used to hold that very disillusion at bay. Tillich attributes the impotence of utopia, and the resulting tendencies to cynicism or terror, to utopia's 'inability to surmount its transitoriness'.[56] But this forces the question of whether this inability should be laid at the door of utopia itself, or whether this ascription and its partial truth is itself contingent. For Tillich, the transcendence of utopia's suspension between positive and negative characteristics requires us not to abandon commitment, but to commit ourselves without idolatry, that is to 'recognize that we are not committed to something absolute but to something preliminary and ambiguous'.[57] In Chapter 6, the shift both in utopian writing and in its criticism in the decades following the publication of Tillich's essay suggest that provisionality and contingency became deeply embedded in the later utopian imagination and in our retrospective reading of earlier works. Modernity, let alone postmodernity, enforced the understanding of the contingency of imagination and thereby enforced an element of reflexivity and provisionality.

The difficulties which Tillich identifies can be overcome by understanding utopia as a method rather than a goal – and this time as a constructive rather than hermeneutic method. Utopian thinking in this sense is not about devising and imposing a blueprint. Rather, it entails holistic thinking about the connections between economic, social, existential and ecological processes in an integrated way. We can then develop alternative possible scenarios for the future and open these up to public debate and democratic decision – insisting always on the provisionality, reflexivity and contingency of what we are able to imagine, and in full awareness that utopian speculation is formed always in the double squeeze of what we are able to imagine and what we are able to imagine as possible. The Imaginary Reconstitution of Society means envisioning the social institutions and social relations of a better society, and thus making a shift from the aesthetic and existential to the social and political – or rather, acknowledging (as critical theory has always done) the interdependence of the existential and the political. For if, to paraphrase John Ruskin, we are concerned with what kind of life is good for human beings and makes them happy, we are necessarily concerned with society as structure, not (just) with the realm of aesthetics. And yet we are still concerned with aesthetics, *both* because the reading of the aesthetic realm in terms of the utopian impulse involves a philosophical anthropology, a claim about what it is to be fully human, *and* because the ultimate criterion of judgment of our social arrangements is how far they can deliver the satisfaction of human longing. This raises core questions about the social construction and satisfaction of human needs and the potential for human flourishing, as well as the construction of the subjects and agents of utopia. It is the holism and institutional specificity of the social utopia that provide the critical link between utopia and sociology (discussed in Chapter 4) and that are important in considering utopia as method in this second sense of IROS. Now, however, we turn to two illustrations of utopia as a hermeneutic method, in relation first to the colour blue, and then to music, where grace is present as both metaphor and substance.

2
Riff on Blue

In Dennis Potter's *Pennies from Heaven,* Bloch's theme of lack and longing, the origin of the utopian impulse, is diffracted through the popular culture of the 1920s and 1930s. The central protagonist, Arthur Parker, is a travelling salesman hawking the sheet music of popular songs, who identifies the longing at the core of them and hence their utopian quality as 'looking for the blue'.

> Months and months I've been carrying this stuff around – these songs – all these lovely songs – I've always believed in 'em. But I didn't *really* know how it was or why it was that I believe in what's in here. There's things that is too big and too important and too bleed'n simple to put into all that lah-di-dah, toffee-nosed poetry and stuff, books and that – but everybody feels 'em. ... It's looking for the blue, ennit, and the gold. The patch of blue sky. The gold of the, of the bleed'n' dawn, or – the light in someone's eyes – Pennies from Heaven, that's what it is.[1]

The utopian character of the colour blue is also noted by Bloch: 'that so often so intractable blue, the fleeting promise of that which is missing'.[2] Like Potter, he links it to gold, even in the more abstract forms of utopian expression: 'Azure day-dreams range from everyday conceits of self-assertion, from commonplace reveries of gold linings and gold brocade, all the way to plans that are no longer merely focussed on the deserving ego of the dreamer-anticipator'.[3] Why blue? What is peculiarly utopian about blue or gold? Or what does blue denote or connote in twentieth-century Western culture that makes this convey intensity of feeling and longing more effectively than if Potter had written, 'it's looking for the green, ennit, and the red. The green of the leaves. The red of the ripe apple, or the colour in someone's cheek.'?

The point is not, of course, to suggest an isomorphic relation between utopia and blue in which blue is always and exclusively utopian or utopia is blue. Rather, the understanding of utopia as the expression of desire enables us to see the utopian aspect of blue and, in Chapter 3, the utopian aspect of (some) music. Through these explorations, the prevalence of utopian desire across different cultural forms becomes visible. However, the apparently abstract domains of colour and of music return us inexorably to questions of social relations and social processes, and thus to utopia as the Imaginary Reconstitution of Society in Parts II and III of the book.

Both in popular meanings and more esoteric contexts, blue maps on to Bloch's conjuring of the double aspect of utopia: lack and longing counterposed to the imagination of fulfilment. In contemporary Western societies, blue is overwhelmingly chosen as people's favourite colour, whether selected by name or from colour charts. Common turns of phrase emphasize how 'blue' figures separation from the mundane, as in 'blue skies thinking' or when things disappear into or appear out of the blue. Blue has a range of positive associations including spirituality, emotional intensity and depth. Thus '[t]he color meanings of blue are related to freedom, strength and new beginnings. Blue skies mean optimism and better opportunities. Blue is cooling and relaxing. Blue symbolizes water, the source of life'; indigo or dark blue signifies spiritual depth or 'wisdom, self-mastery and spiritual attainment'; it 'has an inward rather than an outward orientation', connecting 'the conscious and unconscious minds'.[4] And '[w]hile blue is the colour of communication with others, indigo turns the blue inward to increase personal thought, profound insights, and instant understandings'. Blue is also seen as 'trustworthy, dependable and committed … As the collective color of the spirit, it invokes rest and can cause the body to produce chemicals that are calming'.[5] Yellow is associated with 'enthusiasm, cheerfulness, sense of humor, fun, optimism and intellectuality'.[6] Or '[y]ellow shines with optimism, enlightenment, and happiness. Shades of golden yellow carry the promise of a positive future'.[7] Jenny Balfour-Paul, writing about indigo both as a dyestuff and a colour, says:

> [Blue] echoes the infinite richness of the sea, the midnight sky, the shadowy dusk and early dawn, and represents the elusive seventh colour of the rainbow which some people simply cannot see. In the medieval and Byzantine worlds blue was associated with divinity and humility, and in India with the capricious God Krishna. Many see it as a spiritual or reassuring colour, standing for loyalty, as opposed to the colour of cowards, yellow.[8]

Yet if the dominant trope here is spirituality, blue also has a melancholy aspect. It is associated with low mood and with 'feeling blue' – perhaps the longing that precedes transcendence.

The popular science writer Philip Ball asserts that 'colour, like music, takes a short cut to our senses and our emotions'.[9] In Max Luscher's colour tests, the affective meaning of colour preference is the basis for psychological diagnosis. Proponents argued that these were more effective than verbal tests, revealing aspects of the unconscious and being less susceptible to manipulative self-presentation. For Luscher, blue represents depth of feeling and is 'concentric, passive, sensitive, perceptive, unifying', while its affective aspects are 'tranquility, tenderness, and "love and affection"'.[10] Colour is also used as the basis of healing systems in chromotherapy, where blue is associated with the throat and fifth chakra, and is 'the colour of peace and infinity ... claimed to profoundly relax us', while 'our bodies and minds are conveyed to a state of peace, repose and softness'. Yellow again takes on a utopian character, echoing Bloch's orientation to horizon and *Vor-Schein*, for yellow is 'the symbol of sun at the horizon', thus of dawn and that which is coming into being.[11]

John Gage suggests that the Luscher system, in wide use in the second half of the twentieth century, represents not an account of the intrinsic meanings or effects of colours but 'a universal urge to attribute affective characters to colour'.[12] Gage argues that both the identification of colours and the meanings attributed to them are historically variable, and he provides detailed accounts of these changes. Greek and Roman antiquity, for example, placed more emphasis on light and dark than on hue, and there was no agreement on the range of identifiable colours. Convention now defines the seven colours of the rainbow as red, orange, yellow, green, blue, indigo and violet. But in the seventeenth century, Isaac Newton vacillated over the number of distinct colours achieved through the prismatic refraction of light, since these are a continuum rather than bands with defined boundaries. He eventually settled on seven chiefly because it enabled him to map the colour scale onto the musical octave in the form of the Dorian mode. Applied colour has different characteristics from spectral colour because surface texture affects its perceptible quality and because of the problems of synthesizing different hues. Johann Wolfgang von Goethe, whose 1810 *Theory of Colours* was highly influential among artists, was primarily interested in the human perception of colour. *Contra* Newton, for whom all colour is contained in light and revealed through refraction, Goethe argued that colour arises at the boundary of light and dark as a result of their interaction – rendering colour itself a liminal and thus potentially utopian phenomenon. Goethe also attributed moral and affective properties to colours, although the associations of blue are not self-evidently utopian. The blue side of the spectrum represented negation, shadow, darkness, weakness, coldness, distance and attraction; the yellow side signified the polar opposites of action, light, brightness, force, warmth, proximity and repulsion.[13]

If the identification of colours is historical, so too must be the connotations of the colour blue. Its association with spirituality comes into twentieth-century Western culture through diverse routes, including the emergent medieval convention of representing the Madonna in blue robes and the use of intensely blue stained glass in the thirteenth century, particularly in the cathedrals of northern France. At this point, the dominant meaning of blue shifted from dark to light. And indeed Potter's formulation locates the utopian essence both literally and metaphorically in light: blue sky, golden dawn, the light in someone's eyes. The emphasis on the utopian qualities of blue is intensified in nineteenth-century Romanticism, exemplified in and reproduced through the influence of the 1800 novel by Novalis, *Heinrich von Ofterdingen*. In a dream, the hero embarks on a quest for a blue flower, which takes him through landscapes of blue light and blue rocks. His aide on the quest is a shepherdess Cyane (blue), who claims to be the daughter of Mary. When he finds the flower it has at its centre the face of his beloved, who has 'light sky-blue eyes and blue veins in her neck'.[14] Sometimes the blue of utopia and the blue of the eye reflect one another, in its double attribution to dreams and dreamers. Schulz says of his dreamer-anticipator that '[h]is eyes were an improbably vivid sky-blue, not made for looking outward, but for steeping themselves in the cerulean essence of dreams'.[15]

Historicizing the cognitive understanding of colour's character and effects does not necessarily refute the claim that colours work directly on the emotions. In part it reproduces the disjunction between the possibilities of perception and of naming or talking about colour, a particular form of unutterability which Gage describes as 'a radical imbalance between sensation and language'.[16] The imputed utopianism of colour lies partly in its transcendence of the verbal and cognitive, a claim made forcibly by Aldous Huxley. Recording the effects of mescalin, Huxley notes the 'enormous heightening ... of the perception of colour':[17] 'All colours are intensified to a pitch far beyond anything seen in the normal state, and at the same time the mind's capacity for recognizing fine distinctions of tone and hue is notably heightened'.[18] He was, he writes, '[c]onfronted by a chair which looked like the Last Judgement – or, to be more accurate, by a Last Judgement which, after a long time and with considerable difficulty, I recognized as a chair':[19]

> Where the shadows fell on the canvas upholstery, stripes of a deep but glowing indigo alternated with stripes of an incandescence so intensely bright that it was hard to believe they could be made of anything but blue fire. For what seemed an immensely long time I gazed without knowing, even without wishing to know, what it was that confronted me. At any other time I would have seen a chair barred with alternate light and shade. Today the percept had swallowed up the concept.[20]

Huxley likens this effect to the visions of mystics and contemplatives, suggesting also that there may be a common physiological basis in the reduction of the sugar supply to the brain similarly produced by fasting and by mescalin. But he also argues that the effect is that 'the eye recovers some of the perceptual innocence of childhood, when the sensum was not immediately and automatically subordinated to the concept'.[21] What mescalin offers is 'a gratuitous grace', enabling us to 'intensify our ability to look at the world directly and not through that half-opaque medium of concepts, which distorts every given fact into the all too familiar likeness of some generic label or explanatory abstraction'.[22] His own account suggests that this is not wholly possible, for the visual intensity of blue is described by reference to an everyday object (a chair), and to an abstract and apocalyptic concept (the Last Judgement) – and of course it is a verbal rendering. Nevertheless, Huxley is insistent on the possibility and desirability of experience beyond the utterable:

> At the antipodes of the mind, we are more or less completely free of language, outside the system of conceptual thought. Consequently our perception of visionary objects possesses all the freshness, all the naked intensity, of experiences which have never been verbalized, never assimilated to lifeless abstractions. Their colour (that hallmark of givenness) shines forth with a brilliance which seems to me praeternatural, because it is in fact entirely natural – entirely natural in the sense of being entirely unsophisticated by language or the scientific, philosophical and utilitarian notions, by means of which we ordinarily re-create the given world in our own drearily human image.[23]

'That hallmark of givenness'. French Impressionism aimed at truth to externally-produced sensory perception and at recording colours

as directly perceived rather than derived from knowledge of characteristics of the object 'represented'. Huxley suggests that 'what the rest
of us see only under the influence of mescalin, the artist is congeni-
tally equipped to see all the time'.[24] And blue often predominates in
Impressionist painting, for example in the work of Claude Monet and
of Camille Pissarro, while Paul Cézanne claimed that 'blue gives other
colours their vibration'.[25] Indeed, this prevalence was criticized at the
time as 'indigomanie', 'la manie de bleu', and even evidence of the reti-
nal disorder 'daltonisme'.[26] Many of the meanings of blue were clearly
historically specific. It signified opposition to the dominant conventions of art and the bourgeois conventions they represented. It could
also denote political allegiance with the working class, since blue was
the dominant colour of peasants' and workers' clothing: William Morris
habitually wore a blue suit. Pissarro's paintings include such explicitly
political iconography, but also the extensive use of blue shadows. Paul
Smith interprets this distinctive use of blue as directly political and
intrinsically linked to Pissarro's anarchist beliefs and involvements.
Moreover, he argues that they carried this meaning when it could not be
verbally articulated. Far from being simply a representation of utopian
aspiration (in Bloch's sense abstract utopia), it had transformative consequences in encouraging his anarchist colleagues to effective political
action (thus making a transition to more concrete utopia). It was able
to do this, Smith argues, because of its non-verbal and preconceptual
form: 'Empirically, the precise sense of the blue pictures could not be
expressed so easily or so completely in terms of their enacting a
simple negation of Salon conventions. And their entry into public sense as
paradigms of the particular feelings they exemplified was complicated ...
by the fact that nobody (including the artist) had words with which to
describe this effect. They were not empty of meaning because of this,
but laden with (as yet) pre-linguistic meaning'.[27]

A different kind of aspiration to the pre-conceptual and non-figurative,
and a different attribution of properties to the colour blue, is to be found
in the work of Wassily Kandinsky, pioneer of artistic abstraction and
co-organizer with Franz Marc of the Blaue Reiter exhibitions in Munich
in 1911 and 1912. Whether there was any particular utopian content
to the name Blaue Reiter (Blue Rider) is debatable: Kandinsky said it
was chosen 'simply' because they both liked blue, he liked riders and
Marc liked horses. But in *Concerning the Spiritual in Art,* he argues that
'[t]he power of profound meaning is found in blue ... The inclination
of blue to depth is so strong that its inner appeal is stronger when its
shade is deeper'. He continues: 'Blue is the typical heavenly colour. The

ultimate feeling it creates is one of rest. When it sinks almost to black, it echoes a grief that is hardly human. When it rises towards white, a movement little suited to it, its appeal to men grows weaker and more distant'. He adds that the feeling of rest is of '[s]upernatural rest, not the earthly contentment of green'.[28] White means joy and purity but is beyond us, a 'symbol of a world in which all colour has disappeared' and which 'is too far above us for its harmony to touch our souls'.[29] Kasimir Malevich, the leading figure in Suprematism, disagreed: 'blue does not give a true impression of the infinite. The rays of vision are caught in a cupola and cannot penetrate the infinite. The Suprematist infinite white allows the beam to pass on without encountering any limit'.[30] And 'the blue of the sky has been defeated by the suprematist system, has been broken through, and entered white, as the true, real conception of infinity, and thus liberated from the colour background of the sky … Sail forth! The white, free chasm, infinity, is before us'.[31]

The leading proponents of artistic abstraction in the early twentieth century, including Kandinsky, Malevich, Piet Mondrian and Paul Klee, were strongly influenced by Theosophy. This provides an additional source for the privileging of blue as a signifier of a utopian condition or state of grace. Theosophy may be best understood as the new age philosophy of the late nineteenth and early twentieth century. It was inaugurated in 1875 by Helena Petrovna Blavatsky (1832–91) with the foundation of the still extant Theosophical Society and was responsible for the early influence of Eastern philosophies in the West, especially Hinduism and Buddhism. It is a syncretic system which claims that all religions are directed to the same end, the unity of humankind and the knowledge of God, and all have partial understanding of truth. In its belief in the possibility of individual access to the divine or to the ground of all being, it is a version of the perennial philosophy. Theosophy had a specific system of meanings attributed to colour, mediated chiefly through the works of Rudolf Steiner. Blue conveyed spirituality or devotion to a noble ideal, reinforcing Christian and Romantic meanings but incorporating also the spiritual associations of blue in, for example, Hinduism. The contrasting yellow stood for the highest intellect.[32]

The congruence of early twentieth-century artistic abstraction and Theosophy does not reside solely or even primarily in the presumed affective characteristics of colour. A deeper connection lies in their desire to express an inner reality deemed to be beyond words and beyond figuration. They share a concern with access to, revelation of and progress towards infinity and the absolute, and thus the intuition and expression of utopian desire. They have in common a belief in an inner light and truth which prefigures a utopian state of being and of the world. Where art is concerned, these utopian qualities, even when they are described and experienced as spiritual, are not necessarily religious in any conventional sense. Indeed, they may be seen as an attempt to reclaim through art a dimension of human experience alienated to the supernatural. In the preparation of *Der Blaue Reiter Almanach*, published to accompany the first Blaue Reiter exhibition in Munich in 1911, Kandinsky argued that 'Theosophy must be mentioned briefly and powerfully'.[33] Exhibition brochures summarized the group's 'grand utopian programme': 'Through this small exhibition we do not wish to propagate a *single* precise and special form, rather we intend to demonstrate through the *diversity* of the represented forms how the *inner desire* of the artists manifests itself multifariously'.[34] For Kandinsky, this inner necessity had three aspects, personal, cultural and eternal,[35] the last corresponding to Bloch's cultural surplus, or that which transcends the individual and social context of production.

Kandinsky refers back to his own difficulty in recognizing one of Monet's haystack paintings as a painting 'of' a haystack, causing him to wonder how far one could take the dematerialization of the object. Impressionism is concerned with the perception and recording of external stimuli; conversely, expressionism is concerned with the communication of inner experience. Thus Kandinsky's concern with disembedding colour from figuration was directed towards conveying a preconceptual spiritual essence which would transform human experience and usher in a new world, rather than by a desire to record preconceptual impressions of the outside world. If abstraction in this sense refers to the intentional liberation of art from subordination to an object of representation, it is different from, and opposed to, abstraction in a cognitive sense. For even as art reaches to the ineffable and inexpressible, it depends wholly on the embedded materiality of the human body, its sensory perceptions and affective responses, including the perception and meaning of colour. But bypassing the rational and cognitive remains critical: in *Der Blaue Reiter Almanach*, Schoenberg writes of the arts overcoming 'the belief in the power of intellect and consciousness', and insists that 'in ... translation into concepts, into the language of man, which is abstraction, reduction to the visible, the essence is lost, the language of the world, which perhaps has to remain unintelligible, only perceptible'.[36]

Bloch refers, with direct reference to the Blaue Reiter initiative, to 'visible-invisible expeditions towards the essential'.[37] And he concludes his discussion with 'the self-understanding of such artists themselves', quoting first from the sculptor Naum Gabo, and then from Marc:

> 'If this art should survive any longer period of time, or if this art should grow into something which might be taken as important by the coming age as the old arts were for their age, then this is only attainable if the artist of the future is able to manifest in his medium a new imago, in painting or in sculpture, so that it expresses the true spirit of what the present mind tries to create and that will be the receiving imago of life in the universe'. Or, as Franz Marc expressed it in much simpler terms, devoted in a utopian sense to the exodus of the imago rather than the imago of the exodus, 'Painting is our surfacing at some other place'.[38]

The Blaue Reiter project itself was short-lived because of the outbreak of the 1914–18 war. Kandinsky returned to Moscow until 1921, when he returned to Germany and taught at Bauhaus until its closure by the Nazis in 1933. Marc is a less well-known figure than Kandinsky, partly because he, like his friend and colleague August Macke, was killed in the conflict. But nearly a hundred years later, the work of Mondrian, who shared the belief that 'art could transform not just the quality of life but the whole future of humankind', was presented in the opening displays at London's Tate Modern Gallery under the heading simply of 'Utopia'. In 2006, Tate Modern's exhibition *Kandinsky: The Path to Abstraction*, emphasizing his quest for an alternative spiritual reality, drew record crowds. The 'surfacing at some other place' is directly echoed in contemporary work, this time sculpture, by Anthony Gormley's installation at Crosby beach, *Another Place*. A hundred scattered figures stare out to sea, separate and isolated in this vast space. Their loneliness carries the loss and longing of utopia. Yet there is transformation implied here too. The figures originate in a cast made by Gormley from his own body. Clones then, identical at the start. But they weather to individuality: reddening with corrosion, thickening and greening with accretions of barnacles and weed, sinking and drowning in shifting sands, drowning and resurfacing in the ebb and flow of tides. They look out over the Mersey channel, route of immigration and emigration, movements looking always to another place, a new life, a changed subject, the hope of a better life.

The Theosophical system of colour meanings was not adopted by the Blaue Reiter group in its entirety. Malevich departs from a Theosophical palette of meanings and invokes an earlier black/white/red system: in Suprematism, black represents the worldly or economic; white, pure action; and red, revolution.[39] Mondrian, the most strongly affiliated to Theosophy, was concerned to balance the blue-yellow polarity of spirit and intellect against the material red – but the polarity of blue and yellow is also present more widely, notably in Goethe. For Marc, blue and yellow are both opposed and gendered:

> *Blue* is the *male* principle, sharp and spiritual, *yellow* the *female* principle, soft, cheerful and sensual, *red* the *material*, brutal and heavy and ever the colour which must be resisted and overcome by the other two. If, for example, you mix the serious, spiritual blue with red, then you augment the blue to an unbearable mourning, and the reconciling yellow, the complementary colour to violet, will be indispensable (the woman as consoler, not as lover!).[40]

Kandinsky's claims about the properties of colour also diverge from those of Theosophy. He sees colour as dynamic, shifting with different shades and combinations so that its effects vary with context.[41] He notes the propensity of blue to move away from, and yellow to move towards, the viewer. However he associates yellow not with intellect but with an aggressive, disturbing effect, with 'the sour-tasting lemon and shrill-singing canary' and with 'violent raving lunacy'.[42] And there are other sources for his understanding of blue: Franz von Stück, who taught both Kandinsky and Klee in Munich, also associated blue with mystery, eternity, intellectuality and poetic worth.[43]

Intense blue remained a colour with utopian associations throughout twentieth-century art, and not only in Europe. In 1924, Stanton Macdonald-Wright produced his own *Treatise on Colour* for the benefit of his students in Los Angeles: blue is, he says, 'highly spiritual', the colour of 'ethereality' and 'anti-materialism'.[44] Sometimes the anticipation of possible or impossible colour may itself be utopian. Its intensity is not yet. 'The painter of the future', wrote Vincent Van Gogh, 'will be *a colourist such as has never yet been*'.[45] Kim Stanley Robinson's utopian *Mars* trilogy hypothesizes a distinctive blue. Fredric Jameson describes this as 'color … defamilarised and made strange', an 'unnamed blue that almost speaks to you, like a word on the tip of the tongue'. Robinson writes:

> There was an intensely blue forget-me-not. The petals so suffused with warming anthocyanins that they were nearly purple – the color that the Martian sky would achieve at around 230 millibars … It was surprising there was no name for that color, it was so distinctive. Perhaps that was cyanic blue.[46]

David Lindsay's 1920 novel *A Voyage to Arcturus* posits two new primary colours, ulfire and jale, which can be described only in terms of their emotional characteristics: 'Just as blue is delicate and mysterious, yellow clear and unsubtle, and red sanguine and passionate, so he felt ulfire to be wild and painful, and jale dreamlike, devilish and voluptuous'.[47]

In Yves Klein's case, the inadequacy of actually existing colours provoked his quest for a sufficiently vibrant blue, one in which the solvent did not diminish the intensity of pigment – an intensity that can be seen in Anish Kapoor's sculptural use of piles of powdered pigment, in red, yellow and blue. Klein's quest resulted in a distinctive ultramarine which he trademarked in 1957 as International Klein Blue (IKB). Its quality was intended to be 'close to pure space', and for Klein, who created as series of nearly two hundred monochrome blue paintings, it was 'associated with immaterial values beyond what can be seen or touched'.[48] He asked 'What is blue?', and answered his own question: 'Blue is the invisible becoming visible ... Blue has no dimensions. It 'is' beyond the dimensions of which other colours partake'.[49]

Blue dominates the paintings of the Cornish artist John Miller (1931–2002), which most familiarly 'depict' a streak of golden sand across sea and sky of intense blues. His other landscape and seascape paintings, often semi-abstract, are also often predominantly blue. They include a series of paintings entitled 'Sunrise of Wonder', with a horizon of light and just emergent sliver of sun where the blues of sea and sky meet – reminiscent of the horizon of light in August Strindberg's darker seascapes. Miller was always drawn to mysticism and monasticism, and some of the paintings (notably those inspired by the canticle of St Francis, which are either blue or flaming orange) have an explicitly spiritual referent, while he writes of a series of 'interior landscapes' painted after his parents' deaths as 'intuitive representations of the journey of the soul'.[50] In many paintings, two colours join at the horizon, at infinity. Miller says, '[t]he joining of those two colours is about somewhere beyond my reach. Whether it's a beach, or a passage in the interior landscapes, or that thin line of light under a cloud and beyond the sea ... If I reached it, I would probably stop painting'.[51] Miller's work is undoubtedly popular: in 2003 a survey of sales of reproductions of landscape artists ranked him in the top four alongside Monet and fifth in the current best-selling deceased artists across all genres.[52]

Derek Jarman, reflecting on colour in 1993 as he lost his sight and his life to AIDS, wrote that 'Blue is the universal love in which man bathes – it is the terrestrial paradise', and 'I present you with the universal Blue/ Blue an open door to soul/ An infinite possibility/ Becoming tangible'. He recalls 'the fathomless blue of Bliss' even as 'Blue is darkness made visible'.[53] More recently, in the twenty-first century, the photographer Daniel Thistlethwaite has created a remarkable series of blue photographs, variously taken in the Camargue and along the Dorset and Devon coasts. These exceptionally beautiful images are taken on very long exposures, sometimes as long as eight minutes, in fading light. The camera therefore reveals that which cannot be seen, rather than recording what is evidently present. Darkness made visible. But while fixed landscape features have a precise clarity, moving elements such as clouds blur at the edges. Elements such as boats dematerialize entirely, the trajectory of travel appearing as a line, the movement of a secured, rocking boat simply as a dark area.[54]

If landscape painting and photography draw on and reproduce the utopian resonances of blue, these are also directly present in the built environment. There are blue mosques in Egypt, Armenia and Turkey and Iran, where blue and blue-green symbolize paradise. In Europe, the utopian association of blue is especially apparent in contemporary stained glass. Here, the influences of abstraction and the older forms of ecclesiastical glass coincide in the use of pure colour, exemplified in the work of Marc Chagall and of John Piper. In England, the artists John Piper and Myfanwy Evans (later Piper) were at the heart of the promotion of abstraction in the 1930s. Piper (who is described as having exceptionally blue eyes)[55] referred back to William Blake's question: 'Shall painting be confined to the sordid drudgery of facsimile representations of merely mortal and perishing substances and not be, as poetry and music are, elevated to its own proper sphere of invention and visionary conception?'.[56] He also wrote in 1933 that '[w]e do not hear enough of Kandinsky in London in spite of *The Art of Spiritual Harmony*, now twenty years old, which has proved prophetic and still makes lively reading'.[57] But Piper himself moved away from abstraction towards the representation of place, echoing W. H. Auden's 1936 *Seascape*, 'Look, stranger, on this island now'. The centre of gravity of abstraction in British art moved to St Ives in Cornwall, a place whose legendary quality of light was recently established as consisting of an unusually high proportion of blue wavelength. As a war artist, Piper produced paintings for the 'Recording Britain' project – as well as being despatched to Coventry to record the aftermath of the destruction of the medieval city and its cathedral in November 1941.

Piper's change of style was widely seen at the time as a betrayal of the modern movement, but his capacities as an abstract artist infuse his topographical painting and printmaking both in composition and colour. As he put it, abstraction 'taught me something of the value of clear colours, one against another, when they have no goods to deliver except themselves'.[58] In Piper's most sought-after prints, such as *Long Sutton*, there is a strikingly intense blue, which is also to be found in much of his stained glass. In his commissions carried out in collaboration with Patrick Reyntiens, abstraction remains dominant, and the link between pure colour and existential effect is explicit. Indeed, there is a direct link here between the meaning attributed to the blue of thirteenth-century glass and Piper's own twentieth-century practice. Recording his intentions in the design of the Baptistry window for Basil Spence's new cathedral for Coventry in the 1950s, Piper wrote:

> Ever since I was taken to Canterbury Cathedral as a child, my heart beats faster when I see blue glass in church windows, especially when it predominates in a window in the thirteenth century manner. ... That excitement, that heightening of emotion, always occurs: the blue seems to be *there* in the window, firmly there in its painted glass form, and yet not there at all, as a symbol of infinity, but infinity that has become intensely real instead of an abstraction.[59]

He went on to link this directly to Coventry, where the intention was to work solely through the medium of colour:

> This is what one hoped to convey by the mass of blue at the top of the window, with its star-like and comet-like splinters and echoes of yellow and red. The blue here, of course, is intensified in its blueness by the red of the outer borders, which counterchange downwards, through purples, to blue at the bottom, against the cushion of reds and browns in the main lower part of the window. The central blaze of white and yellow is also cushioned by the dark yellows, ochres, golds, umbers and siennas that surround it.[60]

The only symbolism in the window acknowledged by Piper is 'a great burst of light and grace'.[61] Frances Spalding endorses the effectiveness of the outcome irrespective of matters of belief:

> Whether or not the visitor accedes to the symbolism of the light of Christ or the Holy Spirit, this sun-like effect reaches across the divisions often created by religious beliefs in its communication of regenerative, transformative power. ... [A] deep logic of reparation and reconstruction connects [Piper's] 1940s paintings [of Coventry] with the elemental trumpet call of the Baptistry window.[62]

In 1967, Piper and Reyntiens designed the glass for Liverpool Metropolitan Cathedral, with its central lantern of three areas of colour, red, yellow and blue, each pierced by an area of white light conveying, rather than representing, the Trinity. The inspiration for this was Reyntiens' reading of Dante's fourteenth-century *Paradiso*, which uses colour and light as symbols for God. At Liverpool, the panels around the entrance are a golden yellow, but the glass panels in the surrounding walls are predominantly blue 'in order to create an otherworldly light'. The experience created by this light is for Piper the fundamental purpose of glass design: 'the function – the flesh and blood and bones of stained glass – its whole *being* – is to qualify light and to intensify atmosphere in a room or building, not necessarily to provide colour or a message'.[63] Certainly they succeeded at Liverpool, where the effect is of being cradled in grace.

In another Piper-Reyntiens collaboration for Churchill College, Cambridge, on the theme of 'Let there be light', 'the blue windows at the east end ... represent the human search for truth and God's revelation; the gold and green windows north and south, the human search for beauty and love and God's response'.[64] Bloch reads this colour combination in general as utopian, referring to 'the blue and gold in [a] window as a ... utopian characteristic of a great work of art'.[65] Similar colour iconography, and a similar intention to qualify light and intensify atmosphere, is present in Chagall's set of windows for the small church of All Saints, Tudeley in Kent. Intense blue, which Chagall regarded as the colour of love, is, of course, a feature of his paintings, but it again acquires an added intensity in the medium of stained glass. The windows of the North Aisle are predominantly blue ('an intense, spiritual blue'),[66] while those in the South Aisle representing hope and resurrection are a deep golden yellow. The only set of Chagall windows in England, and within easy reach of the Channel Tunnel, Tudeley is often overly full of visitors. But to walk into the space when it is empty, again produces, through surrounding you in light, an existential shift that displaces the mundane.

Colour and music

Kandinsky was insistent both on the parallels between colour and 'feelings [that] are the material expressions of the soul', and on the inadequacy of words:

> Shades of colour, like those of sound, are of a much finer texture and awake in the soul emotions too fine to be expressed in words. Certainly each tone will find some probable expression in words, but

it will always be incomplete, and that part which the word fails to express will not be unimportant but rather the very kernel of existence. For this reason words are, and will always remain, only hints, mere suggestions of colours.[67]

One consequence of the 'radical imbalance between sensation and language' is that it is difficult to talk or write about either colour or music other than through metaphor. [68] The metaphors for colour (and artistic composition) are frequently musical: composition, rhythm, harmony, tone, timbre are all terms used to describe the arrangement and quality of colour and form in painting. Similarly, metaphors for music are often visual. And the most obvious crossing from colour into music is the designation of a specific musical style, the blues, with roots in American slave plantations. The imputed connection between art and music was more than metaphorical. The relation between colour and music, and more broadly between art and music, preoccupied both painters and composers from the mid-nineteenth century, including Eugène Delacroix, Paul Gaugin, James Whistler and Claude Debussy. As Peter Vergo puts it, 'the musicality of colour would become a question of ever more absorbing interest for writers and artists who regarded painting as an art that was expressive in itself rather than by virtue of any subject or narrative that it might represent'.[69] Kandinsky quoted the composer Schumann: 'To send light into the darkness of men's hearts – such is the duty of the artist'.[70]

The basis of the connection was, in part, social: the transition and exchange between cultural forms was helped both by social networks and by a more polymathic engagement with art and culture. This was true even in England where musical literacy was less widespread, for Myfanwy Piper wrote libretti for Benjamin Britten's operas, while John Piper designed for the stage and was an accomplished pianist. But it was more extensively characteristic of continental Europe. Vergo describes Delacroix as someone for whom 'the enjoyment and appreciation of music were an indispensable part of civilized life'.[71] This attitude, which was even more pronounced in central European culture, involved both musical appreciation and musical performance. Delacroix played both piano and violin. Paul Klee, whose paintings have explicit musical reference, played the violin, performing with the Berne municipal orchestra from the age of 11. Schoenberg, now best known as a composer, showed paintings in the first Blaue Reiter exhibition, although his discontent with how they were hung led him to not participate the following year. The Lithuanian Mikalojus Čiurlionis was both composer and painter and a key figure in the construction of Lithuanian national identity: he

too was invited to exhibit with the Blaue Reiter group but died of pneu-
monia in 1911.[72] And of course it was partly music which propelled
Kandinsky (who played the cello) along the road to abstraction. His
painting 'Impression III: Concert 1911' was a response to a concert by
Schoenberg which Kandinsky attended with Marc and in which he
perceived exactly the disembedding of elements from conventional
relations and harmonies for which he was striving in painting.

Kandinsky's disquisition on colour and affect in *Concerning the Spiritual
in Art* reflects a belief in the direct access to the emotions as a common
characteristic of sound and colour but also in their synaesthetic relation,
or the direct connection of visual and aural senses. This spills over into
the associated tonal qualities and the musical timbre of different instruments: 'In music a light blue is like a flute, a darker blue a cello; a still
darker a thunderous double bass; and the darkest blue of all – an organ'.
'Light warm red' is 'a sound of trumpets, strong, harsh and ringing',
producing 'a feeling of strength, vigour, determination, triumph'. 'Cold,
light red' parallels the 'singing notes of a violin'; orange the note 'of the
angelus, or of an old violin'; violet is a 'sad and ailing' colour which is
'worn by old women' and expressed in music by the English horn or deep
woodwind instruments.[73] *Der Blaue Reiter Almanach* includes the script
for Kandinsky's abstract stage work *Der gelbe Klang* (*The Yellow Sound*)
which begins and ends with blue. Although this was not performed
until the 1960s, it was one influence on Oskar Schlemmer who designed
the sets for the production of Schoenberg's *Die Glückliche Hand* and the
Kroll Opera in the 1920s. This 'includes a crescendo of lights changing from a dull red to yellow, through dirty-green, violet, blue-grey and
blood red'. [74] As we shall see in the next chapter, the Kroll Opera connects
Kandinsky and his circle to Bloch, who was intimately involved in its
work and wrote programme notes for several of its productions.

The social and artistic links were strengthened by the aspiration to
synthetic works of art. In his seminal 1850 essay on *The Artwork of the
Future*, Richard Wagner argued that:

> Artistic man can be wholly satisfied only by the unification of all
> forms of art in the service of the common artistic endeavour. Any
> fragmentation of his artistic sensibilities limits his freedom, prevents
> him from becoming fully what he is capable of being. The highest
> form of communal art is drama; it can exist in its full entirety only
> if it embraces every variety of art ... When eye and ear mutually
> reinforce the impression each receives, only then is artistic man
> present in all its fullness.[75]

The idea of the *Gesamtkunstwerk*, or total work of art, was widely aspired to and was celebrated by, amongst others, Charles Baudelaire.[76] Such attempts at synthesis did not meet with universal approval. Adorno was sceptical about the merits both of elision between art forms intended here and about the politics of the total work of art. He criticized the former for its inadequate attention to the particularities of different artistic forms and the constraints placed upon them by the internal logics and material means of their production. The latter, at least in relation to Wagner's ambitions, he thought 'foreshadowed the totalitarian administration of society'.[77] E. M. Forster put the question of form more simply:

> What is the good of the arts if they're interchangeable? What is the good of the ear if it tells you the same as the eye? ... Wagner ... has done more than any man in the nineteenth century towards the muddling of the arts.[78]

The intention behind *Der Blaue Reiter Almanach* was not exactly to establish the interchageability of the arts as Forster suggests, but to demonstrate their intrinsic connection in terms of the congruence of the inner light they expressed. Thus it contained musical scores (which are visual representations of music), reproductions of paintings, poetry and essays. Indeed, given the claim that music and painting convey a reality that is beyond words, there is a great deal of verbal documentation of intended meanings. It included an essay by the Russian critic and composer Leonid Sabaneiev on Alexander Scriabin's *Prometheus*. Sabaneiev noted that the pursuit of ecstasy, a utopian spiritual state, has historically depended on the synthesis of artistic forms:

> Mystical-religious art, which expresses all of man's secret abilities and leads to *ecstasy*, has always used *all* available means to affect the soul. We find as much in our contemporary church service – the descendant of classical mystical ritual – on a smaller scale the idea of uniting the arts is preserved. Don't we find there music (singing, sounds of bells), plastic movements (kneeling, ritual of the priest's actions), play of smells (incense), play of lights (candles, lights), painting. All arts are united here in one harmonious whole, to attain one goal – religious exaltation.[79]

Scriabin's work is also the strongest expression of the synaesthetic relation between colour and music, with each key having a specific colour and eleven colours mapped onto a circle of fifths. F sharp is blue.[80]

Prometheus is scored for a very large orchestra, and a keyboard of coloured lights. At the time, Scriabin was working on the never-completed work *Mysterium*, of which he wrote:

> There will not be a single spectator. All will be participants. The work requires special people, special artists and a completely new culture. The cast of performers includes an orchestra, a large mixed choir, an instrument with visual effects, dancers, a procession, incense, and rhythmic textural articulation. The cathedral in which it will take place will not be of one single type of stone but will continually change with the atmosphere and motion of the Mysterium. This will be done with the aid of mists and lights, which will modify the architectural contours.[81]

As Schulz put it, 'The man with the sky-blue eyes is no architect. He is, rather, a director of cosmic landscapes and sceneries'.[82] The aspirations for Scriabin's multi-media production were explicitly utopian and transformative. The seven-day production was to be staged in the foothills of the Himalayas, when the world would dissolve in heavenly bliss and inaugurate the new spiritual era envisaged in Theosophy. But although belief in synaesthesia was common in the early decades of the twentieth century, and is demonstrably experienced by some individuals, there is no agreement on the relations between particular colours and sounds. Again, therefore, the musical resonance of blue may be culturally determined rather than intrinsic, a relationship described by Simon Shaw-Miller as cultural synaesthesia. Blue may be associated with compositions in a wide variety of styles, from Arthur Bliss's 1922 Colour Symphony, *Blue, the colour of Sapphires, Deep Water, Skies, Loyalty and Melancholy* to Miles Davis's *Kind of Blue*, while Abbey Lincoln's line 'Everybody knows songs come out of the blue' reprises the blue as simultaneously the sphere of the imagination, deep yearning and a place beyond us.

The return to the social

The hermeneutic method of utopia can be used to draw out the utopian resonance of blue as a colour bearing spiritual depth and inner desire in specific historical and cultural contexts. The utopian qualities of blue revealed by this method are predominantly existential and immaterial. Yet they also depend on the material and social processes involved in the creation and production of cultural artefacts, so that the identification of the utopian moment leads always back to the social and to embodied humanity. Ball suggests that blue was used for the Madonna's robes because it was expensive. The best blue pigment ultramarine (beyond the seas) was made from the finely ground semi-precious stone lapis lazuli, obtainable only from Afghanistan and more expensive than gold. It was used because it was rare and valuable, creating the spiritual association.[83] The development of blue stained glass in the thirteenth century depended both on the diffusion of technical skills in the manufacture and use of glass and on trade with the East. Fabric dyes were derived from indigo, a plant source imported in processed form along trade routes, while the cobalt used for the rich blue glass was similarly imported. More generally, Ball emphasizes the intertwining processes of the material production of pigments from natural materials and their later chemical synthesis, and changing artistic practice. The use of coloured light in stage design and the possibility of productions integrating sound and colour in temporary spaces without stained glass were greatly assisted by, if not wholly dependent on, the development of electric lighting. A very specific technology generates the distinctive blue of LED lighting, incorporated into architectural form in, for example, the Spectrum building in Bristol. Piper's own stained glass commissions, especially the Liverpool lantern, pushed at the limits of technical possibility and necessitated collaboration with the best of craftsmen.

The musical instruments whose differing timbres Kandinsky perceives as colours are of course cultural artefacts (and specifically Western ones at that – no mention here of the Oud, a traditional Eastern instrument, or the saxophone, invented in 1840). Even the term 'the blues', usually assumed to be a metaphor mediated by the melancholy effect of flattened or 'blue' notes, may itself be deeply rooted in material culture and the social relations of its production. Indigo was cultivated on plantations worked by slave labour in Central America and in the Southern States. The dominant understanding of the trade triangle of slavery and the main uses of slave labour in the Americas involve cotton, tobacco and sugar. Yet indigo was also a major economic crop. Initially it was mainly imported from India, with seventeenth-century references to the East India Company's 'Blue Warehouse' in London. By 1775, it formed thirty-five per cent of South Carolina's total exports. Slaves were traded for indigo between Georgia and the Windward Islands as late as 1790. Most British production was moved back to India in the nineteenth century, when indigo remained an immensely valued commodity since the colour was not synthesized until 1897. Moreover, there are 'blue songs' or laments associated with indigo production in both Tamil and Indonesia.[84]

And indeed sometimes the colour blue has a directly social reference, signifying loyalty or solidarity, and drawing on one of its heraldic meanings to conjure an ideal form of social relation. In *Oracle Night*, Paul Auster considers the emotional and moral qualities of colours but then returns us from the existential to the social. '[B]lue is a good colour. Very calm, very serene. It sits well in the mind'. It is ambiguous, associated with both positive and negative feelings:

'... But what does blue stand for?'
'I don't know. Hope, maybe'.

'And sadness. As in, I'm feeling blue. Or, I've got the blues'. [85] But then he suggests that blue is also the colour of loyalty, and the colour of what one might call being a mensch. The Blue Team is 'a kind of secret society, a brotherhood of kindred souls'. The Blue Team 'represented a human ideal, a tight-knit association of tolerant and sympathetic individuals, the dream of a perfect society'. Importantly, however, 'Blue team members did not conform to a single type, and each one was a distinct and independent person'. And again, 'I can't pin it down for you and say it's one thing or another'. It implies 'a connection ... a bond of solidarity'.[86]

Sometimes, too, this solidarity pushes forward to transformation. In one of his earliest formulations, Bloch construes the quest to make a future society adequate to full humanity in terms of blue:

> Only in us does the light still burn, and we are beginning a fantastic journey towards it, a journey toward the interpretation of our waking dream, toward the implementation of the central concept of utopia. To find it, to find the right thing, for which it is worthy to live, to be organized, and to have time: that is why we go, why we cut new, metaphysically constitutive paths, summon what is not, build into the blue and build ourselves into the blue, and there seek the true, the real, where the merely factual disappears.[87]

Schulz's 'Republic of Dreams' is 'a sovereign realm of poetry', 'the exclusive domain of the fictive'. And yet 'The possibility suggests itself that no dreams, however absurd or senseless, are wasted in the universe. Embedded in the dream is a hunger for its own reification, a demand that imposes an obligation on reality'. Thus the dreamer-anticipator 'invites everyone to keep on working, fabricating, jointly creating: we are all of us dreamers by nature, after all, brothers under the sign of the trowel, destined to be master builders'.[88]

3
Echoes of Elsewhere

Dennis Potter, reflecting on *Pennies from Heaven*, connects 'looking for the blue' to a more conventional understanding of utopianism as the quest for an ideal world:

> I picked the Thirties ... because the popular music was, perhaps, at its most banal and its most sugary, least challenging – and yet it also encapsulates, somehow, some diminished image of the human desire for there to be a perfect and beautiful and just world.[1]

And:

> [You] can almost lick them they are so sweet, and yet they have this tremendous evocative power – a power which is much more than nostalgia. Those songs stood together as a package in that they seemed to represent the same kinds of things that the psalms and fairy-tales represented: that is the most generalized human dreams, that the world should be perfect, beautiful and loving and all of those things. A lot of the music is drivel, in that it's commercial and never too difficult, but it does possess an almost religious image of the world as a perfect place.[2]

These songs are utopian both in their expression of desire and in their promise of consolation. Music critic Laura Barton suggests this quality crosses musical genres. Reggae and rock'n'roll make overt reference to Zion as an 'embodiment of yearning' but this '[seeps] into all those stories of desire and escape and belonging, into all those tales of getting out of town and hitting the road and finding true love, unearthing great passion'. There is 'this dirty commonplace Zion, in all these songs that speak of the great unmeetable yearning of the soul'.[3] But this raises an immediate question: how much of their utopianism derives from the words and how much from the musical settings? Franz Schubert's *An die Musik* celebrates music's capacity to transport us to a better world or to reveal a heaven of better times; the words claim a utopian power for music, but it is less obvious how the music conveys this. In Kurt Weill's *Youkali*, the words (by Roger Fernay) reprise the ambiguity of More's pun: 'Youkali, c'est le pays de nos desires/.../ Mais c'est un rêve, une folie/ Il n'y a pas de Youkali' (Youkali is the land of our desires... But it is a dream, a foolishness; there is no Youkali). Weill's tune was used both before and after the song-setting for instrumental pieces; again, it is harder to pin down the utopian aspect of the music. The same is true of John Lennon's iconic *Imagine*. Yet claims about the utopian character of music echo through sources as diverse as Bloch's *Principle of Hope*, contemporary music criticism and Ian McEwan's novel *Saturday*. They relate variously to the music itself, its interweaving with text, and the process of performance. Potter himself uses song and dance routines to signal a shift from the relative realism of spoken drama to a realm of fantasy and imagination. And performance returns us to the social relations enacted in or imputed to music-making as a prefigurative practice. Utopia as hermeneutic method allows us to explore the significance of music to questions of loss, longing, fulfilment and redemption in these different ways.

The music itself?

In *The Principle of Hope*, Bloch argues that music is the most utopian of cultural forms 'by virtue of its so immediately human capacity of expression', and yet music is the most socially conditioned of all arts. This potential contradiction is resolved by the idea of cultural surplus, the general capacity of art to overflow its historical location and conditions of production and point towards that which is not yet. Music excels here: 'no art has so much surplus over the respective time and ideology in which it exists'.[4] It has a particular capacity to produce the sense of the fulfilled moment. As Fredric Jameson puts it, for Bloch '[t]here exist ... existential experiences which may be understood as foreshadowings of what the plenitude of ... an ultimate Utopian instant might be like: this ... is the most genuine function of music as a limited and yet pure feeling of that unity of outside and inside which Utopia will establish in all the dimensions of existence'.[5] Bloch goes further: through its capacity to communicate that which is not (yet) utterable, music is uniquely capable of conveying *and effecting* a better world; it invokes, as well as prefigures, that world.

> [M]usic as a whole stands at the frontiers of mankind, but at those where mankind with new language and the *call-aura around captured intensity, attained We-World,* is still only forming. And precisely the order in musical expression intends a house, indeed a crystal, but from future freedom, a star, but as a new earth.[6]

and

> Musical expression as a whole is thus ultimately a *vice-regent for an articulation which goes much further than anything so far known* ... Thus music is that art of pre-appearance which relates most intensively to the welling core of existence ... of That-Which-Is and relates most expansively to its horizon; – *cantus essentiam fontis vocat* [singing summons the existence of the fountain].[7]

Bloch does not claim that all music possesses this quality and would agree that it can be present in distorted or diminished form. Just as incipiently utopian wishes may be only those the powerful want people to have, Bloch notes that for every *La Marseillaise* which calls people to transformative action 'there are a hundred thousand "folk songs" of the nineteenth century, designed to leave no room for any thought', and that '[d]runken music ... sustains an unconsolable life by administering consolation' in ways that sustain divisions between poor and rich.[8] We should add that music has been and is used as an instrument of torture, a support to oppressive regimes, an accompaniment to spectacle and a commodity within market capitalism. Nor is this an issue of 'good' versus 'bad' music as Bloch seems to suggest. The ambiguous role of seductively beautiful and splendid music is figured in the utopian tradition itself. Ursula Le Guin's 'The Ones Who Walked Away From Omelas' contrasts the exquisite flute playing of a young boy with the misery of the imprisoned child on whom that possibility, and the society itself, depend. *Slaves of the Mastery*, the second volume of William Nicholson's *Wind on Fire* dystopian trilogy, portrays a dictatorial regime that suppresses dissent by murdering the relatives of troublemakers. It is nevertheless a beautiful place, and a spectacular public event involves choreographing massed choirs and orchestras to produce wonderful music amid splendid architecture – as well as fights to the death.[9]

For Bloch, music remains a vehicle of possibility even in the face of death, that greatest barrier to utopia: 'If death, conceived as the axe of nothingness, is the harshest non-utopia, then music measures itself against this as the most utopian of all arts'.[10] It is an idea with deep roots in Western culture, expressed in the Orpheus myth. Orpheus went down into the underworld to bring back his lost wife from the dead. The beauty of his playing on the lyre won him leave to restore Eurydice to life, on condition that he did not look at her until she reached the surface of the earth. Orpheus guided Eurydice up to the sunlight with the sound of music, but he turned too soon and lost her forever. The myth affirms the power of music in the face of death, yearning and ultimately irreparable loss, while the name of Orpheus recurs through musical history.

Bloch turns not to Orpheus but to the requiem to explore music's capacity to carry the deepest sense of loss and redemption, again claiming 'the symbols of expectation which are at work in the requiem' are 'inscribed in the music'.[11] Neither of the works Bloch makes central is a requiem mass. He reads (hears?) Beethoven's opera *Fidelio* as a secular requiem with iconic utopian status: *'If one seeks musical initiation into the truth of utopia, the first, all-containing light is Fidelio'*.[12] He interprets the trumpet call which overtly announces the arrival of a key character as announcing 'the arrival of the Messiah', and quotes Verdi's Requiem, *Tuba mirum spargens sonum* (The trumpet scattering its amazing sound).[13] His own messianism is reflected in his response:

> Every future storming of the Bastille is intended in Fidelio, an incipient matter of human identity fills the space in the sostenuto assai … Beethoven's music is chiliastic … more than anywhere else music here becomes morning red, militant-religious, whose day becomes as audible as if it were already more than mere hope. It shines as pure work of man.[14]

Bloch quotes from Brahms's German Requiem, which has a biblical rather than a liturgical text. 'For here we have no continuing city, but we seek one to come'; 'Behold I shew you a mystery: We shall not all sleep, but we shall all be changed'; 'Therefore the redeemed of the Lord shall return, and come with singing unto Zion; and everlasting joy shall be upon their head'.[15] The music, he argues, signals something more profound:

> all music of annihilation points to a robust core which, because it has not yet blossomed, cannot pass away either; it points to a non omnis confundar. In the darkness of this music gleam the treasures which will not be corrupted by moth and rust, the lasting treasures

in which will and goal, hope and its content, virtue and happiness could be united as in a world without frustration, as in the highest good: – *the requiem circles the secret landscape of the highest good.*[16]

Music and narrative content

Bloch emphasizes music's utopian content. But the parallels between music and colour or art coalesce into three strands: their inherent orderliness; their abstraction; and their transcendence of concept and language and consequent direct route to and from emotion. Colour and music are patterned wavelengths of light and sound, structured and ordered into visual and aural compositions, and form itself may be utopian. Johann Sebastian Bach's music, especially in the construction of the fugue, is often seen to constitute perfection of form, while the fugue itself had a distinctive place in artistic abstraction, exemplified in the paintings of František Kupka and in attempts by the Bauhaus circle to represent the structure of Bach's music both graphically and sculpturally.

Music's 'abstraction' in the sense of transcending verbal language is critical for Bloch: it has a 'latent expressive power which goes beyond all known words'.[17] Music succeeds where words fail, as Gustav Landauer insisted they must: 'Doesn't everyone who has tried to put dreams into words know that the best is dissolved and destroyed when they are cast into a language?'[18] Bloch argues that words are always music's poor relation: 'the note actually *draws* ... whereas the word is just used'.[19] The claim is the same as that made for colour. Musical expression and reception are preconceptual: 'the ear perceives more than can be explained conceptually'.[20] Even in opera and music dramas which constitute a large proportion of Bloch's musical examples, 'the whole of the action that can be spoken is latently overtaken ... by the sounds originating in us, by the subjective streak in the note'.[21] Thus:

> The dark primordial sound of music dissolves every word, even every drama within itself, and the deepest transformations, a multitude of mysterious shapes concealing future revelations, are crowding past us in the singing flames of great music. Hence there is no *great* music at all ... whose prerequisites do not exceed the limits of even the most masterly and polished poetry.[22]

Music can of course be described as a language, but the central point is that it is non-verbal. Thus Daniel Barenboim endorses the view that music's abstraction enables the expression of that which is otherwise literally or politically unutterable: 'Music is ... an abstract language of harmony ... which makes it possible to express what is difficult or even forbidden to express with words'.[23]

It is extraordinarily difficult to separate the utopian resonances of music itself from that of text embedded in it. Tia De Nora rejects the dualism of attempting this, arguing that 'musical and textual meanings are interrelated, co-productive', so that we cannot speak of or decode the 'music itself'.[24] Bloch similarly argued that where text and music work together, the approach of music to the absolute is enhanced. But even he often finds the verbal content more accessible and explicable, so that his practice in identifying the locus of utopian substance is contradictory. His reference to the 'sublimely rich expression' of the duet of the cranes in Bertolt Brecht and Kurt Weill's *Aufstieg und Fall der Stadt Mahagonny* is to the words: 'poetry of extraordinary value and not unworthy of late Goethe'.[25] The musical figure is not mentioned. The centrality given to *Fidelio* (echoed by Adorno, Barenboim and Edward Said) rests on the plot and on the music. Barenboim insists that the focus must be on the music itself. *Fidelio* is a struggle for freedom and a movement from darkness to light; but this same movement is present in Beethoven's non-choral music, not least in his symphonies. Yet he also suggests that Beethoven's purpose in adding the choral and textual element to his Ninth Symphony was in part to make the message of liberation more accessible. At the same time, bringing together such a large number of singers enacts the message of human solidarity.[26]

Privileging a particular artistic form is problematic. Similar claims of utopian power are made for other non-verbal and indeed verbal forms of expression. Moreover there are many cases of the interplay between artistic forms, suggesting that the Blaue Reiter's belief in an underlying inner light, transcendent quality or utopian content can be found elsewhere. T. S. Eliot's *Four Quartets* was inspired by the late Beethoven quartets, while John Miller cites Eliot's poem and the mysticism of St John of the Cross which it reflects as an influence on his painting, especially his interior landscapes. Images inspired by or accompanying words are often more than 'illustration'. In Terry Frost's series of prints accompanying poems by Federico García Lorca, his own desire to communicate emotion through colour and form was intensified by Lorca's words: 'Lorca awakened something in me ... [H]e probes the distance between each emotion'.[27] In the 1930s Christopher Caudwell made strong claims that poetry has a utopian power, possessing both an expressive and an instrumental function and the potential to transform agency and thence the world.[28] George Steiner argues for both music and language. '[M]usic puts our being as men and women in touch with that which transcends the sayable, which outstrips the analysable ... It has long been, it continues to be, the unwritten theology of those who lack or reject any formal creed';[29] yet language, despite its vulnerability to debasement, is the primary 'vessel of human grace'.[30] Steiner describes the (changing) literary and cultural canon as 'the tested and accredited assets of grace',[31] and argues that 'great literature *is* charged with what grace secular man has gained in his experience'.[32]

Music and narrative context

The indivisible relation between language and music is present also in the narrative context – that is, in writing about music. The 'impossibility' of this is widely claimed. Benjamin Korstvedt suggests that Bloch's musical philosophy struggles to verbalize essentially non-verbal experience.[33] Claude Lévi-Strauss regarded music and myth-making as homologous, with music unique among languages in being both immediately intelligible and untranslatable.[34] Even Steiner writes that '[w]hen it speaks of music, language is lame', although this is qualified and historicized by his observation that this idea that music is 'more universal, more numinous than speech, haunts the western imagination'.[35] The music critic Alex Ross insists that it is not 'especially difficult' to write about music, but still says that '[e]very art form fights the noose of verbal description. There is a fog-enshrouded border past which language cannot go'.[36] Perhaps something is always missing, lost in translation. We are, perhaps, looking again at Gage's radical imbalance between sensation and language. Nevertheless, there is a vast amount of writing about music, some of it very fine, including by Adorno, Barenboim, Said, Maynard Solomon and a younger generation including Ross, Barton, Dorian Lynskey and Rob Young. Bloch's own work here conjures rather than describes that which is not yet. It is difficult to separate the utopianism of evocative writing about music from the utopianism of the music itself. And Ross warns of the risks here, of attributing too much to, and expecting too much from, music: 'when we speak of its ineffability we are perhaps protecting it from our own inordinate demands'.[37]

The general lack of overlap between the skills of musicologists and social theorists compounds the problem, although there are notable exceptions. Solomon's analysis of the utopianism of Mozart's *The Magic Flute* addresses both its narrative content and the music. He makes both general and particular claims for the utopian function of Mozart's music: 'The unprovable premise ... is that musical form is capable of symbolizing the process whereby creativity resists the natural tendency of all things to go out of existence, that a composition can stand for a discrete and rounded universe of experience carved out of a surrounding field of tonal disorder and silence'.[38] This is utopia as form, but utopia is also present as content. Solomon cites Schubert, who wrote: 'As from afar the magic notes of Mozart's music still gently haunt me ... They show us in the darkness of this life a bright, clear, lovely distance, for which we hope with confidence. O Mozart, immortal Mozart, how many, oh how endlessly many such comforting perceptions of a brighter and better life hast thou brought to our souls!'[39] Solomon himself makes the general claim that: 'As wish [Mozart's] music tells of the landscapes he wants to inhabit, modelled out of the mythic imagery of the pastoral and Arcadian. As memory, his music tells of what he has experienced. As desire, his music tells of what he wants to enfold in his arms'.[40] More specifically, 'the formal rounding off of Mozart's adagios and andantes may be emblematic ... of the repair of every possible kind of fractured wholeness – a healing of woundedness, a balm to a convalescent soul, a reparation of injustice, a resurrection of those we have lost'.[41] Solomon also argues that Mozart subverts 'the artist/patron/audience compact that provided an easy utopia of present contentment rather than an unreachable utopia of things that are not-yet'.[42] Ross (who remarks that 'Mozart's most striking feature was a pair of intense blue-gray eyes') refers to the 'complex paradise that he created in sound', to the recurrent motif of rising and falling phrases as 'an archetype of love and longing', and to 'the counterpoint and dissonance [which] are the cables on which Mozart's bridges to paradise are hung'.[43] It is precisely the refusal of resolution of dissonant chords that Adorno endorsed in Schoenberg's music, while Schoenberg himself reacted against the romanticism of Max Bruch's 1881 *Kol Nidrei*, a sonorous adagio based on a Hebrew prayer for the Day of Atonement. His own setting of the *Kol Nidrei* in 1938, first performed just over a month before Kristallnacht, was very different. The contrast between them illustrates different possible modes of utopian expression in and interpretation of music. Yet Adorno also responds to music in terms of the double movement of grief and deferred consolation, as in this passage on Schubert:

> In the face of Schubert's music, the tear falls from the eye without first asking the soul: it falls into us, so remote from all images and so real. We weep without knowing why; because we have not yet reached the state promised by the music, and in our unspoken joy,

all we need is for it to assure us that we one day will. We cannot read it; what it holds up to our fading, overflowing eyes, however, are the ciphers of an eventual reconciliation.[44]

Ross also uses utopian language to describe Schubert's music. The principal theme of his B flat sonata 'bestows grace for seven measures'; the String Quintet in C is like 'light pouring in from another world'.[45] Steiner points to the same work, echoing Bloch's claims for the *non omnis confundar*:

> There is music which conveys both the grave constancy, the finality of death and a certain refusal of that very finality. This dual motion ... is made transparent to spiritual, intellectual and physical notice, in Schubert's C-major Quintet. Listen to the slow movement.[46]

Proximity to death recurs in the idea of late style. Adorno defines this not in relation to a composer's biography, but in terms of musical archaisms which have a fracturing effect and which, in Ross's terms, 'suggest alienation from the present or a position outside the flow of time'.[47] But Ross suggests that '[i]n old age, certain composers reach a state of terminal grace in which even throwaway ideas give off a glow of inevitability, like wisps of cloud illumined at dusk'.[48] In late Brahms, the 'tone of late-night consolation' gives way to apocalypse and grace, with several of the late chamber works marked *grazioso*.[49] Brahms's own melancholy utopianism may be reflected in his quotation from Novalis that '[o]ur life is no dream but ought to be and perhaps will become one'.[50] For Ross, the late works contemplate Job's question 'Why is light given? Why go on? What do we have that is better than death?'.[51]

Abstraction, embodiment, duende

Music, like colour, is abstract only in the sense of being non-linguistic. It is also essentially concrete and embodied. In *The Principle of Hope*, Bloch locates the origin of music in the panpipe or shepherd's pipe, invented to call to the distant beloved. He reprises the myth of Syrinx as told by Ovid. Pan pursues Syrinx, who escapes leaving only reeds in Pan's hands, which he fashions into pipes: Syrinx has both vanished and not vanished, remaining in, or as, the sound of the flute. 'Thus music begins longingly and already definitely as a *call to that which is missing*. ... The panpipe ... is the birthplace of music as a human expression, a sounding wishful dream'.[52] The mysterious character of music is also here at the start, originating in a hollow space, and the product of literal disembodiment. But in his earlier essay on *The Philosophy of Music*, which forms a large part of his early work *Geist der Utopie* (*Spirit of Utopia*), Bloch provides a more embodied account of the origins of and the response to music. Here, the human voice is central, and music is precisely 'unabstract' in its dependence on 'the act of utterance' or performance and the equally physical process of hearing.[53] Thus '[t]o become music [the note] is absolutely dependent on the flesh and blood of the person who takes it up and performs it'.[54] In response, we find our way about the musical beat 'by virtue of breathing'; our 'pulses throb audibly'; we understand inflexion in song because 'our own throat, gently innervated in sympathy, permits us to see and understand from within, as it were, what is being directed at us, what is speaking here'.[55]

Barenboim similarly insists on the embodied nature of hearing and listening: 'Music has a power that goes beyond words. It has the power to move us and it has the sheer physical power of sound, which literally resounds within our bodies for the duration of its existence'.[56] Jay Griffiths describes collective singing as 'embodied empathy', as each member of the group feels 'the same music reverberating in their individual bodies'.[57] In a very literal sense, the experience of rhythm and melody in the human voice may be part of our pre-verbal experience. Recent work on human parent-infant bonding suggests that melodic inflection is fundamental here, underlining the relational element in music and musical response. Baby-talk uses pitch variation (together with facial expression and eye contact), not randomly, but in repeated patterns, engaging an infant's attention and connection with the parent.[58] This early experience may contribute to music's continuing emotional appeal.

For early Bloch, the humanly created sound conveys crucial meaning: 'What it contains of the actual person singing, and thus what quality the singer or player "puts into" the note, is more important than what his song contains purely in terms of note-values'.[59] The emphasis on the capacity of the human voice to move us is inscribed in the West Papuan word for soul, *etai-eken*, literally 'the seed of singing'.[60] Ross discusses with the singer Björk the difficulty of simultaneously maintaining accurate pitch and deep emotion, a rare ability. In describing the quality of Lorraine Hunt-Lieberson's voice, his metaphors take messianic and utopian form: loveliness, passion, pain, 'a fearsome kind of anger'; a 'prophet-in-the-wilderness quality', an 'unearthly tranquility', a range from 'angelic serenity to angelic wrath'; voice as 'a kind of moral weapon', 'seared round the edges, raised up like a flaming sword'. [61]

This emotional depth is close to what Lorca calls duende, although for Lorca this is a demonic earth spirit rather than angel or muse. An angel sheds grace from another world, but the duende is a spirit with whom the artist struggles, rising from the soles of the feet through the body with visceral passion, shaking both performer and audience in spontaneous communication. Brook Zern's account recalls Huxley's description of the effects of mescalin: duende 'dilates the mind's eye, so that the intensity becomes almost unendurable. ... There is a quality of first-timeness, of reality so heightened and exaggerated that it becomes unreal, and this is characterized by a remarkable time-distortion effect which is frequent in nightmares'.[62] The power of duende derives from embodiment, from the confrontation with mortality: 'the duende does not come at all unless he sees that death is possible'.[63] It expresses a yearning beyond visible expression, opens the possibility of human communication, understanding and love, and announces 'the constant baptism of newly-created things'.[64]

The use of 'otherworldly' or utopian metaphors may illustrate the limits of language. It may also suggest that, as with colour, music's affective character is associational rather than intrinsic. Some elements of response to music may result directly from our embodied nature. Ross notes that '[t]he music of dejection is especially hard to miss. When a person cries, he or she generally makes a noise that slides downward and then leaps to an even higher pitch to begin the slide again'. This, as David Crystal notes, is the universal pattern of the pain cry of human infants. Ross goes on to identify this pattern in musical laments all over the world. The falling fourth, following the steps of the chromatic scale or minor mode is, he says, 'the same four-note descending figure that has represented sorrow for at least a thousand years'. And:

> Those stepwise falling figures suggest not only the sounds we emit when we are in distress, but also the sympathetic drooping of our faces and shoulders. In a broader sense, they imply a spiritual descent, even a voyage to the underworld ... At the same time, laments help guide us out of the labyrinth of despair.[65]

This musical figure is used for the cry from the cross in *La Pasión Segú San Marcos* by the Argentinian Jewish composer Osvaldo Golijov: 'Abba, Abba, Abba, Abba' is set to descending minor thirds over a basso lamento which repeatedly drops a fourth from tonic or keynote. The same figure characterizes the siguiriya, a Gypsy lament that Lorca identifies as the prototype of Andalusian 'deep song' or *canto jonde*. It carries both loss and longing, and the promise of fulfilment, confronting both love and death. Notice, says Lorca, 'the transcendence of deep song'. It is, he says, 'truly deep, deeper than all the wells and the seas in the world, much deeper than the present heart that creates it or the voice that sings it, because it is almost infinite ... It comes from the first sob and the first kiss'.[66] Deep song 'shoots its arrows of gold right into our hearts. In the dark it is a terrifying blue archer whose quiver is never empty'.[67] As for Bloch, in both duende and deep song, the encounter with death is also the origin of the utopian promise, the *non omnis confundar*, of love.

A similar chromatic downward slide characterizes the blues, another musical form combining grief and loss and their antidote – or even *as* their antidote, for Branford Marsalis describes the blues as 'a kind of emotional vaccination'.[68] For Ross, it is 'full of resilience, even as it heeds the power of fate. The gesture of lament annuls itself and engenders its opposite'.[69] The central protagonist of McEwan's *Saturday*, a highly successful neurosurgeon called Henry, muses on his response to his son Theo playing the blues: 'At the heart of the blues is not melancholy, but a strange and worldly joy'. But Theo's playing also reminds Henry of the limits of what he himself has settled for, and that something is (always) missing:

> Theo's guitar pierces him because it also carries a reprimand, a reminder of buried dissatisfaction in his own life, of the missing element. ... The music speaks to unexpressed longing or frustration, a sense that he's denied himself an open road, the life of the heart celebrated in the songs. ... Theo's playing carries this burden of regret into his father's heart. It is, after all, the blues.[70]

Solomon suggests that 'there is something within each of us that wants to limit the power of the imaginative to touch us, for that may open us to our deepest fears and most regressive yearnings', but also, as perhaps Henry's response suggests, that it 'is only when we feel the power of ... music to bruise us that we can discover its enchanted healing power as well'.[71]

Music as performance

Music is evanescent. It depends upon performance – or, as Barenboim prefers, realization. It is 'sonorous air'; duration and temporality are of its essence.[72] For Barenboim, this gives music its own narrativity towards change: 'The inevitable flow in music means constant movement – development, change, or transformation'.[73] It exists only in relation to the silence against which we hear it and into which it disappears. Bloch identifies the motif of the vanished Syrinx in Berlioz's *Symphonie Fantastique* as the vehicle of 'the unenjoyed … the Not-Yet, indeed even the Never'.[74] The evocation of absence rests on the notes, but only in relation to the silences and pauses around them: for Lorca, all arts are capable of duende, but it 'manifests itself principally among musicians and poets of the spoken word … for it needs the trembling of the moment and then a long silence'.[75]

Not yet. Suspension. Terry Eagleton refers to textual meaning as 'a kind of constant flickering of presence and absence together', and suggests that in reading, the meaning of a sentence is 'always somehow suspended, something deferred or still to come'.[76] Musical suspension is doubly utopian. It occurs within the music itself: Schoenberg's music is said to reflect 'the hollow space of this age and the atmosphere brewing in it, noiseless dynamite, long anticipations, suspended arrivals'; Mahler's *Song of the Earth* 'moves with an unresolved suspension into an immense Eternal, eternal'.[77] But there are recurrent claims that music alters the experience of temporality, takes the listener out of time, suspends time itself. Ross says of John Dowland that 'his forlorn songs have about them an air of luxury, as if sadness were a place of refuge far from the hurly-burly, a twilight realm where time stops for a while'.[78] Richard Dyer says of Hunt-Lieberson that 'time itself stopped to listen'.[79] Potter's plays use musical shifts to suspend reality. Robert Hunter describes Weill's Crane duet as a suspension of *Mahagonny*'s dystopian tableaux, in this case entailing suspensions within the music itself.[80] Luis Romero reflects on the way the musical incursion in the film *The Shawshank Redemption* serves to suspend the oppressive reality of incarceration.[81] Both Hunter and Romero echo an element of the Orpheus myth, where the music of the lyre temporarily suspended the tortures of the damned. And both insist, as does Bloch, that the music is not simply an interlude of consolation, but one which drives forward to transformation, rebellion and revolution.

Ross describes Hunt's voice 'beautiful enough to stop a war if anyone thought to try'.[82] The idea that music can make time stand still and effect peace is utopian indeed. In Nicholson's *The Wind Singer*, which precedes *Slaves of the Mastery*, this is exactly what happens. The city of Aramanth is a meritocracy in which different strata of society are defined by annual examination results and identified by the colour of their clothes and the districts where they live. It also contains a strange ancient construction which makes groaning noises in the wind. After a successful quest, three children return with its silver 'voice', but are pursued by a supernatural army of Zars. Shinning up the tower and re-inserting the voice into the wind singer has a magical effect, suspending enemy action and breaking the spell of the repressive regime of Aramanth itself:

> The wind singer turned in the breeze, the air flowed into its big leather funnels, and found its way down to the silver voice. Softly, the silver horns began to sing. The very first note, a deep vibration, stopped the Zars dead in their tracks. ... And all around the arena, a queer shivery sensation ran through the people. The next note was higher, gentle but piercing. As the wind singer turned in the wind, the note modulated up and down, over the deep humming. Then came the highest note of all, like the singing of a celestial bird, a cascade of tumbling melody. The sounds seemed to grow louder and reach further. ... And all the time, the song of the wind singer was reaching deeper and deeper into the people, and everything was changing. Examinees could be heard asking each other, 'What are we doing here?' ... The families in the stands began to intermingle, and there was a great mixing of colours, as maroon flowed into grey and orange embraced scarlet.[83]

The different utopian representations of music in this trilogy merit a longer discussion than is possible here. The use of music as a means of suspension 'teaches' the child reader about its utopian power. But (like the lesson of the mirror of Erised) it works only because it will be understood – either as a real attribute of music, or its culturally attributed power.

Performance is not unique to music. It spans theatre, musical theatre, opera and dance, as well as readings of poetry and prose and oral traditions of story-telling. But the emphasis on performance underlines the uniqueness of each live event and its historical specificity. Bloch was acutely aware of this. Between publishing *The Philosophy of Music* in 1918 and drafting *The Principle of Hope* in exile in the United States in 1930s, he was closely involved with the Kroll Opera in Berlin. This immersed him in controversial and avant-garde productions. The Kroll's programmes embraced both new music and opera, and new interpretations and stagings of classical and recent works, including both *The Magic Flute* and *Fidelio*. Indeed, Bloch wrote the introductory programme article for the Kroll's opening production of *Fidelio* in 1927. This was an adaptation of Otto Klemperer's 1924 Weisbaden production designed by Ewald Dülberg, who aimed 'to provide a visual accompaniment to the score by means of form, colour and space'. In the closing sequence of the 1924 production, '[t]he prisoners formed an undifferentiated mass with shorn hair and whitened faces and in the finale the chorus was again deployed in static blocks, this time against a brilliant, blue background'. Critics claimed that '[a]ll historical accretions, all implausibilities of plot and text are swept away. Myth emerges from anecdotal story, archetypes out of operatic characters. Most splendid of all, Beethoven is reborn out of the experience of our own time, fashioned out of our feeling for space and sound'.[84]

This practical involvement made Bloch sensitive to the difficulties of cultural reproduction of classic works. If utopian resonance is present 'in the work', it is only communicated in and through a particular production in a particular historical moment, requiring fresh stagings, fresh realizations. Both *The Magic Flute* and *Fidelio* possess cultural surplus. Both works are 'immortal because of their continuing relevance, their ongoing call to action, their posing of new problems'. [85] Precisely for this reason, they cannot simply be reproduced but must be reworked so that the surplus is grounded in the historical conditions of production and reception. When this is successful, as with Klemperer's production of *The Magic Flute,* 'the listeners feel themselves to be not on historical ground but on living earth, and this earth trembles like children do when a fairytale is told'.[86] So also, perhaps, with Peter Brook's and Bouffes du Nord's stripped-down production of the opera in 2011, staged only with movable bamboo poles and focusing attention on the text and the music in an attempt to realize the inner core of the work.

Hunter discusses this problem of the cultural reproduction of utopian content in relation to two collaborative works by Kurt Weill, *Mahagonny* and *Der Silbersee*. In both, meaning is co-produced by music and text, but their utopian functioning differs. *Mahagonny* presents a negation of capitalism rather than an illustration or prescription of an alternative; *Silbersee* prefigures a reconstituted humanity and social order. Both were originally composed and performed in Weimar Germany, although Klemperer's vacillation meant that *Mahagonny* was not, as originally intended, premiered at the Kroll. Hunter asks how, and in what sense, these works can have a utopian function eighty years later, especially where audiences are unaware of the original historical context or where they have been rewritten to make them more 'relevant', more 'accessible' or simply less political. The question is not whether, but how, to update. Some adaptations make no real sense of the original work or of its relationship to the present; the challenge is to demonstrate the recurrent relevance of a work's themes to the lived present.

Music-making as prefigurative practice

Music may also be construed as utopian beyond particular compositions and performances, as a field of cultural production riven by fissures and divisions and competing claims about the relative merits of different musical genres. Ross, who moves between different genres with ease, aspires to the erasure of such boundaries, so that music is just music. This is what he reads as utopian in Björk's music:

> What's most precious about her work is the glimpse it affords, in flashing moments, of a future world in which the ideologies, teleologies, style wars, and subdivisions that have so defined music in the past hundred years slip away. Music is restored to its original bliss, free both from the fear of pretension that limits popular music and of the fear of vulgarity that limits classical music. The creative artist once more moves along an unbroken continuum, from folk to art and back again. So far, though, this utopia has only one inhabitant.[87]

It does, however, have other aspirants. Cellist Yo Yo Ma's Silk Road Project pursues a utopian goal of transcultural understanding through musical fusion. Sixty musicians from twenty-four countries constitute an ensemble working from multiple musical traditions. They work with young people inside and outside formal educational settings, using a variety of techniques: one workshop used the history of indigo to explore themes of cultural diffusion and exchange. The core idea is that collaborative music-making drawing on contrasting traditions enables new music to emerge, and at the same time entails a process of cultural exchange that has wider implications. Ma says: 'By listening to and learning from the voices of an authentic musical tradition, we become increasingly able to advocate for the worlds they represent'.[88]

It is often the social practice of performance as much as the music itself that is ascribed prefigurative or transformative utopian qualities. The imputed relationship between the performers is an ideal form of non-conflictual human connection. McEwan has Henry ponder on:

> these rare moments when musicians together touch something sweeter than they've ever found before in rehearsals or performance, beyond the merely collaborative or technically proficient, when their expression becomes as easy and graceful as friendship or love. This is when they give us a glimpse of what we might be, of our best selves, and of an impossible world in which you give everything you have to others, but lose nothing of yourself.[89]

Henry's musings continue in anti-utopian vein: 'Out in the real world there exist detailed plans, visionary projects for peaceable realms, all conflicts resolved, happiness for everyone – mirages for which people are prepared to die and kill. Christ's kingdom on earth, the workers' paradise, the ideal Islamic state'. But he returns to the assertion of the prefiguration or instantiation of utopia in musical performance: 'But only in music, and only on rare occasions, does the curtain actually lift on this dream of community, and it's tantalisingly conjured, before fading away with the last notes'.[90]

McEwan privileges improvised jazz as the model of this relation, again picking a particular musical genre. Eagleton similarly sees the jazz group as an embodiment of the good life 'where there is no conflict between freedom and the good of the whole'.[91] Holloway uses the metaphor of improvised jazz for ethical social practice.[92] The implicit reference is to the superiority of improvisation over the imputed 'reproductive' character of classical music, misunderstanding both genres. Not all jazz is improvised, and classical music does not simply reproduce what is written: as Barenboim and Said agree, 'the score is not the piece'.[93] Moreover, the connection between players is equally palpable in performances by string quartets, or musicians from folk or other genres. In *Electric Eden: Unearthing Britain's Visionary Music*, Rob Young explores a century of the folk tradition and its transformation: this is utopia as archaeological method. The idea of Albion that flickers through the music is, perhaps, *Heimat*. The story involves recovery and revival, but also a search for alternative musical forms loosely bound up with a quest for a different way of being, the forging of a collective subject and a wider social transformation.[94]

For McEwan, the audience – the subject position of both Henry and the reader – is outside the charmed circle, an observer of the possibility of human connection through music rather than a participant in it. For others, the observer is also participant: the saxophonist John Harle refers to a 'point of grace between audience and performer' which 'only happens live'.[95] Barenboim links the connection between orchestral players and with the audience to the utopian or 'mystical' quality of the music itself:

> [W]hen all things are right on the stage – when the playing, the expression, everything becomes permanently, constantly, interdependent – it becomes indivisible. And this is ... mystical ... that there's suddenly something that you cannot divide any more. The experience of music-making is that ... And when this actually happens ... the active listener ... can communicate with that.[96]

The question of (temporarily) reconstituted relations between musicians and audiences sometimes involves the demarcation of utopian spaces or heterotopias. Rudolf Serkin's annual meeting of musicians at Marlboro Music was intended to 'create a community, almost utopian'.[97] More broadly, music festivals may have this quality of a space out of time, out of the ordinary run of events. Think Woodstock, but also Glastonbury or Womad.

On music education

If music enables qualitatively different forms of social relation that are transformative of people as subjects and agents, music education takes on a utopian quality as a prefigurative practice. Music and dance played a central role in Robert Owen's project for the simultaneous transformation of society and of character at New Lanark in the early nineteenth century. Owen believed that 'any general character, from the best to the worst, from the most ignorant to the most enlightened, may be given to any community, even to the world at large, by the application of proper means'; and physical education was an integral part of the development of character. Observers described both the social cooperation necessary to collective dance displays and the effect on individual children, who are upright, poised, polite, and direct rather than deferential.[98] The endorsement of the 'upright gait', a metaphor of freedom and dignity recurrent in Bloch, is here given literal embodiment. The significance of this is all the greater in historical context – those very times when, as Marx describes in *Capital*, the bodies of child workers elsewhere were being bent, broken and distorted.

Music education still doubles as social education. Venezuela's 'El Sistema' was initially set up in 1979 to prevent poor children from becoming involved in crime and drugs, and to give every child in Venezuela the opportunity to learn a musical instrument, through a network of children's orchestras. Major international attention was attracted when the Simon Bolivar Youth Orchestra played a 2007 Promenade Concert in London conducted by Gustavo Dudamel. In 2008, Richard Holloway, former Bishop of Edinburgh, set up a similar project in Raploch with the arts charity Sistema Scotland. The Big Noise operates in partnership with the BBC Scottish Symphony Orchestra, who perform concerts in the community, and whose individual members mentor the children. Like its Venezuelan model (with which there is a formal knowledge exchange programme), children play and learn collectively in orchestral groups from the outset – although each child also has some individual tuition. The programme is intensive: primary-aged children play for over seven hours a week in term time and twenty hours a week in school holidays. Its objectives include raising aspirations, improving empathy and cooperation, as well as training musicians. An independent evaluation conducted in 2010 concluded that the children involved were happier, more confident, had improved social skills and concentration; that their families were also happier; and that these improvements were more noticeable in children with particular difficulties.[99] The impact was considerable and unequivocally positive, if the long-term aims which included transforming lives, or even effecting social transformation, remain aspirations for the future. In 2012, as part of the Cultural Olympiad surrounding the London Olympics, the Raploch children played alongside members of the Simon Bolivar Orchestra. The evaluation report stresses that the effects derive from this being *music* education: the utopian force lies both in the social process and the musical content. Holloway would demur at the suggestion the project is in any way utopian, for (as we have seen in Chapter 1) he shares the kind of antipathy to utopia exemplified by Gray. But still, the music matters, and Holloway argues that music 'offers to its disciples … moments of grace and transcendence' as well as 'opportunities for protesting against the powerful'.[100]

Just as there is a danger in reading textual utopias as didactic exercises rather than improvisations on the education of desire, there is a risk of reducing the utopian potential of music-making to examples of good behaviour or idealized social relations. Although three pilot projects were set up in England in 2009, the umbrella site emphasized its social character: 'In Harmony will be as much about building life skills, aspirations and self-esteem as it is about nurturing musical talent';[101] 'In Harmony aims to use music as a tool to promote children's personal and social development'; 'The In Harmony programme recognizes the many benefits playing an instrument and playing in an orchestra can bring: concentration, commitment, creativity, teamwork, raising aspirations and self-esteem'.[102] In the public presentation of this programme, there was little sense of music as a source of joy or delight, or of its importance to individual children. The In Harmony pilots were expected to show results within two years, which they did. But the music education review set up by the incoming Coalition government in 2010 expressed doubts about whether this was really 'music education' at all. Rather, it was social action 'which uses music as a tool to deliver change in particularly deprived communities', even if 'the benefit of developing musical skills among the children involved … is an excellent by-product of the programme'. And it was too expensive.[103]

Music education is more than a training ground for social cooperation. In her memoir *All Made Up,* Janice Galloway recalls music, music
lessons and the school orchestra as a protected formative space for both
personal expression and social participation.[104] Music plays a large part
in the second of Edgar Reitz's three epic films *Heimat, Die Zweite Heimat,*
and *Heimat 3. Heimat* is based in the small rural town of Schabbach,
whose communal and familial bonds belong to childhood. 'Home is
something "lost", a longing which never allows itself to be satisfied'.
The twenty-six-hour sequel *Die Zweite Heimat* is set in Munich. The title
translates as 'the second home', one that we choose, find and make for
ourselves as adults. This involves love, friendship and profession – but
these are fragile, rendering the second home always precarious. For the
student artists, it is music rather than Munich that becomes Heimat, the
place where they are at home in the world.[105]

The indivisibility of the social relations of performance and the
place of the music itself pervades Barenboim's accounts of the West-
Eastern Divan Orchestra (WEDO). In 1999, Barenboim and Said set
up the West-Eastern Divan workshops to bring together young musicians across the political divide in the Middle East, initially in Weimar.
The orchestra was subsequently given a permanent home in Seville,
reflecting Andalusia's historic significance as a place where Muslims,
Jews and Christians co-existed peacefully for centuries. The purpose
of WEDO is primarily musical, not the solution of the political problems: for Barenboim, music as 'sonorous air' does not 'solve any problems'.[106] But it can foster a different way of thinking and enable the
construction of a different subject position on the part of the player.
Barenboim argues that music is inherently dialogic. There are different
voices within compositions. Dialogue arises in a complementary way
in the process of performance, because members of a musical ensemble must necessarily play and listen simultaneously. Thus '[i]f you wish
to learn how to live in a democratic society, then you would do well
to play in an orchestra. For when you do so, you know when to lead
and when to follow. You leave space for others, and the same time you
have no inhibitions about claiming a place for yourself'.[107] Orchestral
playing is 'not simply a common activity ... but an existential process
that encourages reflection and understanding'. This becomes utopian
in both a visionary and a transformative sense: 'Through music it is
possible to imagine an alternative social model, where Utopia and prac-
ticality join forces, allowing us to express ourselves freely and hear each
other's preoccupations'. And '[t]he idea of music ... could be a model for
society; it teaches us the importance of the interconnection between

transparency, power and force'. In the end, 'Music teaches us ... that everything is connected'.[108] Barenboim's position here seems close to Adorno's, who, comparing Franz Kafka and Samuel Beckett with the 'engaged' stance of Jean-Paul Sartre and Bertolt Brecht, argued that '[t]he inescapability of their work compels the change of attitude which committed works merely demand'.[109]

Transforming the subject and the world

There is something here, too, about what it means to be human, about what we most deeply are, and what we might become. In *The Principle of Hope*, Bloch refers back to the 1918 edition of *Geist der Utopie* in which he claimed that 'music is one great subjective theurgy' and adds that this theurgy 'proposes to sing, to invoke, that which is essential and most like proper human beings', that which expresses 'adequateness to our own core'.[110] It is partly that 'experience of music provides the best access to the hermeneutics of the emotions, especially the expectant emotions', but also that it touches on the subject as agent, or as the agent that is still forming, is not yet.[111] It is the music, not just the social process of its realization, that is active here. The relation to the latent subject is a key element of music's importance, and a contributory reason why the 'language sought and intended in music ... lies much further beyond existing designations ... than any other art'.[112] It conveys 'intensive root, signalled social tendency', and moves 'towards the *wellspring sound of as yet unachieved self-shaping in the world*'.[113] This reaching to a latent subject does not presume an essential human nature so much as a route to possibility, a 'cracked, cracked-open nature, a nature illuminable into regnum hominis'.[114] Or as Leonard Cohen put it, '[t]here is a crack, a crack in everything: that's how the light gets in'.[115] Music drives towards the 'core of human intensity'.[116] Or again:

> this world is not that which has already become but that which circulates within it, which, as the regnum hominis, is imminent only in future, anxiety, hope. The relation to this world makes music, particularly in social terms, seismographic, it reflects cracks under the social surface, expresses wishes for change, bids us to hope.[117]

Beethoven is central in terms of the pre-appearance of a particular human subject whose 'voice becomes cries for help and of outrage', 'whom nothing in this illusory life satisfies, who stands above even the highest level of what the real world can encompass, who like the genius of music itself is exemplified or welcomed nowhere in the world'.[118] Bloch clearly saw music as a revolutionary force, but a revolutionary force mediated by this transformation of subjects and agents. In his review of *The Threepenny Opera,* he wrote:

> But whereas music cannot change a society, it can, as Wiesengrund [Adorno] rightly says, signalize an impending change by 'absorbing' and proclaiming whatever is decomposing and re-forming beneath the surface. Most of all it sheds light on the impulses of those who would be marching towards the future in any case, but can do so more easily with its help.[119]

There is a chorus of assent. De Nora insists that music is constitutive of agency, seeing it as a resource with and through which people construct and configure themselves as agents. Golijov says that 'Music is a way to map, in sound, the human soul'.[120] For Ross, '[t]he difficult thing about music writing in the end, is not to describe a sound but to describe a human being'.[121] Steiner claims 'the matter of music to be central to that of the meanings of man', so that '[t]o ask 'what is music?' may well be one way of asking 'what is man?''.[122] Barenboim goes beyond musical performance as social education, or the claim that the relations between players prefigure those of a better world. Rather, there is something *in the nature of music itself and our making of it* which reforms us as subjects and agents, and thus both conjures the possibility of a new world and moves towards it. Hunter suggests that the whole social and cultural formation, not just the immediate space of the work's production, is implicated in the possibility of articulating this utopian power: it is 'necessary for artists, producers, critics, and cultural commentators to share that same sense of mission that Weill and his fellow artists had about the possibility of influencing a new cultural formation. They ... need to be joined ... with a social movement informed with the hope of an attainable future, one brought under our collective control'.[123] This is declared again in song. Blake's *Jerusalem* – 'bring me my bow of burning gold, bring me my arrows of desire' – is revisited by Jim Boyes in a call to action, a demand for the instauration of a new utopia: 'Bring back the voice of burning gold/ Stifle the Silver Tongues with fire/ We'll join our hands across the world/ To reclaim what we most desire/ We shall not cease from mental strife/ For Unity is our demand/ And bound together we will rise/ To make this Earth a promised land'.[124]

Part II

4
Between Sociology and Utopia

Wells's claim that 'the creation of utopias – and their exhaustive criticism – is the proper and distinctive method of sociology'[1] implies a different utopian mode from the hermeneutic exploration of desire and of what is missing. If Bloch allows for the expression of utopia to be fragmentary or fleeting, Wells points to an outline of a good society set out with some degree of institutional specificity – in other words, the imaginary reconstitution of society – embedding a normative claim of how society should be. But hermeneutic and constructive methods are connected, for the imaginary reconstitution of society is always essentially an attempt to establish the institutional basis of the good life, of happiness, and the social conditions for grace. This chapter demonstrates the interpenetration of sociology and utopia around the end of the nineteenth century. Chapter 5 shows how the institutional development of sociology, whose onset in the early years of the twentieth century formed the context of Wells's claim, forced the separation of these modes of thought. It led to the expulsion of utopian currents, entrenching the polarities between is and ought, between science and utopia, between thought and feeling, as well as separating the understanding of social life from environmental concerns and limiting the critical power of social theory. In Chapter 6 we will see that a similar retreat to critique afflicted utopia and utopian theory; but in recent years, as Chapter 7 shows, there have been tentative challenges to the entrenched dualism between sociology and utopia, allowing utopia to re-enter social theory but raising questions about its nature and role.

Both utopian and sociological sensibilities informed fictional and non-fictional texts in the late nineteenth and early twentieth centuries. Some of these works written between 1888 and 1905 have become canonical texts in sociology, in the history of utopian thought, in

Marxism, or in feminism. They include Edward Bellamy's *Looking Backward* (1888) and *Equality* (1897); William Morris's *News from Nowhere* (1890); Emile Durkheim's (1893) *De la Division du Travail Social (The Division of Labour in Society)*; Friedrich Engels's *The Origin of the Family, Private Property and the State* (1895); Charlotte Perkins Gilman's *Women and Economics* (1898); and H. G. Wells's (1905) *A Modern Utopia*. The parallels are explored here primarily through the utopian content of Gilman's and Durkheim's sociologies, and the sociological content of the utopias by Bellamy, Morris and Wells, demonstrating the intrinsic relation between the two approaches.

This discussion requires working definitions of both sociology and utopia. In 1959, the American sociologist C. Wright Mills argued that sociology was fundamentally concerned with the relationship between private troubles and public issues and with the intersection of biography and history – how our personal lives are shaped by wider, structural characteristics of our social context and its trajectory in time. What he called the sociological imagination was by no means confined to sociology and was often alarmingly absent from it. For Mills, the core questions concern social structure, history and 'human nature': 'What is the structure of this ... society as a whole? What are its essential components, and how are they related to one another?'; 'Where does this society stand in human history? ... What is its place within and its meaning for the development of humanity as a whole'; and 'What varieties of men and women now prevail in this society and in this period? ... In what ways are they selected and formed, liberated and repressed, made sensitive and blunted?'[2] These questions are directly addressed by the fin de siècle literary utopias, which typically contrast the writer's own society with a better alternative, proffering a holistic account of history, social structure and persons.

Utopia asks additional questions: how might it become and be otherwise, and how *should* it be? Utopia concerns what is not (yet). It is intrinsically evaluative, concerned with what ought to be and the process of conforming the world to that standard. The problematic polarity between 'is' and 'ought' later becomes definitive of sociology. This generates a vantage point in which sociology is the dominant narrative, explaining the various forms and expressions of utopianism in their social contexts as part of cultural anthropology or the history and sociology of culture. If utopia is the expression of what is missing, of the experience of lack in any given society or culture, then a proper understanding of any society must include the consideration of unfulfilled aspirations which it produces. The sociology of utopia defines the legitimate relation between the two. Wells suggests something else. He argues that '[s]ociologists cannot help making Utopias; though they avoid the word, though they deny the idea with passion, their very silences shape a Utopia'.[3] We must consider the utopian assumptions, the assumptions about what should be, in sociology. That is, rather than confining ourselves to the sociology of utopia, we must consider sociology as utopia, as well as utopia as sociology.

Sociology as utopia: Durkheim and Gilman

To describe sociology as utopian is simply to assert without derogation that it contains implicit and sometimes explicit ideas of a good society. It is uncontentious that the origins of sociology, socialism and utopia were intertwined in nineteenth-century Europe, and the emergence of sociology in the United States was equally bound up with utopianism and with forms of prefigurative practice.[4] My argument is that this relationship was not an accidental historical phase which sociology somehow grew out of, but a fundamental congruence, even if the later development of sociology resisted recognizing it. The word sociology itself was coined by Auguste Comte (1798–1857), who, together with the utopian socialist Henri de Saint Simon (1760–1825) and the social Darwinist Herbert Spencer (1820–1903), is commonly identified as a founder of the discipline. Comte was a positivist, arguing that the proper role of sociology was uncovering the laws of development of human history, both in relation to statics (social order) and dynamics (social change). He also argued for a scientific organization of society matching individual aptitudes to occupational roles, a view shared by Durkheim, Bellamy and Wells. In this new social order, economic or temporal power would need to be balanced by spiritual power, so Comte proposed a new religion of humanity with a priesthood of social scientists that would fulfil this function. Raymond Aron reads Comte as both anti-utopian and utopian: 'hostile to … the utopias of the reformers' because of their voluntaristic suppositions about social change, but '[a] utopian, dreaming of a future more perfect than any known society',[5] one who made 'an exact diagram of his dreams'.[6]

The opposition between science and utopia to the detriment of the latter is reflected in the term utopian socialism, applied by Marx and Engels to Owen, Fourier, Saint Simon, and others. Those same 'utopians' accepted the antinomy but regarded themselves as wholly scientific. Fourier insisted: 'What is Utopia? It is the dream of well-being without the means of execution, without an effective method. Thus all philosophical sciences are Utopias, for they have always led people to the very opposite of the state of well-being they promised them'.[7] It is common now for Marx to be described as utopian: this is a recurrent element of the conventional anti-utopian case, where Marx is held responsible for all the (real and imputed) negative consequences of the Bolshevik Revolution. It is also problematic, certainly in Aron's terms, because Marx held that the historical determination of human nature made it impossible to define the needs and wants of future generations. Consequently he refused to spell out the institutional forms of future society, as well as rejecting idealist and voluntaristic models of social change. Nevertheless, together with the still most powerful analysis of the structures and processes of the capitalist society we inhabit, there are identifiable elements of the good society detectable in Marx; and all of his writing is infused with the passionate desire for the world to be otherwise.

It is less conventional to describe Durkheim as utopian, and Durkheim, like Marx, was explicitly antipathetic to utopia. But in *The Division of Labour in Society*, which is a canonical work in the history of sociology, Durkheim construes the actual state of the world as pathological, contrasted with a benign normality which should have emerged, and which must and will. He argues that society evolves from simpler to more complex forms as population pressure drives an increasing division of labour. This produces a change in the basis of social cohesion. Mechanical solidarity deriving from the similarity of constituent individuals and their social function gives way to organic solidarity deriving from their differentiation and interdependence. The change is both economic and moral. In complex societies the shared beliefs, attitudes and dispositions that characterize earlier modes do not disappear, but they become general and abstract rather than specific and prescriptive. This leads to greater generality and abstraction in legal codes, and a shift from purely repressive law and punishment to a predominantly restitutive framework.

The last section of Durkheim's book is subtitled 'abnormal forms'. The very idea of normality and abnormality deployed here is utopian. The 'normal' is hypothetical and exists nowhere in reality. It is anticipatory, appealing to a better future state against which present reality can be judged. The anomic division of labour deriving from lack of regulation, the forced division of labour, and the reduction of economic activity resulting from lack of coordination are all presented as observable aspects of contemporaneous society, but as 'devious forms' or departures from the right. Understanding these pathological forms 'in which the division of labor ceases to bring forth solidarity' is a route to understanding the conditions of the 'normal' state.[8] The anomic division of labour manifests as economic crises and industrial conflict, revealing that organic solidarity – social cohesion through interdependence – depends on 'adequate regulation', juridical rules, and an enforcing state. It also indicates the need for intermediary institutions between individual and state, for 'there must ... exist, or be formed, a group which can constitute the system of rules actually needed'. These should be modernized versions of guilds or corporations, in which people are grouped 'according to the particular nature of the social activity to which they consecrate themselves', as the occupational milieu rather than the family becomes dominant.[9]

Conflicts between capital and labour also result from the forced division of labour, in which 'the distribution of social functions' does not correspond to 'the distribution of natural talents'.[10] Durkheim argues that occupational aptitudes are cultural rather than hereditary and advocates perfect social mobility. One necessary foundation of this is perfect equality of condition, including the radical abolition of inheritance. All external inequality compromises organic solidarity through the maldistribution of workers to occupations and through its effect on contracts: 'as long as there are rich and poor at birth there cannot be just contract' nor 'a just distribution of social goods'.[11] The issue is not just the ownership of wealth but 'the regulation of the activity to which these riches give rise'; this means that '[i]t will be necessary that in each occupation a body of laws be made fixing the quantity of work, the just remuneration of the different officials, their duties towards each other and towards the community'.[12]

The third abnormal form, lack of coordination, results in unemployment and underemployment, which are wasteful. The normal effect of the division of labour is to increase the continuity and intensity of work, so the 'deplorable loss of effort' undermines social cohesion.[13] Solidarity declines because the activity of each worker, and therefore their participation in the whole, is lower than 'normal' – and this notwithstanding Durkheim's recognition that 'work is still for most men a punishment and a scourge'.[14] Maintaining a proper level of economic activity again requires regulation by the state.

Can the idea of organic solidarity be globalized? Durkheim notes that '[m]en have long dreamt of finally realizing in fact the ideal of human fraternity' and that such aspirations 'can be satisfied only if all men form one society, subject to the same laws'. At present there are too many 'intellectual and moral diversities ... on the earth' for such a thing to be possible. But '[i]f the formation of a single human society is forever impossible, a fact which has not yet been proved, at least the formation of continually larger societies brings us vaguely nearer the goal'. It would depend on the further development of functional specialization: 'We can then formulate the following proposition: the ideal of human fraternity can be realized only in proportion to the progress of the division of labor. We must choose: either to renounce our dream, if we refuse further to circumscribe our activity, or else push forward its accomplishment'. [15]

Organic solidarity changes people. Here Durkheim's discussions hover on the edge of dystopia. The division of labour is driven by structural processes, the increase in volume and density of population, not by the pursuit of happiness. For Durkheim, happiness depends on the fit between socially generated needs and wants and socially available satisfactions, so that it varies both between and within societies. Consequently 'savages are quite as content with their lot as we can be with ours'; the happiness 'of lower societies cannot be ours'; and 'the happiness of man is not that of woman', since '[b]y constitution woman is predisposed to lead a life different from man'.[16] The division of labour produces changes in the moral order and in the kinds of people needed, and therefore valued, for the cohesion of the whole. It requires specialized functionaries rather than rounded persons. Thus 'in higher societies, our duty is not to spread our activity over a large surface, but to concentrate and specialize it. We must contract our horizon, choose a definite task and immerse ourselves in it completely, instead of trying to make ourselves a sort of creative masterpiece, quite complete, which contains its worth in itself and not in the services that it renders'. The socially constituted nature of man in advanced society is 'to be an organ of society', and the socially sanctioned proper duty that derives from this is to play that role, rather than indulge the egotistical pursuit of a general humanistic culture.[17] As Thomas Carlyle remarked sardonically in *Past and Present*, 'The latest Gospel of this world is, Know thy work and do it'.[18]

This emergent expectation is reflected in a suspicion of the aesthetic. Art is the domain of liberty, a luxury, an end in itself – and thus the antithesis of morality, which implies obligation. 'It might even be contended that in the case of individuals, as in societies, an intemperant development of the aesthetic faculties is a serious sign from a moral point of view'.[19] And '[t]oo much idealism and moral elevation often deprives a man of the taste to fulfill his daily duties. In general, the same may be said of all aesthetic activity; it is healthy only if moderated.

The need of playing, acting without end and for the pleasure of acting, cannot be developed beyond a certain point without depriving oneself of serious life. Too great an artistic sensibility is a sickly phenomenon which cannot become general without danger to society'.[20] Privileging a wide-ranging knowledge of humanistic culture over the practice of a socially useful skill is, from the point of view of the emergent society, flabby dilettantism: '[T]he categorical imperative of the moral conscience is assuming the following form: *Make yourself usefully fulfill a determinate function*'.[21] And be careful what it is: don't put your son on the stage, Mr. Worthington.

Durkheim contends that sociology has a role in social reform: 'Although we set out primarily to study reality, it does not follow that we do not wish to improve it; we should judge our researches to have no worth at all if they were only to have a speculative interest. If we separate carefully the theoretical from the practical problems, it is not to the neglect of the latter; but … to be in a better position to solve them'.[22] But for Durkheim, as for Aron, to be utopian is something else entirely. It means to specify the future good society in detail, to be unrealistic, and to adopt voluntaristic models of social change. Saint Simon qualifies as utopian for offering an overly detailed account of the proper organization of industrial society. Sociologists should avoid utopianism by confining their proposals to 'general principles as they appear from preceding facts'.[23] The boundary between general principles and excessive detail is, of course, debatable. We have 'utopia in the proper sense of the word, when a desirable ideal … is presented as executable by the turn of the hand or with processes of child-like simplicity'.[24] In contrast, Durkheim claims he is realistic, knowing 'only too well what a laborious work it is to erect this society where each individual will have the place he merits, will be rewarded as he deserves, where everybody, accordingly, will spontaneously work for the good of all and of each'.[25] He rejects idealist models of social change. We cannot choose solidarity, because it is an emergent property of social structure rather than the product of ethical commitment. If 'the first work is to make a moral code for ourselves' fit for the realities of modern life, '[s]uch a work cannot be improvised in the silence of the study; it can arise only by itself, little by little, under the pressure of internal causes which make it necessary'.[26]

Nevertheless, *The Division of Labour* contains an image of a good society that can be facilitated by human agency, and it draws this by juxtaposing pathological reality with utopian possibility posited as normality. In *The Rules of Sociological Method*, Durkheim attempts without success to find an objective basis for distinguishing the normal from the pathological.[27] It could be argued that Durkheim is here using a utopian method to reveal the shortcomings of the present, but ultimately he identifies the utopian figure as a goal. *The Division of Labour* concludes that 'the service that thought can and must render is in fixing the goal that we must attain. That is what we have tried to do'. There is a caveat: 'In the present state of knowledge our approximation will be clumsy and always open to doubt'; but this caveat is about the limitations of existing knowledge, not its necessary contingency.[28]

Charlotte Perkins Gilman: *Women and Economics*

Reading Durkheim is exasperating, not because he uses the generic masculine like most writers at the time, but because in his case men means men. The social division of labour is distinct from the sexual division of labour. He assumes that organic solidarity means the interdependence of men through work, with women appended to this through conjugal solidarity based on difference. Women properly take care of the affective functions in society and men the intellectual functions. His argument is largely based on the historical anthropology of *Ancient Societies* (1877) by Lewis Henry Morgan. Both historically and in existing less developed societies, Durkheim argues, there is less physical difference between men and women. Sexual selection means that women have become both relatively weaker and less intelligent.

Not all fin de siècle sociology was quite so androcentric. Charlotte Perkins Gilman's *Women and Economics* was published just five years after *The Division of Labour* and mounts an excoriating critique of the position of women. Gilman defined herself as a sociologist, claiming Lester Ward and Patrick Geddes as two major influences on her work. Her move to the utopian mode both within and beyond *Women and Economics* is more overt than Durkheim's. Her later non-fiction works include *The Home: Its Work and Influence* (1903), *Our Androcentric Culture* (1911) and *His Religion and Hers* (1923). *Herland*, one of a series of utopias, was serialized in *The Forerunner* in 1915, although not published in book form until 1979. Here, a sociologist is among the three male visitors to the all-female society, and the only one who is presented sympathetically.

Women and Economics also makes an evolutionary argument. Gilman sees as peculiar to humans the dependence of females on males for the basic necessities of life. The process of sexual selection involved in this has led to an exaggerated difference between the sexes. Like Durkheim, she argues that in more primitive societies, women are stronger, and more able to run, hunt and provide for themselves. Both sexual selection and social conditions contribute to women's relative weakness and produce their lack of capacity to undertake real work outside the home. Man and woman are forced into the roles of provider and dependant. 'The poet and novelist, the painter and sculptor, the priest and teacher', says Gilman, 'have all extolled this lovely relation. It remains for the sociologist, from a biological point of view, to note its effects on the constitution of the human race, both in the individual and in society'.[29]

Gilman argues that 'a civilized State is one in which the citizens live in organic industrial relation'. However, all human progress has been achieved by men. Women have been excluded, integrated only through their sexual and reproductive function; men are fully human, women 'checked, starved, aborted in human growth'. [30] This gender inequality and the economic dependence of women is bad for them and for humanity as a whole. Women are debarred from productive activity and specialize in consumption, a double waste:

> Much, very much, of the current of useless production in which our economic energies run waste – man's strength poured out like water on the sand – depends on the creation and careful maintenance of this false market, this sink into which human labor vanishes with no return. Woman, in her false economic position, reacts injuriously upon industry, upon art, upon science, discovery and progress ... And, in the external effect upon the market, the oversexed woman, in her unintelligent and ceaseless demands, hinders and perverts the economic development of the world.[31]

Once the sexual division of labour was advantageous; now it is not. As social development increases, the emphasis on woman's role as mother becomes damaging: indeed, Gilman describes as pathological both motherhood and childhood as they are presently constituted and argues that the more women are forced into economic dependency, the more pathological does this relationship become. In reality, says Gilman, women embark on maternity without appropriate education for it, so are unskilled. As homemakers they undertake a range of household tasks, including the selection and preparation of food, in an equally unskilled manner. She sees a less pathological condition emerging in the 1890s marked by women's increasing independence. Gilman, like Durkheim, contends that the forces producing this change are structural, not ideological. Social organization has produced ever greater individualization 'which has reached at last even to women', combined with greater social consciousness, while at the same time women inherit from men a drive to specialization.[32] The women's movement is the result, not the cause, of this social development, entailing a real change in their capacities as part of a wider social progress.

Sociological observation and utopian aspiration are combined in the identification of tendencies within the real. The emergent condition includes the division of labour of women's work, leading to specialized functions (like cooking) conducted outside the home. Gilman's prescriptions draw on a tradition of cooperative housekeeping in the United States in the second half of the nineteenth century, present both as utopian aspiration and as prefigurative practice, and drawing on the influence of Charles Fourier and Arthur Brisbane. Gilman synthesizes rather than invents these themes, presenting them as a move to greater social efficiency.[33] She prescribes and predicts kitchenless houses and apartment hotels, where nutritious and well-prepared meals, far superior to most home cooking, are ordered in as required. Cleaning should become a specialized, commercial and increasingly mechanized function. Children should be cared for by professional nurses and teachers in purpose-built premises. Women will, of course, choose professions compatible with maternity, so home and family will be enhanced rather than undermined by stripping away the present medley of inefficient services it provides. The normal division of labour, increasing specialization and the resultant organic solidarity proposed by Durkheim is here extended to women's work and the domestic sphere. As with Durkheim, we have a historical account of how current conditions have emerged; an account of the present condition of the (sexual) division of labour in society, its faults and how it is changing; and a projection of an emergent utopian state, here the economic independence of women, benefiting all humankind.

Utopia as sociology: Bellamy, Morris, Wells

If sociology embeds utopia, literary utopias similarly involve sociological analysis. Such utopias proliferated after 1870 in the aftermath of the Paris Commune and with the onset of economic depression, declining according to some commentators from the turn of the century, and according to others from the outbreak of the 1914–18 war.[34] Like all forms of nineteenth-century social commentary, from the social realist novel to sociology, utopian writing confronts the problem of understanding a rapidly changing present from within – what Bloch repeatedly describes as the darkness of the lived moment. Krishan Kumar argues that in the case of sociology this difficulty leads to an abbreviation of the historical process, in which future trends are collapsed back into the present.[35] Matthew Beaumont suggests that the utopian perspective solves this problem by offering a base outside, in the future, providing a different vantage point.[36] The present is seen through the lens of a putative future, which both brings into focus particular features of the present, and provides a perspective which tends to stretch rather than compress history. However, Beaumont also argues that fin de siècle texts, with the notable exception of Morris's *News from Nowhere*, represent a premature resolution of conflicts that could not be resolved in reality, so that many of them posit change without change in the fundamental structure of society, preserving the position of the middle classes and allaying their fears.

Reading these texts as sociology emphasizes content over form. In Chapter 6 we will return to the complex issue of how literary form works to inform the content, function or effect of a text, and the limits and merits of straightforward and literal readings. However, these portrayals of utopian societies address Mills's questions about the social and institutional structure, place in history, and human inhabitants of the alternative world. The description as an integrated whole of the social institutions and practices of the new world makes them incipiently sociological. But literary utopias are always intended – and predominantly read – as a criticism of the present, and thus also embed a sociology of the originating society. They represent and explain the institutions and practices of the society from which they arise, offering accounts of how its substantive irrationalities produce negative outcomes. They contain narratives of the place in history of both originating and alternative societies, of how we got *here* and how we might get *there*. They delineate the future as a criticism of the present, and also, as Beaumont emphasizes, reconstruct the present as the prehistory of the future. We need therefore to explore what our key texts claim for the future but also what they claim about the present, and – in so far as they address this – what they claim about the process of transition.

Looking Backward

Bellamy's *Looking Backward* was published in 1888, five years before Durkheim's *Division of Labour*. By 1890, it was selling 10,000 copies a week. By 1898, over a million copies had been sold in Britain and America, and it had been translated into fourteen European languages, as well as Chinese, Japanese and Hebrew.[37] The response was both literary and political. A swathe of fictional responses followed. Others, such as Beatrice Webb's *Looking Forward*, were planned but never written.[38] Nationalist Clubs propagating Bellamy's views sprang up across the United States. The radical London publisher William Reeves issued a series of fictive and factive texts under the banner of a Bellamy Library. There is no evidence that Durkheim read Bellamy, although the French philosopher Charles Secrétan, whom Durkheim quotes in the introduction to *The Division of Labour*, certainly did, writing his own utopia in response; another French sociologist, Gabriel Tarde, had published a utopia, *Fragment d'histoire future*, which he described as a sociological fantasy, in a sociological journal in 1876.[39] Readers and writers moved between fictional and non-fictional forms, and the parallels between Durkheim and Bellamy show the interpenetration of sociology and utopia. Indeed, one critic described *Looking Backward* as 'a philosophical, encyclopedial histoury [sic] reaching searchingly to the core of sociological problems'.[40]

Looking Backward compares the state of Boston with its potential future through the eyes of Julian West. A chronic insomniac, West is placed in a hypnotic trance in a sealed underground vault in 1887. His house is destroyed by fire overnight, and West sleeps on until disinterred and woken in the year 2000. His hosts, Dr and Mrs Leete and their daughter Edith, introduce him to the new rational society. Utopian Boston is a clean, smoke-free city with copious greenery and splendid buildings, including public art galleries whose contents are not described. Bellamy presents a version of state socialism in which most of the functions of the state have withered away in favour of the administration of things. Coordination of production and distribution takes place through the 'industrial army', in which everyone (except mothers) participates between the ages of twenty-one and forty-five. The workforce is differentiated by gender and by occupational specialization, and social solidarity, as for Durkheim, derives from the interdependence of function. Everyone receives the same pay in the form of credits allocated by the state and exchangeable for goods and services. The central administration fixes price and hours of work in different occupations and regulates supply and demand. Household organization is similarly efficient. Most meals are taken at local restaurants, but the nuclear family is preserved, together with private dining rooms. Boston's inhabitants are recognizable as idealized versions of the Victorian bourgeoisie: women shop, and men sit up talking and smoking cigars late into the night.

One contemporary reviewer complained that '[t]he absence of art, literature, privacy, individuality in the pictured life is more than the French critic can bear'.[41] Yet West is told that after completing their required work, Boston's citizens enjoy a long and healthy retirement dedicated to life's proper goals of social, artistic and spiritual enjoyment. Artists and writers (like teachers, doctors and priests) are bought out of the industrial army by public demand for their services. Curiously, musicians are part of organized labour. Professional musicians perform without audiences in the sequestered spaces of acoustically perfect halls. Musical consumption is privatized, with a varied programme available on demand in individual homes and at each bedhead. There is no collective amateur music-making as professional standards makes this pointless, although some do play instruments for pleasure and we are told everyone can sing. There is, however, no live music, so Harle's point of grace between audience and performer does not happen at all. Music-making is a prefigurative social practice only in its consummate efficiency. (In contrast, sport is entirely non-professional, and there are no monetary rewards for prowess.) West's response is that if in 1887 'we could have devised an arrangement for providing everyone with music in their homes, perfect in quality, unlimited in quantity, suited to every mood, and beginning and ceasing at will, we should have considered the limit of human felicity already attained, and ceased to strive for further improvements'.[42]

Bellamy's account of nineteenth-century Boston anticipates Durkheim's discussion of abnormal forms. Recurrent economic and financial crises and strikes have an increasing impact as the size of enterprises increases: this is the anomic division of labour. Polarization between rich and poor and a mismatch of talents to occupations, the forced division of labour, is overcome by the education system in utopia. Substantial proportions of labour and capital lie idle in a lack of coordination mirroring Durkheim's third abnormal form: 'Four-fifths of the labor of men was utterly wasted by the mutual warfare, the lack of organization and concert among the workers'. In the new society, the four great wastes have been abolished: waste by mistaken undertakings; waste from competition; waste by periodic gluts and crises; and waste from idle capital and labour, including parasitic occupations. West asks 'What have you done with the ... bankers? Hung them all, perhaps ...?'. No, merely abolished them; for those who think the financial sector is the core of the economy mistake 'the throbbing of an abscess for the beating of the heart'. [43]

The calm of the new society pervades its inhabitants and contrasts sharply with the old capitalist world, the people in it, and West's own emotional turbulence. In the closing chapter, West dreams himself back in his own time with the perspective of the future – perhaps the intended effect on the reader. He sees extreme inequality, ubiquitous advertising, miles of stores with elaborate window-dressing to attract custom, a complicated financial system, and the anxious faces of all classes. Money is necessary only 'because the work of producing the nation's livelihood, instead of being regarded as the most strictly public and common of all concerns, and as such conducted by the nation, was abandoned to the hap-hazard efforts of individuals'. His growing alienation from visible commercial activities accompanies mounting horror and guilt at the plight of the poorest in Boston's rookeries. Their faces reflect dead souls within, yet 'superimposed upon each ... I saw the ideal, the possible face that would have been the actual if mind and soul had lived' – what might have been, were society otherwise. He counterposes their descendants in utopia, 'stood up straight before God'. When West harangues his fiancée's family about the need for change, he is ejected with cries of 'Fanatic' and 'Enemy of society'.[44]

Nevertheless change happens. The new society evolves peacefully from the old in a process substantially congruent with Durkheim's putative 'normal' course of the division of labour: 'The solution came as the result of a process of industrial evolution which could not have terminated otherwise. All that society had to do was to recognize and cooperate with that evolution, when its tendency had become unmistakable'.[45] Ever larger monopolies produced widespread industrial unrest, and squeezed out the possibility of individual enterprise, so that small businesses were 'reduced to the condition of rats and mice, living in holes and corners'. By rational consent and political action, the progressive concentration of capital led to its eventual efficient consolidation in the hands of the nation: 'The industry and commerce of the country, ceasing to be conducted by a set of irresponsible corporations and syndicates of private persons at their caprice and for their profit, were intrusted to a single syndicate representing the people, to be conducted in the common interest for the common profit'; and 'it is the business of the administration to keep in constant employment every ounce of available capital and labor in the country'. [46]

News from Nowhere

Bellamy suggests that the transformed society of the future would mean that 'the earth would bloom like one garden, and none of its children lack any good thing'.[47] In *News from Nowhere*, Morris presents us with a future in which 'England ... is now a garden, where nothing is wasted and nothing is spoilt'.[48] But these visions of the future and the processes of transformation they describe are radically different. Morris was not a sociologist, despite affirming in 1881 'I am of course much interested in sociology'.[49] He was a writer, poet, artist, craftsman, successful businessman and political agitator. From 1883 he was a member of a series of explicitly revolutionary Marxist organizations: the Democratic Federation, renamed the Social Democratic Federation; the Socialist League, which seceded from the SDF; and finally the Hammersmith Socialist Society. He subsidized the movement's periodicals, wrote, lectured and spoke on street corners. His utopia, a response to Bellamy, was originally serialized in the socialist paper *Commonweal*. He criticized Bellamy's picture of socialism as overly regimented and mechanized, and for concentrating on the machinery of society rather than the life to be lived within it. Morris contended that 'the multiplication of machinery will just – multiply machinery' and that 'the ideal of the future does not point to the ... reduction of *labour* to a minimum, but rather to the reduction of *pain in labour* to a minimum, so small that it will cease to be a pain'. He insisted that 'the true incentive to useful and happy labour is and must be pleasure in the work itself'.[50]

Domestic labour is treated quite differently by Morris than by Bellamy or Gilman, both of whom regard household work as unskilled and unpleasant and are preoccupied with efficiency. Bellamy radically reduces work within the home through technological change, a position intensified in his later *Equality*. Gilman aims to abolish household labour by introducing kitchenless houses, collectivized childcare and mechanized and commercialized cleaning. Morris largely leaves unchallenged the sexual division of labour in Nowhere – although there are women carvers, and he elsewhere suggests that in a better society women might undertake any work they chose. But he insists that in a future society freed from exploitative relationships people will have to do their own work and take an interest in the details of daily life. He consequently treats household work in all its dimensions as skilled and valuable.

This is a decentralized socialist utopia in which the use of machinery has been radically reduced, though not abolished, and work has become pleasure. Politically, it is based on participatory democracy, and *News from Nowhere* has repeatedly been used to challenge the idea that utopia is necessarily totalitarian. But as a sociology of the future, *News from Nowhere* is far less institutionally specific than *Looking Backward*. The visitor is told that although life is much simplified and freed from 'conventionalities and sham wants', it remains 'too complex ... to tell you in detail by means of words how it is arranged: you must find that out by living amongst us'.[51] Whereas Bellamy claims to have abolished buying and selling but in practice makes this a state monopoly, Morris actually does so: food and goods are produced, but 'markets' are simply collection and distribution points where no money changes hands. The very calculus of production and consumption has been transcended.[52] The 'necessary' gap between wants and satisfactions identified by Davis is here closed by a presumption of plenty, based on abolishing artificial wants. Morris, following Ruskin (and like Gilman) regards most of what is produced in capitalist society as 'illth' rather than wealth: luxuries that do not satisfy real needs, or cheap and shoddy goods bought only by those who can afford no better. As Stephen Arata points out, what Morris represents is not renunciation but simplicity. Luxury and asceticism both constitute 'a deformation of the senses, an estrangement of the body from the body of the world'. Nowhere restores this relationship, so that '[t]he spirit of the new days' is 'delight in the life of the world; intense and overweening love of the very skin and surface of the earth on which man dwells'.[53] Art disappears as a separate category, for it is integrated into the whole mode of production, in the maintenance of the beauty of the world, the construction of wonderful buildings, and the making of beautiful things. Morris insists that 'art, using that word in its widest and due signification, is not a mere adjunct of life which free and happy men can do without, but the necessary expression and indispensable instrument of human happiness'.[54]

The visitor, William Guest, makes two journeys in future England. The first heads westward from Hammersmith to the British Museum through a London largely replaced by a series of villages. The Houses of Parliament are used as a store for manure: 'dung is not the worst kind of corruption'.[55] The second traverses the 137 miles of the Thames linking Morris's two houses in Hammersmith and the Oxfordshire village of Kelmscot. The intervening section is a conversation about the nature and structure of nineteenth-century society and the process of transition – a sociology of the old society and an account of its place in history. The capitalist class has been expropriated in a revolution made violent by state forces, followed by a long period of social development. Paul Meier has argued that Morris gives an orthodox Marxist account of this process: after the seizure of state power and the 'dictatorship of the proletariat', the state withers away and full communism is achieved. Indisputably, there is sociological explanation here mirrored in nonfiction texts and informing political practice. Morris's demonstration of the connectedness of work, art, social relations, space and human happiness is also sociological. His holistic approach, and especially the connection between individual biography and history, is the very essence of the sociological imagination.

A Modern Utopia

Wells's first major literary success was his 1895 novel *The Time Machine,*
followed rapidly by others including *The Island of Dr. Moreau, The War
of the Worlds, When the Sleeper Wakes* and *Love and Mr. Lewisham.* In
1901 his series of articles in the *Fortnightly Review,* published collectively
as *Anticipations,* predicted the future course of social development and
looked to the emergence of a new republic. *A Modern Utopia* was serialized in the same journal in 1904 and published in book form in 1905.
Wells describes it as a 'hybrid', between 'the set drama of the work of
fiction you are accustomed to read' and 'the set lecturing of the essay
you are accustomed to evade';[56] Wolf Lepenies describes it as the epit-
ome of the sociological novel.[57] Wells locates his own work in a genre
of utopian literature stretching back beyond More to Plato. Morris is a
contemporary reference point: 'Were we free to have our untrammelled
desire, I suppose we should follow Morris to his Nowhere, we should
change the nature of man and the nature of things together; we should
make the whole race wise, tolerant, noble, perfect – wave our hands to a
splendid anarchy, every man doing as it pleased him, and none pleased
to do evil, in a world as good in its essential nature, as ripe and sunny,
as the world before the Fall'.[58]

Wells implies that his own project is more realistic, yet *A Modern Utopia*
is set on another planet rather than in the trajectory of evolutionary
or revolutionary progress common to Durkheim, Gilman, Bellamy and
Morris. This alternative world shares the natural features of earth and
its inhabitants are doubles of the world's population, but both social
organization and the built environment differ. The world state has a
mixed economy. Enterprises such as energy, water and transport are
state-owned, though sometimes coordinated at regional level. Much
production and work comes from private enterprise, but the state is the
employer of last resort, paying a minimum decent living wage. There is
money, but the basic unit against which value is assessed is energy. The
inheritance of productive property but not of private property has been
abolished. Women have greater equality, but generally earn less than
men (because men are better at most things) unless they are mothers,
who are paid by the state. Technological advance enables global freedom of movement, although this is limited by the availability of work
and monitored by detailed surveillance. The system is governed by the
samurai, an elite echoing Plato's Guardians. Members voluntarily subordinate themselves to a quasi-monastic rule, and anyone of sufficient
education, skill and inclination may join. Like Durkheim, Wells extols
regulation, coordination and the reduction of waste: 'the coordination

of activities this smaller waste will measure, will be the achieved end for which the order of the *samurai* was first devised'.[59]

People in Wells's utopia are of four types. The Poietic, or creative, comprise artists, scientists, entrepreneurs; Wells claims that the recognition of the importance of poiesis distinguishes his utopia from all others. The Kinetic are less imaginative but energetic and competent. The Dull lack both energy and imagination, while the Base, who originate in any of the other three classes, are morally deficient. The eugenicist element in *A Modern Utopia* retreats from the more extreme position of *Anticipations*. Procreation is restricted to prevent the numbers of Dull and Base increasing, an issue discussed at length in the early meetings of the Sociological Society at the time. The narrator, whom Wells calls the Voice, wonders whether this will remain a significant issue with high standards of education and social provision. *A Modern Utopia* also posits greater variation within 'races' than between them. Attributing particular national or racial characteristics, when not just wrong, often confuses contingent outcomes of circumstance with inherent traits. The necessarily synthetic culture and language of utopia must draw from human plurality. Differences of temperament and opinion must be accommodated: 'It is not to be a unanimous world any more'.[60] The cultural and religious variety inherent in the global reach of utopia, Wells suggests, imply more general and abstract rules and laws to accommodate variable particulars of ethnic, cultural and local traditions. Echoing Durkheim, The Voice says that the accommodation of difference means that '[t]he tendency of all synthetic processes in matters of law and custom is to reduce and simplify the compulsory canon, to admit alternatives and freedoms'.[61]

Wells shares Durkheim's suspicion of the arts, echoing Plato's ban on dramatic poets and the fear of artistic creativity as a potentially disruptive force. The samurai are expected to cultivate detachment from 'the little graces and delights ... of the daily world', for '[s]uch an order means discipline'. They are forbidden 'the religion of dramatically lit altars, organ music and incense', together with acting, singing and reciting: 'professional mimicry' is undignified and weakens and corrupts the soul.[62] Despite the ostensible value placed on creativity, art and music are not central. The other London celebrates literature, universities, libraries, museums and overarching glass arcades, but not theatres or concert halls. There are artists. In another oblique reference to Morris, we are told they adopt a voluntary uniform of indigo blue.[63] But they cannot join the samurai. Samurai membership requires the possession of skills, such as those of a doctor or lawyer. Musicians occasionally sneak in, to the disapproval of the Voice's double, who complains it is 'catholic to the pitch of absurdity' that '[t]o play a violin skilfully has been accepted as sufficient for this qualification'.[64] Grace inheres in bodily comportment and architecture rather than in the arts. Again we see the figure of the upright gait: a 'free carriage', and 'unaffected graciousness' are visible across society; all are 'graceful and bear themselves with quiet dignity'. The built environment is similarly described as graceful and gracious. These bear witness to something more profound: 'Convenient houses, admirable engineering that is no offence amidst natural beauties, beautiful bodies, and a universally gracious carriage, these are only the outward and visible signs of an inward and spiritual grace'. [65]

Wells pays much less attention to the transition, but he does suggest the emergence of a hidden party of samurai. The agents of change are already among us. The face of a girl with eyes that dream reminds him: 'After all, after all, dispersed, hidden, disorganised, undiscovered, unsuspected even by themselves, the *samurai* of Utopia are in this world'. A movement will build: 'First here, first there, single men and then groups of men will fall into line ... with a great and comprehensive plan wrought out by many minds and in many tongues'.[66] Samurai groups were set up, although Wells resisted involvement in these.[67]

Sociology, utopia and the social imaginary

What emerges from these textual comparisons is a strong commonality between the concerns of sociology and of utopia at the end of the nineteenth century. They suggest that sociology itself has a strong utopian element, while utopia may be usefully understood as an explanatory sociology of past and present and a speculative sociology of the future. Both sociology and utopia form part of what Charles Taylor calls the social imaginary, the ways in which ordinary people 'imagine the societies they inhabit and sustain'. The social imaginary encapsulates the 'ways in which [people] imagine their social existence, how they fit together with others, how things go on between themselves and their fellows, the expectations which are normally met, and the deeper normative notions and images which underlie these expectations'. For Taylor, the social imaginary is intrinsically evaluative, being 'both factual and "normative"'.[68] It is, like sociology, shot through with implicit, unexamined utopias, as well as assumptions about the real, the possible, the probable, the desirable.

Sociology and utopia are similarly engaged in making explicit the processes and relations embedded in the social imaginary, while themselves forming part of it. But they do this in slightly different ways. Sociology foregrounds what utopia backgrounds, while utopia foregrounds what sociology represses. Sociological models are explicitly holistic, descriptive, explanatory and present (or past) oriented. They are, necessarily, imaginary: any model of how society works entails an imaginary reconstitution of society. Sociological models are sometimes explicitly critical, normative and prescriptive, but more usually implicitly so: our very silences shape utopias. Utopian models are explicitly holistic, imaginary, critical, normative, prescriptive and (often) future-oriented. Nevertheless, most of them contain descriptions of present conditions, not just as a foil for the better utopia but as an explanation of how social processes work and therefore what needs to change. In this sense, they are present-oriented. But utopia involves the imaginary reconstitution of society in a slightly different sense: it is the imagining of a reconstituted society, society imagined otherwise, rather than merely society imagined.

As sociology emerged as a distinct discipline, however, the antinomies between utopia and science and between factual and fictive texts were intensified. The sociological content of utopian writing was generally ignored; the utopian content of sociology was frowned on, denied and repressed as it struggled for recognition as a respectable 'science'. The causes and consequences of sociology's denial of utopia are the subject of Chapter 5.

5
Utopia Denied

The textual comparisons in Chapter 4 suggest that utopia may usefully be understood as a form of speculative sociology of the future and an explanatory sociology of the past and present, while sociology has a strong utopian element. Yet to talk of the interpenetration of sociology and utopia at the fin de siècle is anachronistic, for what Mills later called the sociological imagination was widely diffused, and sociology barely existed as a distinct and identifiable discipline. As sociology became institutionalized within the academy, it became consistently hostile to its utopian content. As Bloch complained of Marxism, the cold stream of analysis persistently overrode the warm stream of desire to make the world a better place. The denial of utopia resulted in a triple repression within sociology: repression of the future, of normativity, and of the existential and what it means to be human. It also involved a retreat from active engagement and involvement with a wider public. Despite this, subterranean utopian currents have contributed to sociology's continuing project of social critique.

Institutionalizing sociology

Durkheim gave the first French university course in sociology in 1887. In Britain, the institutional development of sociology was slower and marked by some hostility from academic and scientific organizations. The Sociological Society was set up in 1903 and held its first meeting the following year. Key participants included Patrick Geddes, Victor Branford, Francis Galton, Leonard Trelawney Hobhouse and Wells himself who is listed as a member of the Society's Council. *Sociological Papers* records the proceedings of the first three years, revealing extensive disagreement about the nature of sociology itself, its appropriate methods and its relationship to eugenics, statistics, civics, ethics, social reform and social evolution. Philip Abrams locates over sixty defini-tions of the nature and aims of sociology in these volumes.[1] The sole point of agreement was that the new discipline was to be understood as a science.

Wells presented his paper on 'The So-called Science of Sociology' to the Society in February 1906, the year after the publication of *A Modern Utopia*. A longer and ruder version addressed to a wider public had appeared in the *Independent Review* the previous May.[2] At this time, Wells was becoming a prominent public intellectual. *Anticipations* triggered his friendship with Sidney and Beatrice Webb and his membership of both the Fabians and the Co-Efficients.[3] Wells was also actively lobby-ing for a Chair in Sociology.[4] In April 1904, he complained to Beatrice Webb that by working for nothing she made life more difficult for those without a private income and suggested she should donate her wealth to the London School of Economics and draw a salary. Thus, 'Who is going to pay £1000 a year to research professors when you had turned out the best work for nothing? ... You make it nearly an impossible industry for unsupported persons like myself, & knock all the stuffing out of the arguments that might find a chair of sociology for me – not [Benjamin] Kidd, not Geddes, not that flimsy thing [Edward] Westermarck, but me to fill'.[5] Four months later he wrote again: 'I presume there is no hope of an endowment for me unless I get it myself, & sociology will have to be considered in suspense with me until I've got a war chest'.[6] In May 1905, he wrote directly to the Prime Minister Arthur Balfour (whom he had met through the Webbs), asking for an endowment of £1000 to free his writing from the demand of the market place. 'I have thought, for example, of a text-book of Sociology that I venture would be a seminal sort of work. There's a good deal of activity in the directions of sociology and a certain amount of irregular disorganized endowment & I believe if I could be let loose in this field for a time I could give things a trend'.[7] Balfour passed this request to his Parliamentary Private Secretary, whose response was that he was not convinced 'that Wells was a true genius' and 'that sociology was not an exact science'.[8]

Wells's lecture is usually either ignored completely or treated as a footnote both in accounts of his life and work and in the history of sociology. But given his ambitions and the contested character of sociol-ogy at the time, we should perhaps take it more seriously as a prospectus for a different *and then potentially possible* kind of sociology – a kind of 'Lenin shot at Finland Station' for the discipline which is less repressive of normative and utopian aspects of social understanding.[9] Wells challenges the one point of consensus, namely that sociology should be regarded as, and should aspire to be, a science. Looking back, he said 'I insisted that in sociology there were no units for treatment, but only one single unit which was human society, and that in consequence the normal scientific method of classification and generalization breaks down'.[10] It is an argument against reductionism, and for respecting the level of the social as something indivisible: 'We cannot put Humanity into a museum, or dry it for examination; our one, single, still living specimen is all history, all anthropology, and the fluctuating world of men. There is no satisfactory means of dividing it, and nothing in the real world with which to compare it'.[11] Comte and Spencer are 'pseudo-scientific interlopers', Spencer coming 'near raising public shiftlessness to the dignity of a national philosophy'. [12] In consequence, 'Sociology must be neither art simply, nor science in the narrow meaning of the word at all, but knowledge rendered imaginatively and with an element of personality, that is to say, in the highest sense of the term, literature'.[13] He distinguishes two appropriate literary forms. One involves 'the fitting of "schemes of interpretation" to history', anticipating later arguments following Clifford Geertz that sociology, like anthropology, is best understood as 'thick description'. The second, both 'smaller in bulk' but altogether 'under-rated and neglected', is the creation and criticism of utopias.[14] Wells suggests a project of utopography to map all the different versions of the ideal society, 'a sort of dream book of huge dimensions' and claims this 'would be the backbone of sociology'.[15] The role of utopia is two-fold, and in both cases the relation with sociology is interpenetrating rather than hierarchical. Given the indivisibility of human society and hence the impossibility of comparative method, utopia provides a virtual point of comparison. Max Weber would not have wholly disagreed with this, since he explicitly describes ideal types or conceptual models as utopias.[16]

For Wells, the comparison is also prophetic and normative, measuring what exists against the direction of social development and (simultaneously) against the ideal society. This underpins his view of social action and what sociology is: in *A Modern Utopia*, he defines sociology as '[t]he study of the aggregations and of the ideals of aggregations about which men's sympathies will twine, and upon which they will base a large proportion of their conduct and personal policy'.[17] He argues that the interpellation of utopias is inevitable, and should be explicit than implicit. Similar arguments were to be made throughout the later twentieth century, as the assumptions embedded in 'value-neutrality' were repeatedly exposed. Wells insists:

> There is no such thing in sociology as dispassionately considering what *is*, without considering what is *intended to be*. In sociology, without any possibility of evasion, ideas are facts. ... I submit it is not only a legitimate form of approach, but altogether the most promising and hopeful form of approach, to endeavour to disentangle and express one's personal version of [the Social Idea], and to measure realities from the standpoint of that idealisation. I think, in fact, that the creation of utopias – and their exhaustive criticism – is the proper and distinctive method of sociology ... Sociologists cannot help making Utopias; though they avoid the word, though they deny the idea with passion, their very silences shape a Utopia.[18]

Wells proposes: 'Suppose now the Sociological Society, or some considerable proportion of it, were to adopt this view, that sociology is the description of the Ideal Society and its relation to existing societies, would this not give the synthetic framework Professor Durkheim, for example, has said to be needed?'[19].

But the future of British academic sociology lay in the hands of the London School of Economics, founded by the Webbs in 1895. In 1907, James Martin White endowed the first Chair of Sociology at the LSE, with some expectation that Patrick Geddes would be appointed. There were other contenders, possibly including Wells himself. Eventually Hobhouse, who had been a tutor at Oxford, and then a journalist at the Manchester Guardian, was appointed.[20] Maggie Studholme argues that the choice of Hobhouse over Geddes effectively prevented the engagement of sociology with wider environmental concerns, and that the dominance of LSE well into the post-1945 era compounded this.[21] Geddes was also more utopian, so the relationship between sociology and utopia in the twentieth century might have been quite other than it actually was. And had Wells been appointed, both utopia and gender relations would have been central to the discipline from the outset. But either choice would have run counter to prevailing trends towards the separation and specialization of academic disciplines, a process which fragmented knowledge, professionalized it, and sequestered its production within universities. This meant differentiating sociology from biology, and especially from eugenics, while struggling to define it as a science and therefore a legitimate form of knowledge. In a context where utopia and science were generally seen as antithetical, sociology increasingly sought alignment with the latter, resulting in the repression of utopian thought and the polarization of social theory and utopia.

Hobhouse's appointment also led to a division between sociology at LSE and outside the academy. Between 1908 and 1910 Hobhouse edited *The Sociological Review*, successor to *Sociological Papers*. He resigned after disagreements with the Sociological Society, which continued to prop-agate the more demotic and utopian sociology favoured by Geddes, Branford and Lewis Mumford, particularly in the regional survey move-ment. Geddesian sociology was influenced by the French sociologist Frederic Le Play, focussing on the triadic relation of place, work, folk. The regional survey movement used multiple methods, carried out or contributed to by local people, to represent the specificity of place, its history, and people's means of livelihood and ways of life – a holistic and interdisciplinary synthesis of social and environmental knowledge. Methods included statistics and geology, but also maps, photographs, interviews and testimony. There are some similarities with Mass Observation, launched in the late 1930s, which also used mixed methods and ordinary people to generate an anthropology of ourselves. But Mass Observation was wildly empiricist, while Geddes had a slightly more coherent and holistic theoretical position.

The purpose of the regional survey movement was also different from Mass Observation. The documentary movement of which Mass Observation was part set out to record what was on the point of disap-pearance. The aims of regional survey were utopian – or rather eutopian, for Geddes and Branford differentiated these terms. Utopia or outopia was unrealistic and bad, while eutopia was 'the good place as it can be made here and now if we set our minds to the task'. Branford argued that '[t]he regional eutopia comes to birth out of the regional survey in the degree and to the extent that the mass of individual players in any given community grow into its orchestra'.[22] The approach risks slipping into utilitarianism, just as the celebration of the orchestra as social edu-cation risks losing sight of the music. It introduces, too, the question of realism, which, as we shall see in Chapter 7, is a recurrent theme in the relationship between sociology and utopia. In their later works, and especially in the 1920s, Geddes and Branford elaborated their goal as a third alternative to state power and rampant capitalism. Branford proposed a sabbatical year for the 'money power' in which all resources above a certain level should be put to the social and public good.[23] The emphasis was on the city and its region, and the potential transition to a better society from this local perspective.

Mumford's 1923 *The Story of Utopias* implicitly adopts the method proposed by Wells. It begins with a critical historical survey of literary utopias, filtered through the lens of place, work and folk, and including Plato, More, Bellamy, Morris and Wells. In common with most such accounts before the 1970s, it ignores the history of utopian writing by women: Mumford's compatriot and fellow-sociologist Gilman is not mentioned. Mumford suggests that Plato's ideal, in which 'the good life must result when each man has a function to perform, and when all the necessary functions are adjusted happily to each other' is 'carried out point for point in the organization of a modern symphony orchestra'.[24] He remarks on the restrictions on the arts in the education of the Plato's Guardians, and especially the taboo on much music and on dramatic mimicry, saying that Plato distrusted the emotional life. He describes Bellamy as having 'descended from literature to sociology', saying that like most utopian writers he shows an excessive concern with the machinery of society.[25] *News from Nowhere* is critically described as a utopia of escape rather than reconstruction, while *A Modern Utopia* is commended, above all as 'an accounting and a criticism'.[26]

Mumford then addresses the dominant tropes in the social imaginary, which he labels idola, or (following Durkheim) collective representations, or (following Georges Sorel) social myths. The Country House, Coketown, and Megalopolis, together with the National State, are subjected to blistering critique. The discussion of the country house anticipates themes later developed by Raymond Williams and Pierre Bourdieu. Mumford notes its orientation to collection rather than creation and its dependence on 'taste' and a 'gourmandizing' habit of mind. These dominate in the country house itself, in its metropolitan equivalent, and in its shrunken, suburban travesty. Consequently '[c]ulture came to mean not a participation in the creative activities of one's own community, but the acquisition of the products of other communities; and it scarcely matters much whether these acquisitions were within the spiritual or material domain'.[27]

In his final section, Mumford endorses the regional survey movement and argues that 'Geddes is the outstanding exponent of the Eutopian method both in thought and practical activity'.[28] Mumford adopts the distinction between utopia and eutopia, insisting on the necessity of eutopia, for '[u]nless we can weave a new pattern for our lives the outlook for our civilization is ... dismal'.[29] The social imaginary affects human action, and new eutopias are necessary to helps us act in ways that overcome the momentum of existing institutions. Mumford contends that '[t]he chief use of the classic utopias ... is to suggest that the same methods which are used by ... utopian thinkers ... may be employed, in a practical way, to develop a better community on earth'.[30] He points to the holism of both sociological and eutopian method, the need to understand the world in its complicated totality, and, in looking towards change, the need to consider human nature and its transformation.

There are two related polarities that pervade these early arguments and that remain current: the opposition between science and utopia and the dualism of 'is' and 'ought', or the question of normativity. Wells does not challenge the distinction between science and utopia. Nor do Geddes, Branford and Mumford. Their distinction between eutopia and utopia is between 'good' and 'bad' utopia, between the real possible future and wishful thinking, between reconstruction based on science and irrational dreaming. Mumford complains that much social science is pseudo-science, or 'disguised literature', 'in which the jargon of science is accepted as a substitute for the scientific method of arriving at factual truth'.[31] What is distinctive about Wells is that rather than devaluing literature relative to science he recognizes both sociology as utopia and utopia as sociology as legitimate and necessary forms of knowledge. He is right that building alternative scenarios and exploring the interrelationships between elements, structures, systems and processes does result in better understanding of both present realities and future options. This holds for qualitative accounts as well as computer simulations, and in terms of human experience within social structures, or biography and history, the qualitative mode is necessary.

A century later, lay audiences and novice students are still presented with the oppositions between science and utopia and science and literature, with sociology on the side of science. Steve Bruce's *Sociology: A Very Short Introduction* refers to 'improvers and utopians' as 'impostors'; utopia is not defined and his principal target is social reform.[32] A. H. Halsey's *History of Sociology in Britain* notes 'the rivalry between science and literature for ownership of the intellectual territory of social criticism and social reform'. As Wolf Lepenies shows, that deep cultural rift had a profound influence on the development of sociology, although its precise effects differed in France, England and Germany. Halsey reproduces this historical dichotomy by arguing that 'the arts formed a significant barrier to scientific sociology' in Europe.[33] He then redraws it in terms of explanation and interpretation. Explanation is aligned with science and quantitative method, interpretation with literature, qualitative methods and cultural studies. Halsey ignores Wells's extensive and popular non-fiction writings and his scientific education, insisting that 'despite the protests of novelists like H. G. Wells, sociology has persisted in its claim to scientific status, offering a rational and coherent account of human action' – as if the non-scientific, non-quantitative, interpretative approach were also non-rational and incoherent.[34]

The question of normativity is related to, but not identical with, that of scientificity. Utopia may be rejected as sociology either because of its literary form or because of its evaluative content. In the 1960s, undergraduates were taught that sociology was concerned with what is, not what ought to be, and that these could and should be rigorously separated. The distinction reprised Hobhouse's inaugural editorial in *The Sociological Review:* 'sociological thinking must start with a clear cut distinction between the "is" and the "ought", between the facts of social life and the conditions on which society actually rests and the ideal to which society should conform'.[35] Less attention was drawn to his following comments on the difficulty of the distinction, to his belief that sociology and social philosophy are intrinsically connected, or to his suggestion that it may sometimes be possible to deduce ought from is. Hobhouse is critical of the danger of collapsing what ought to be into representation of what is actually the case. Again, this suggests that if sociologists are not open about their aspirations for the future, their very silences make utopias. Neither Hobhouse nor Wells thought that the distinction between is and ought implied that sociology should be solely focused on the former. Endorsing the role of utopia as a proper mode of sociological orientation is not to collapse this distinction, but to admit normativity as a proper aspect of sociology itself. More recent writing has challenged the opposition between knowledge and judgement. Martha Nussbaum argues persuasively against the dualism between thought and feeling, or between reason and emotion, which runs through Western culture.[36] Andrew Sayer argues that evaluation and openness to the future are intrinsic to description and explanation, rather than separate from or even antithetical to them.

For sociology, the pursuit of scientific respectability and disciplinary specialization combined to suppress both normativity and utopianism, especially in Britain, which suffered from a deeply anti-intellectual and utilitarian culture. The institutional development of distinct disciplines in the humanities and social sciences simultaneously prevented the coherent accounts possible in a pre-disciplinary era and limited the evaluative role of social science. This process was contested, including by Geddes, who was critical of the way the fragmentation of knowledge impeded understanding. But as Sayer says, '[t]he division between positive and normative thought has become institutionalized with the emergence of the academic division of labour, and the estrangement of social science, dealing with description and explanation, from philosophy and political theory, dealing with normative thinking'.[37] Consequently sociology has been far more antipathetic to the utopian mode than have politics or philosophy; this is one reason why sociology sometimes seems so dull. Mumford complained that social scientists added to the offence of not being good scientists by not being any good at literature.

Wells is surely right that sociologists carry silent utopias in their work, both as substance and as inspiration. Utopia's exclusion was never absolute, but its presence was persistently denied. It was not recognized as sociology, and the utopian content of sociology was seen as a serious flaw. But sociology contains repressed utopias. Some are conservative, seeking to preserve the status quo and disguising values behind claims of an avowed scientific neutrality and making the error Hobhouse identifies, representing the real world uncritically as if it already corresponds to a utopian vision. Others are oppositional, seeking to politicize 'bourgeois' or patriarchal sociology. Most sociologists who work in fields of social inequality – economic inequality, class, gender, ethnicity – are driven by a critical conviction that these inequalities are damaging and wrong; underpinning this is always an implicit idea of a good society in which such inequalities are absent. These two opposing tendencies echo Mannheim's distinction between ideology and utopia.

Only six years separate Mumford's book from Karl Mannheim's *Ideology and Utopia*, published in German in 1929 and in English translation in 1936. This remains the only well-known discussion of utopia in mainstream sociology. Entries on Utopia in dictionaries of sociology from the 1960s and 1980s generally name only Mannheim and More, although one 1950s source does also note the merits of utopia as a form of 'creative political and sociological play' – that is, utopia as sociology.[38] For Mannheim, both ideology and utopia are incongruous with reality. They are distinguished in terms of their function in relation to social change; ideology operates to sustain the status quo, utopia to transform it. Thus '[o]nly those orientations transcending reality will be referred to by us as utopian which, when they pass over into conduct, tend to shatter, either partially or wholly, the order of things prevailing at the time'.[39] Importantly, though, for Mannheim utopia is not a representation of a better way of being, still less a description of an alternative society. While such fantasies may sometimes have a utopian function, they are just as likely to be compensatory. Mannheim reads as ideological those elements that Bloch construes as incipiently utopian:

> Wishful thinking has always figured in human affairs. When the imagination finds no satisfaction in existing reality, it seeks refuge in wishfully constructed places and periods. Myths, fairy-tales, other-worldly promises of religion, humanistic fantasies, travel romances, have been continually changing expressions of that which was lacking in actual life. They were more nearly complementary colours in the picture of the reality existing at the time than utopias working in opposition to the *status quo* and disintegrating it.[40]

The distinction between ideology and utopia has appealed to many utopian scholars seeking to separate good and bad utopianism, sometimes failing to register that Mannheim is not talking about utopias in the conventional sense, but about transformative political ideas. It is a mistake, however, to treat the distinction between ideology and utopia as a binary opposition, for Mannheim also suggests that it is impossible, other than in retrospect, to distinguish between the two; and that in reality, utopian and ideological elements are often intertwined. Angelika Bammer illustrates this through the blindness of some feminist utopianism to issues of race and class, just as socialist utopias are often blind to race and gender. But Mannheim also develops a typology of utopian thought, which includes the idea of a conservative utopia, otherwise a potential oxymoron. This account of the changing forms of utopia emphasizes the different historical orientations to time and to social change. He argues that different utopias are mobilized by social groups or classes in their struggle for social power; in this process a distinctive conservative utopia arises as a countervailing force. This is very much the sociology of utopia. But Mannheim's importance within the sociological canon has rested less on these discussions than on his general approach to the sociology of knowledge. In the 1970s Mannheim was regarded as having 'dealt with' the question of utopia rather than opening it up: as a doctoral student I was told there was no more to be said. Social theory has not adopted his distinction. Utopia has generally been treated as a form of ideology rather than its opposite, and both ideology and utopia have been contrasted with reality and science.

In 1958, Ralf Dahrendorf launched a critique of functionalist sociology, which explained social institutions and processes in terms of their function in sustaining the system as a whole. 'Out of Utopia' castigated this approach for its tendency to represent actually existing society as a smoothly-operating, conflict free system – that is, in Dahrendorf's terms, as a utopia. Unlike the utopian tradition which at least intends critique of the status quo, such a collapse of utopia and reality is conservative in effect – in Mannheim's terms, ideological. However the terms of Dahrendorf's critique of sociology as utopia are substantially negative about the utopian mode itself, which he reads as intrinsically static: utopias are 'monolithic and homogeneous communities, suspended not only in time but in space', free from 'conflict and disruptive processes', places marked by consensus and harmony. Utopia is 'a world of certainty', 'paradise found', where 'utopians know all the answers'. Collapsing Huxley and Orwell, Dahrendorf writes:

> All utopias from Plato's Republic to George Orwell's brave new world of 1984 have had one element of construction in common: they are all societies from which change is absent. Whether conceived as a final state and climax, as an intellectual's nightmare, or as a romantic dream, the social fabric of utopias does not, and perhaps cannot, recognize the unending flow of the historical process.

Dahrendorf knows this is contentious: he adds that he would defend it even of Wells, despite quoting him as saying that '[t]he Modern Utopia must not be static but kinetic, must shape not as a permanent state but as a hopeful stage, leading to a long ascent of stages'.[41]

As sociology expanded, so it diversified. The growth of British universities in the 1960s entailed founding twenty-eight new sociology departments and thirty new chairs of sociology. The number of sociology graduates rose from under 200 in 1952, to 724 in 1966, to 1768 in 1971, the year of my own graduation.[42] Students may have been attracted by the hope of a critical perspective on society, or, especially around 1968, its imminent transformation; such expectations were generally disappointed. However, the expansion did result in the appointment of many young staff, and sociology did become more critical. Marxism was more widely taught, while feminism, anti-racism and anti-colonialism added further critical viewpoints on the discipline, the academy and society itself. The overt project was critique, not utopia, for 'utopian' remained a derogatory term on almost all sides.

Curiously, this was also partially true of feminism. Curiously, because feminism is fundamentally informed by the view that the world should be otherwise, and that critical knowledge is important as a route to women's emancipation. Feminism's challenge to academic practices was both substantive and methodological. Feminists complained that sociologists ignored women and their distinctive experience. They sought to explain and challenge unequal gender roles, and the social construction of gender and sexuality themselves. They challenged hierarchical research practices, preferring the term research participants to subjects or respondents and recognizing them as co-producers of knowledge. The need for this demonstrates the distance between conventional sociology and the earlier social survey movement or Mass Observation.

The interpenetration of feminism politics, feminist theory, and feminist utopianism in the 1970s is documented in Angelika Bammer's *Partial Visions*. A surge of feminist utopian fictions in the 1970s and the reissue of earlier works, including those from the nineteenth century, as still relevant to contemporary experience and politics was inextricably bound up with the rise of the feminist movement itself. Those works included Ursula Le Guin's *The Dispossessed* and *Always Coming Home*, Marge Piercy's *Woman on the Edge of Time*, Joanna Russ's *The Female Man*, and Sally Miller Gearhart's *The Wanderground*, which was an iconic radical feminist text in the United States.[43] Yet the suggestion that feminism is an intrinsically utopian perspective was unpopular within the academy, largely because feminism struggled so hard for recognition and acceptance. This acceptance remains incomplete notwithstanding feminism's transmutation into gender studies. Harriet Bradley, like Bammer, argues that academic interest in gender arose out of the politics of the 1970s and the rebirth of feminism. In *Gender*, Bradley provides a critical synthesis of the main academic debates in the field. But she is also at pains to demonstrate the impact of gender on lived experience – and does this through a series of vignettes set in a different font from the main text. One of these includes a brief discussion of utopias as counter-narratives to the global prevalence of violence against women, drawing on Gilman, Le Guin, Russ and Piercy. The presentation of Bradley's discussion both enacts a tentative rapprochement between academic sociology and utopia through feminism and indicates the continuing rift between utopian and experiential modes and conventional academic discourse.[44]

But, as Bradley also notes, the link between sociology and political activism that characterized 1970s feminism was largely broken in the 1980s. By the end of the decade, sociology was again under attack. The 1979 Conservative government in Britain slashed university funding; for the following decade there were to be very few new academic appointments, still fewer sociologists. The Social Science Research Council was symbolically renamed the Economic and Social Research Council – removing the term science and privileging economics over sociology. Small amounts of money were made available for 'new blood' appointments especially in the natural sciences, paid for by cuts in the social science research budget. Margaret Thatcher declared that there was no such thing as society, only individual men and women and families. Graffiti appeared over toilet rolls declaiming 'sociology degrees – please take one'. The 1960s was blamed for all social ills, and sociology was somehow implicated in this. Even in 2012, the political commentator Melanie Phillips could declare on national radio in Britain that sociology professors were responsible for the break-up of the family.[45]

The postmodern turn added fuel to the anti-utopian fire. Here, it is important to distinguish between postmodernity and its cultural correlate, postmodernism. Postmodernity refers to a structural change in the nature of the society we live in, for which some prefer terms such as late or liquid modernity or late capitalism, and sometimes to a broad cultural, political and theoretical condition which results from this structural change. This cultural condition also manifests as a narrower artistic or aesthetic movement more properly termed postmodernism. Thus Jameson argued that postmodernism is the cultural logic of late capitalism.[46] In all three senses this is an intensification and continuation of trends within modernism as much as a sharp break from it. Modernity itself has been held responsible for totalitarian politics in the twentieth century, embedding the fear of utopia as blueprint.

Cultural changes were far-reaching. Modernism entailed the recognition of contingency and the significance of literary form, while later cultural and deconstructive turns focused more intently on modes of representation rather than the overt content of texts, undermining literal readings. Postmodernism went further. Its epistemological and moral anti-foundationalism constituted a challenge to utopia in so far as the latter entails claims about truth and about morality. Jean-Francois Lyotard's challenge to 'grand narratives' argued that overarching representations or explanations of historical process oriented to past or future are suspect. This did not augur well for answering Mills's sociological question about the place of any given society in history. Still less did it encourage projecting wholesale schemes of social transformation into the future. The 'deconstruction of the subject' undermined the possibility of discussing interests beyond the self-defined identity and identification of individuals, so that collectivities became theoretically disintegrated into selves, and further into fragmentary selves. Moral and ethical absolutes were deemed impossible; substantive claims about human flourishing and the claim that one society is better than another – claims fundamental to the utopian project – were undermined. Even the idea of society itself as in some sense a totality, a concept which underpins the whole notion of social science, as well as utopia as a society transformed, was called into question. If we understand utopia to be a totalizing (though not therefore totalitarian) representation which is holistic, social, future-located, unequivocally better and linked to the present by some identifiable narrative, and one which embeds a view of human flourishing, then postmodernism is profoundly anti-utopian. These positions implied not just a loss of hope in the social, but a loss of belief in it. The quest for utopia in this reading is an irretrievably modernist, and therefore irredeemably flawed, project. Krishan Kumar used utopia as an analytical lens to reveal the view of a better world subsumed and anticipated in classical, postindustrial and postmodern social theory.[47] He argued that if postmodernists are right, 'it is not simply that "there aren't any good or brave causes left" to fight for anymore' but there cannot be.[48]

Sociology as critique

If sociology has been overtly suspicious of utopianism other than as an explanandum, its relationship with critique has been more ambiguous. For the last four decades, Marxism and critical theory have been core components of the field of sociology. Critical theory refers primarily to the tradition of the Frankfurt School, and especially to the work of Max Horkheimer, Theodor Adorno, Walter Benjamin, Herbert Marcuse, and Jürgen Habermas, as well as others including Erich Fromm and Bloch himself. Horkheimer argued in 1937 that traditional social theory was concerned only with explanation and understanding, whereas a properly critical social theory was oriented to critique and to social transformation.[49] There are strong utopian currents in this tradition, and the 1968 slogan, 'Be Realistic: Demand the Impossible', was accompanied by the popularity of the more utopian critical theorists such as Marcuse and Fromm, as well as Bloch. These writers were most explicitly concerned with delineating a better society; they were also the most willing to engage with existential questions about human nature. Marcuse is sometimes travestied as advocating a utopia of sexual libertinism;[50] rather, he saw libidinal energy as the source of potential challenge to domination, imposed scarcity and unnecessary labour. Repression might be deeply introjected into the psyche, but there was a chink of light in human nature itself which could emerge into a new reality principle and social transformation. Bloch too saw the unconscious as the source of creativity and the utopian impulse; Fromm's work is unequivocally about the conditions for human flourishing.

Marcuse and Fromm have ceded prominence to Adorno, Benjamin and Habermas, whose work is more compatible with the critical and deconstructive character of postmodernism. More broadly, the term critical theory can be applied to (or claimed for) any work which fits Horkheimer's category. Few sociologists would not regard themselves as critical; 'uncritical' is a criticism verging on the insulting. But there is an important distinction between intellectual acuity and political critique. Horkheimer's formulation implies a distinction from (and superiority to) 'ordinary' social theory and sociology, and that difference lies in the explicit normativity of critical theory, as well as its claims to greater explanatory power. Yet if, as Adorno says of Kafka and of *Mahagonny*, critical theory views the world 'from the secret position of redemption',[51] that utopian place remains secret, remains repressed.

More recently, the French sociologist Luc Boltanski has argued that sociology itself is inherently about critique. Critical theories are both based in the 'discourse of truth adopted by the social sciences' (the 'is') and have a necessarily normative orientation (the 'ought'), a combination Boltanski describes as perilous. The foot firmly planted in social scientific knowledge entails an explicit acceptance that 'reality does not provide sufficient purchase to sketch with precision what society would be once released from the alienations that hamper it, or even to identify clearly the goods that underlie the critique'. Thus critique is not utopian, for utopias are 'based exclusively on moral exigencies' and 'can free themselves from the reality principle'.[52] Boltanski distinguishes, though, between the world and the real, which refers to socially constructed accounts (including those of social science). These are tested and contested through truth tests and reality tests which may reinforce existing hierarchies or unmask contradictions or reveal repressed elements of reality.

Boltanski distinguishes between positions of exteriority and interiority in relation to social structure: 'The project of taking society as an object and describing the components of social life or, if you like, its framework, appeals to a *thought experiment* that consists in positioning oneself outside this framework in order to consider it as a whole'.[53] He argues that the bulk of sociological work the world over is generated from this position of expertise, and subordinates sociology to management. There is a tension between sociology as description and explanation and critical sociology which involves a normative dimension, but, says Boltanski, 'even in the case of sociologies that do not foreground their critical dimension, it can be said that this tension is ever present, at least in a way, *by default*'.[54] A critical sociology may occupy this position of exteriority, but in so doing holds itself at a distance 'from the critical capacities developed by actors in the situations of everyday life', and thus from the sociology of critique. The latter concerns itself with the actions and experiences of agents rather than the abstractions of structure.

The focus on agents throws up a different kind of test which has not yet undergone institutionalization, the existential test. This acquires centrality because there is always a gap between the experiences of actual embodied people and their necessary practice in the world, and the collective accounts and institutional forms within which those practices take place – that is, between the world and the real. This gap generates unease. 'Existential tests', says Boltanski, 'are based on experiences, like those of injustice or humiliation, sometimes with the shame that accompanies them, but also, in other cases, the joy created by transgression when it affords access to some form of authenticity'.[55] Such experiences are difficult to articulate precisely because they have not yet been formulated in a collective and thus collectively sanctioned frame. Hence the importance of the aesthetic realm, for it is here that these potentially radical bases of critique may find expression: 'radical critique is frequently based, at least in its early stages, on expressions used in forms of creation – such as poetry, the plastic arts, or the novel – where is it socially more or less permissible (at least since Romanticism) to confide to the public personal experiences and feelings, and whose aesthetic orientation makes it possible to bypass the constraints of consistency and legal and moral justification imposed on argumentative discourse'.[56]

The gap between critique and utopia narrows here. It is precisely in the fissure Boltanski designates as unease, in the crack where the light gets in, that the sense of 'something's missing' arises; and utopia too is projected into the aesthetic sphere and other non-political forms of praxis. The dissonance between experience and expressibility recalls that radical imbalance between sensation and language identified by Gage in relation to colour and running through claims for music's utopian quality. Notwithstanding the social construction of the real, as embodied beings rather than disembodied minds we live also in the world. Discourse cannot capture all of our experience. There is always something left over.

In so far as the sociology of critique intends to make the existential experiences of ordinary people visible and intelligible, sociology, rather than the radically critical or incipiently utopian responses in question, remains the dominant narrative. But Boltanski's aim is not only the sociology of emancipation (the subtitle of the book); sociology and critique are emancipatory forces. Such a critique needs to restore 'the links that might connect it to the experience of actors – that is to say, to the sufferings and desires they have experienced, and also to the moral sense they have applied in order to interpret these tests'.[57] Sayer points in the same direction, in ways we will return to in Chapter 9 which reflects on utopia as ontology. He argues that the dualism between explanation and evaluation obscures the human condition:

> The distinction between is and ought, that has dominated thinking about values in social science, allows us to overlook the missing middle, the centrality of evaluation. It obscures the nature of our condition as needy, vulnerable beings, suspended between things as they are and as they might become, for better or worse, and as we need or want them to become.[58]

Such evaluation, Sayer argues, should involve 'careful analysis and attentiveness to the object, an orientation to what is, albeit one which includes needs, lack and becoming, suffering and flourishing, and hence also an orientation to future possible states'.[59] Boltanski argues that critique needs also to 'seek to weather' these experiences 'by giving them a political orientation, so as to transform sorrows and dreams into demands and expectations'.[60] There is a utopian aspiration here, but it is disowned by Boltanski's own distinction, remaining (for him) a question of critique because of the absence of identifiable substance to the utopian content and the rejection of the utopian mode, at least in the holistic sense.

Sociology is comfortable with utopia only as an element in the social imaginary that is the object of explanation. It repeatedly approaches utopia and retreats from it. And yet the impulse towards social transformation, there at the origin of the discipline, does not go away. The warm stream runs underground. Both the general diffusion of utopia across culture (in Bloch's sense) and the parallels between sociology and utopia (in Wells's sense) would lead us to expect this. For the excitement and promise of sociology lies in this presence; the disappointment lies in its recurrent repression and denial. Substituting sociology for politics in Patrick Hayden and Chamsy el-Ojeili's defence of utopia, we might say that:

> To be utopian ... is the stuff of [sociology], and it first involves subjecting the [society] of the present to critique. Secondly, it involves imagining human communities that do not yet exist and, thirdly, it involves thinking and acting so as to prevent the foreclosure of social possibilities in the present and future. [61]

6
Utopia Revised

The trajectories of utopia and sociology in the twentieth century were largely separate. From the 1970s utopian studies emerged as a distinct interdisciplinary academic field, but it has until recently been dominated by historical and literary orientations and a tendency to define utopia itself in terms of form, as a literary genre. Historical accounts of utopian thought and utopian literature both predate and follow Mumford's *The Story of Utopias*, beginning at least as early as 1879 with Moritz Kaufmann's *Utopias* and continuing to the present through such works as Frank and Fritzie Manuels's 1979 *Utopian Thought in the Western World*, Krishan Kumar's 1987 *Utopia and Anti-Utopia in Modern Times*, and Gregory Claeys's 2011 *Searching for Utopia: The History of an Idea*. All of these approach their subject matter as a relatively straightforward history of ideas. By the 1970s, however, change was overtaking both utopian literature and utopian commentary. These were affected by same intellectual and political challenges as social theory, with similar results. An upsurge of political activism in the 1970s stimulated utopian thought, and the very nature of those politics altered both its content and its form. This brought contingency, provisionality and reflexivity centre-stage. But this political impetus overlapped with and gave way to the postmodern turn, in which sociological and systemic analyses were downplayed in favour of questions of representation and literary form. This signalled a retreat from reading utopias as programmatic proposals for social transformation; issues of process rather than structure and form rather than content, or form as content, took priority, while 'openness' was preferred to 'closure'. The risk here is that utopia becomes a vehicle only of critique rather than of transformation. The best work implied a dialectic of openness and closure, transcending that binary through an implicit though not yet conscious treatment of utopia as method.

Utopia challenged

This raises again the definition of utopia, its identification in social theory and its potential social purposes and effects. The broader analytical definition of utopia as the expression of the desire for a better way of being or living better enables us to explore historical shifts in the content, form, location and function of utopia, and the ways in which specific social and historical circumstances encourage or block different kinds of utopian expression and sensibility. As a hermeneutic method, it reveals the desire that the world be otherwise within social theory itself, even when that theory is overtly hostile to a particular form of holistic utopian depiction taken to exhaust the meaning of utopia itself. The tension between these two definitions means that the impact of postmodernism on the relationship between social theory and utopia was ambiguous: it undermined utopia in the sense of a specification of an alternative social structure, but simultaneously intensified concern with the very desire that is the motive force of utopia in its analytic sense.

Tobin Siebers argued that 'utopia has emerged as the high concept of postmodernism'. For Siebers, aesthetics becomes central to postmodern theory because objects of art are 'allegories of desire' and postmodernism, like utopia, turns on questions of desire.[1] This is endorsed by Gilles Deleuze and Félix Guattari in *Anti-Oedipus*, one of postmodernism's founding texts.[2] Deleuze and Guattari contest both Freudian and Lacanian psychoanalytic theory. The Oedipal triangle, they argue, is a formulaic representation which does not describe the 'natural' development of desire, frustration, and healthy transcendence or otherwise. Rather, Freudian psychoanalysis demands that we understand our blocked desires in terms of the Oedipus myth, which both constrains and denies our experience, and proves our desires to have been illegitimate in the first place. Desire should be understood as a much more variable complex of libidinal flows. It is not oriented solely sexually, nor to parental figures, but to fragmentary, partial objects. They argue against Lacan that the centrality of the phallus, like the oedipal triangle, is a totalizing myth, which denies the fragmented character of flows of desire; and it intrinsically links desire to lack, which Deleuze and Guattari repeatedly oppose.[3]

Bloch, of course, does connect desire with lack: utopian imagining, even as abstract utopia, is important because it is difficult to articulate lack or desire other than in terms of potential fulfilment. As Raymond Williams argues, 'We cannot abstract desire. It is always desire for something specific, in specifically impelling circumstances'.[4] Consequently utopia requires the representation and objectification, of desire. This is the first step to fulfilment, even if representation is usually, and perhaps necessarily, misrepresentation. In Siebers's collection, utopia is focused on the body as the locus of desire and human happiness. Such utopianism might be seen as expressive of desire rather than instrumental and transformative. More accurately, it changes what is to be transformed: postmodern aesthetics involves the willed transformation of the body by ornament, diet, exercise and surgical intervention. As David Morris argues, 'utopia in the postmodern era has largely fixed its new location in the solitary, private, individual body', reflecting 'a belief that the only valid remaining space of perfection lies ... in our own individual flesh: a paradise of curves and muscle'.[5] If utopian thought of all kinds is expressive of a desire for a better way of being, its projection onto the body rather than the body politic is a retreat from hope, at least social hope, to desire. It is a retreat from understanding desire, as Deleuze and Guattari, Reich, and Marcuse did, in terms of a libidinal energy suffusing the realm of the social, and thus fuelling capitalism and fascism as well as their potential utopian alternatives. For these writers, desire may emanate from the body in an essentialist, vitalist way; but it does not stay there. And for David Harvey, body politics may also be the start of a move from abstract to concrete utopia, for the campaign for a living wage is a politics concerned directly with the body and the struggle for social provision for its sustenance.[6] Adorno's comment on utopia resonates here: 'There is tenderness only in the coarsest demand: that no-one shall go hungry any more'.[7]

Sociologists did note shifts in the utopian accents of the social imaginary contingent on the postmodern turn. Jürgen Habermas posited a move from content to process, arguing that the conditions of late modernity made it possible to propose only the processes by which utopia might be negotiated rather than the structural features or content of utopia itself.[8] The utopian problematic shifts away from questions of production, consumption and distribution and becomes primarily or even exclusively processual and communicative. In practice, this sneaks in claims about the actual character of utopia by the back door: Habermas outlined the conditions of non-coercive dialogue as the ideal speech situation, which may be read either as aspiration or as a regulative ideal exposing the way in which domination is exercised in debate and consultative processes. Ulrich Beck argued that at least in the affluent West, concern moved from questions of distribution to often invisible risks. These risks affected everyone. Since economic security was more widespread, class society was replaced, at least discursively, by risk society.

Safety trumped distributive equality.[9] The ecological crisis is predominantly represented in terms which endorse Beck's argument. Carbon emissions, global warming, melting ice-caps, rising sea levels, reductions in habitable land mass, acidification of the oceans, pollution, resource exhaustion and depletion affect the whole social system in which all of us inhabit the earth, so we are all in this together. From this viewpoint, the utopian assumption of overriding common interests is plausible and partially true. But class is a structural feature of a capitalist society inherently geared to growth. Concentration of wealth and wide dispersal of poverty never disappeared. The economic crises following 2008 put questions of inequality, ownership, capitalism and class back on the political agenda, expressed in popular demonstrations, in the Occupy movement and in accessible social scientific books such as Richard Wilkinson and Kate Pickett's *The Spirit Level* and Owen Jones's *Chavs*.[10]

Zygmunt Bauman also posited a shift in the character of utopian thought. Bauman's own overt engagement with the question of utopia began with his 1976 *Socialism: The Active Utopia*. This, perhaps Bauman's least-known and least-cited book, follows Mannheim in construing political struggle as a contest between competing class-based projects for the future.[11] Utopia recurs in Bauman's later work, informed by his concept of liquid modernity. He proposes that '[t]o measure the life "as it is" by a life "as it *should* be" ... is a defining, constitutive feature of humanity'; and that the 'urge to transcend' is a universal feature of the human condition.[12] Not so the articulation into 'projects'. Programmes of change and visions of life in the form of elaborations of an alternative world are, he argues, specific to 'solid' modernity. His characterization of such utopias is familiar. They are blueprints, marked by territoriality and finality, invoking the expectation of a perfectly orderly society. They are also intrinsically linked to the spatial form of the nation-state, and to a degree of engagement within such spaces by all classes of society. But globalization has undermined the autonomy of the nation-state and allowed global elites to disengage. Here, Bauman echoes Wells himself. Shortly after witnessing Bleriot's first flight across the English Channel, Wells argued that mobility would sever people's connection to place, anticipating globalization, mass migration, and what sociologists eighty years later described as space-time compression and disembedding. Already, said Wells, increasing numbers of people were uninterested in their own locality and oriented to a wider arena. Wells predicted an extended conflict between the globalizing implications of air travel, useful international finance and business, and the existing national structures of government.[13] Bauman contends this leaves utopia with no topos, no place. Loss of territoriality and finality make impossible utopia as an imagined future state of the world. The pursuit of a better tomorrow or an alternative physical or social space has been nullified. Transgressive imagination takes a different form: an 'unending sequence of new beginnings ... and the desire for a different today', and a quest for happiness not as a steady state but a series of fleeting moments.[14] This is, perhaps, a reversal of Bloch's move from concrete to abstract utopia, a return to utopian desire manifest only in its pre-social and often unarticulated forms. Again, what is suggested here is a sociology of utopia – an argument about the changing forms and contents of utopian desire and the historical and social conditions that underpin these – although Michael Hviid Jacobsen argues that a subterranean utopian impulse, a desire for the world to be otherwise, infuses all of Bauman's work.[15]

These changes have implications for the function of utopia, and, as suggested above, for the relationship between desire and hope. Utopia has at least three potential functions: compensation, critique and change. These are, of course, frequently intertwined in practice, and the line between critique and transformation is particularly difficult to draw. The compensatory role of utopia is widely noted: Mumford distinguishes between utopias of escape and those of reconstruction; Ricoeur regards the compensatory utopia which imagines a harmony of desires as pathological; Mannheim views compensatory fantasies as ideological rather than utopian. Bloch is more sympathetic, regarding even the most trivial imaginings as proleptic social critique. He recognizes that utopian longing is not necessarily profound: 'Most people in the street look as if they are thinking about something else entirely. The something else is predominantly money, but also what it could be changed into'.[16] A shop window proclaims 'Utopia: Everything Five Pounds'. People may take refuge in daydreams about winning the lottery and having the resources for more substantive escape. Most lottery winners buy a new house. This creation of a personal utopian enclave is underscored in twenty-first-century Britain by the prevalence of television programmes dedicated to property transformation on all scales, including the renovation of the Country House and (as Mumford noted a hundred years earlier) its miniature suburban imitation. Such programmes also emphasize the reciprocal process of the conversion of utopian capital back into its economic form. The travel industry constitutes another repository of compensatory utopianism, advertised in explicitly utopian and paradisical terms. Both dreams imaginatively transform only the dreamer's place in the world, not the world itself, although property markets, the DIY industry and the travel industry of course have profound physical, social and economic effects both locally and globally.

Utopia may do more than articulate through compensatory fantasies the unsatisfactory nature of present reality. As critique it foregrounds and makes explicit this inadequacy, identifying the source of dissatisfaction as something more systemic, more general than one's own place in the world. A sociological imagination is brought into play and personal troubles become public issues. This is a necessary though not sufficient condition for utopia's strongest function, that of change. For many, utopia's importance lies its capacity to embody hope rather than simply desire and to inspire the pursuit of a world transformed. Williams argued that this willed transformation of the social world was an essential characteristic of the utopian mode, and that without it, there was the danger of utopia settling into 'isolated and in the end sentimental 'desire', a mode of living with alienation'.[17] Such willed transformation is the target of political and ideological anti-utopianism. But it demands a holistic, sociological approach, normative judgement and political commitment, all called in question by the social and cultural conditions of late modernity.

The feminist turn

None of the changes remarked on by sociologists such as Habermas, Beck and Bauman registered the transformative impact of feminism on utopian writing and thinking in the 1970s; feminism remained marginal to sociology. But this period saw a recovery of feminist utopian writing, hitherto excluded from historical accounts of utopia, leading Angelika Bammer to observe that, in terms of a literary genre, one might perhaps start not with More, but with Christine de Pizan's *The Book of the City of Ladies*, written a century before *Utopia*.[18] Bammer's *Partial Visions: Feminism and Utopianism in the 1970s* is primarily concerned not with historical recovery, but with the theoretical relationship between feminism and utopianism, and in particular the impact of feminism on the idea of utopia itself. She argues that '[c]umulatively, the feminisms of the 1970s recuperated the concept of the utopian as a vital dimension of a radical politics. They did so by redefining what the "utopian" meant and challenging their readers to do likewise'.[19] Influenced by Bloch, her objective is explicit:

> My goal is to replace the idea of 'a utopia' as something fixed, a form to be fleshed out, with the idea of 'the utopian' as an *approach toward*, a movement beyond set limits into the realm of the not-yet-set. At the same time, I want to counter the notion of the utopia as unreal

with the proposition that the utopian is powerfully real in the sense that hope and desire (and even fantasies) are real, never 'merely' fantasy. It is a force that moves and shapes history.[20]

Bammer locates particular texts and textual strategies in the different politics of the United States, France and East and West Germany, noting that actual utopias are always historically situated and thus contain both utopian and ideological elements; the focus on gender inequality is sometimes accompanied by alarming blindness to questions of ethnicity and class. Utopian writing by women has not, however, typically taken the form of the fictional utopia as conventionally understood; in itself this requires a broadening of the concept of utopia from a literary genre to the more diffuse Blochian not yet. Her foil is a classical form of utopianism characterized by stasis and perfection, a 'changeless state outside of history',[21] against which she posits a shift from timelessness into time that is also a move towards agency in which women become the subjects of history.

For Bammer feminism itself is intrinsically utopian. It is driven by anticipation, by the recognition of patriarchy as an unnatural state, and by the belief in and pursuit of an alternative. But the nature of that alternative is hard to define because women have first to experience and articulate their authentic experience in the world. As we struggle to find this, questions of embodiment and of language become central, and utopia is redefined in a new and critical way, as a journey and not a goal. This demands an open and indeterminate future, which refuses the 'illusory coherence' of a fully worked-out alternative. Bammer argues that conventional utopias are inherently conservative by virtue of their form; their transformative potential is undermined by their closure, their 'apparatus of self-containment'.[22] Feminist utopianism, as Lucy Sargisson also argues, thus opens up both the concept and the content of utopia.[23] The openness, the radical indeterminacy of consciousness and of the future, are seen as feminism's contribution to a new utopianism. Bammer's characterization of the place of utopia within the process of social change implies utopia as method: we should think of utopia not as antithesis, but as 'a series of utopian moments within the shifting configurations of the possible'.[24]

Utopia goes critical

Bammer establishes beyond doubt that feminism produced an upsurge of utopian writing in the 1970s; that this writing took new forms; and that it grew out of and intended political transformation. *Partial Visions* was published five years after Tom Moylan's hugely influential book *Demand the Impossible*. Like Bammer, Moylan sees the new utopianism as a product of the politics of the 1960s and 1970s. Authors like Marge Piercy were politically involved and trying to live differently; texts, like Sally Miller Gearhart's *The Wanderground*, were part of the building of the political movements themselves. Moylan also argues that the utopias published in the 1970s, many of them feminist, differ in both form and content from those of the fin de siècle. These works, for which Moylan coined the term 'critical utopias', have a more fragmented narrative structure than earlier utopias. The discrete register of plot and character is foregrounded; the iconic register, describing the social structure of both utopian society and its foil, recedes. Again, the emphasis is on subjects and on agency. As sociology, the combination of discrete and iconic registers is a double perspective on structure and agency; in Boltanski's terms, it combines exteriority and interiority. For Moylan, the societies portrayed are decentralized and differentiated. Their values and institutions are interrogated within the utopian society and less unequivocally endorsed. The gap between individual experience and public discourse in utopia itself, Boltanski's unease, is opened up: this is a strong theme in Le Guin's *The Dispossessed*. Many novels contain possible dystopian as well as utopian futures, breaking down the sense of an inevitable move towards utopia and refusing grand narrative. Such texts 'reject utopia as blueprint while preserving it as dream'.[25] As Williams said 'the utopian impulse now warily, self-questioningly, and setting its own limits, renews itself'.[26]

In the late twentieth century, critical utopianism was sustained in the work of writers like Kim Stanley Robinson and China Miéville. But dystopian accents dominated. Cinema in the 1990s was replete with images of utopia as dystopia, as in *The Truman Show* and *Pleasantville*, or straightforward dystopias such as *Dark City* and *The Matrix*.[27] Moylan, in collaboration with Raffaella Baccolini, tracks this turn to dystopia.[28] Dystopia portrays the darkness of the lived moment, the difficulty of finding a way out of a totalizing system. It is not necessarily anti-utopian: anti-utopianism actively opposes the imagination and pursuit of alternatives. Much hangs on whether the dystopia points to unremitting closure or to another possible future, and the ending and framing of the dystopia is crucial here. Baccolini and Moylan argue that these are dystopian 'texts that maintain a utopian impulse'. Their emphasis on totality and transformation, argues Moylan, is one of the key distinctions between the critical and the classical dystopia. They both intend political change and inscribe it in the text by way of eutopian enclaves and appendices that indicate the dystopian world is history. But if the critical dystopia can be a vehicle of resistance, it is much less able to register transformation and redemption. It may point to the exit, but it does not suggest what we might find, or make, when we leave.

The 'critical utopia' does not offer an unequivocal alternative. It is, for Moylan, critical in three senses: it implies an Enlightenment sense of critique; a postmodern reflexivity and provisionality; and a political critical mass leading to change – the latter existing by implication outside the text. My own more pessimistic view is that the political impetus and intent of the critical utopia is not necessarily matched by political effectiveness. This depends on the conditions of cultural reproduction. A politically quiescent context and reading enables them to function only as critique. On the other hand, the very reflexivity and provisionality means they can be seen as examples of utopia as method – the self-conscious promotion of interrogation of possible alternative futures from a position which registers both the necessary indeterminacy of the future and the plurality of the agents who will create it.

We are all pluralists now. The recognition of the contingency of our moral and conceptual frameworks is now commonplace. If utopia is intrinsically evaluative, the recognition of cultural difference poses a problem. Fin de siècle texts by Durkheim, Morris and Wells acknowledge the issue. In *News from Nowhere,* we are told that nation states have been abolished, allowing for the flourishing of cultural difference between peoples. But the text endorses pluralism only outside itself. Diversity lies elsewhere: 'Cross the water and see. You will find plenty of variety: the landscape, the building, the diet, the amusements, all various'.[29] Political difference is resolved through direct democracy. The system works for differences of opinion about the common interest; no fundamental differences of interest arise. Marge Piercy's *Woman on the Edge of Time*, an exemplar of the critical utopia, brings cultural difference and conflicts of interest into the utopian society, Mattapoisett, itself, with cultural pluralism deliberately and actively separated from any connection with 'race'. She posits the need for institutional processes to address differences of interest. The process of conflict resolution is extended discussion: 'We argue. ... How else?'.[30] This continues until agreement is reached; after a major dispute, the winners have to feed and give presents to the losers. *Contra* Gray, there is here no claim that utopia is a perfect world where all desires and all interests are harmonized. But the problem with 'we argue, how else?' – especially in a society which is not culturally homogeneous – is the presumption that agreement will be reached. This assumes that shared interests will override conflicting ones. It also assumes agreement over the terms of the debate, the procedures of discussion, the frame of the argument. Indeed, if these difficulties are successfully managed within Mattapoisett, its external affairs are less consensual: it is engaged in a defensive war with its neighbours.

A more radical challenge to the utopian imagination arises if the frame of argument is contested. How can utopia handle absence of agreement on the rules of the game as well as conflicts of interest? This difficulty contributes to the dystopian turn. If utopia is a space for the fictional resolution of problems that humankind has not (yet) solved, incommensurability can only enter as a dystopian shadow. Language and translation provide a vehicle for such questions, as in Suzette Elgin's (1985) novel *Native Tongue,* or the Irish singer Christy Moore's (1994) lament *Natives*, which begins 'For all of our languages, we can't communicate; for all of our native tongues, we're all natives here...'.[31] The biblical figuration is the Tower of Babel, which recurs in novels which are not part of an explicitly utopian/dystopian genre, such as A. S. Byatt's (1996) *Babel Tower* and Paul Auster's (1987) *The New York Trilogy.*[32]

The shift to a greater pluralism, provisionality and reflexivity in fictional utopias is paralleled in a theoretical commentary which treats utopia as heuristic rather than telic. Like the utopias themselves, this focuses on process rather than content, but the process is of dialogue with, rather than within, the text. Neo-Marxism, critical theory, postmodernism, and feminism converge in exploring utopia in terms of desire, in terms of form and process rather than content, in terms of how the text works rather than what it means. It is a move which has encouraged rich and deep readings of literary texts, surfacing utopian surplus and dystopian shadows that overspill the conscious intentions of authors. But this preoccupation with representation rather than figuration, or with the process of representation rather than what is represented, again tends to limit the possible function of both utopia and literary and social theory to one of critique. For Bammer, the two movements of feminism and deconstruction that converged in the 1970s are presented as unproblematically congruent. But the postmodern and deconstructive turn can also pull in the opposite direction, away from the political intention of the critical utopia. It also raises the question of whether there has, in fact, been a profound change in the nature of utopian writing, or whether utopian texts are simply read differently in the context of late modernity.

Miguel Abensour: educating desire

The best example of this is Miguel Abensour's re-reading of *News from Nowhere* which emphasizes its reflexivity, provisionality and openness. Morris's letters, lectures and political writing demonstrate his own appreciation that the utopian mode is necessarily provisional. Images of the future are necessary because it is 'essential that the ideal of the future be kept before the eyes of the working classes, lest the *continuity* of the demands of the people be broken, or lest they should be misdirected'.[33] However, we cannot predict the needs and wants of later generations: 'it is impossible to build a scheme for the society of the future, for no man can really think himself out of his own days'.[34] Morris warns against literal readings: 'The only safe way of reading a utopia is to consider it as the expression of the temperament of its author'. The danger is that 'incomplete systems impossible to be carried out but plausible on the surface are always attractive to people ripe for change, but not knowing clearly what their aim is'.[35]

Abensour posits a significant disjuncture in utopian thought around 1850 between a 'systematic' mode which involves constructing blueprints and a 'heuristic' mode, in which utopias become exploratory projections of alternative values sketched as alternative ways of life. He approaches *News from Nowhere*, and by extension the proper function of utopia itself, in terms of desire. Desire, as throughout postmodernism, involves a libidinal energy rather than simply a cognitive preference for a better society. What matters is less the portrayal of objects of desire in the text, but how the text itself acts on the act of desiring. We should not approach it as a naturalistic representation of the good society. Rather, we should understand it as the catalyst of a process, in which the reader is an active agent, of disrupting the normative and conceptual frameworks of mundane experience. As noted in Chapter 1 above, utopia does not simply illustrate the meeting of familiar wants unmet by existing society, the meeting of already experienced lack. It creates a space that enables us to imagine wanting something else, something qualitatively different. It offers not simply cognitive distance, but existential and affective estrangement through the experience of transformed desire. For Abensour, the 'education of desire' is the 'organizing function' of *News from Nowhere*. It depends on the presence of a particular quality in the text, the utopian marvelous. He quotes Pierre Mabille in terms which recall the utopian charge of colour and music and the moment of grace:

> The marvelous expresses the need to bypass empirical limits, imposed by our structure, to attain a greater beauty, a greater power, a greater pleasure, a greater duration. The marvelous wants to bypass the limits

of space and time, it wants to destroy all barriers, it is the struggle of freedom against everything which reduces, destroys and mutilates; it is a tension, that is to say something different from routine mechanical work, an impassioned and poetic tension ... It is the strange lucidity of the delirium, the light of the dream and the green light of passion; it burns above the masses at the time of revolt. But the marvelous is less the extreme tension of being than the juncture of desire with external reality. The marvelous is, at a specific moment, the troubling instant in which the world gives us its assent.[36]

The presence of the utopian marvelous 'intensifies the ambition of Morrissian utopia to awaken and energize desires so that they might rush toward their liberation'. This is 'action on the movement of passion', or 'affective formation'.[37] It withdraws libidinal energy from productive, rational and useful concerns, orienting it in a radically different direction of 'a new principle of reality whose desire and foretaste can be communicated only by means of a *simulacrum'*.[38]

Literary form is central: 'the structure of the narration involves putting utopia to the test'.[39] The contrast between the old systematic, didactic utopia and the new, experiential utopian spirit is embedded in this structure, which counterposes the dialogues of the central section with the drama of the journeys in the outer sections, especially the final journey up the river. It is there in Morris's subtitle, 'An Epoch of Rest', implying the suspension of time, and in the fluidity of the river itself. The openness and indeterminacy of Morris's utopia transcends both conventional utopian writing and Marxist antipathy to dreaming about the future. *News from Nowhere* is often criticized for its lack of institutional specificity: Darko Suvin says that '[u]nfortunately the absence of socio-political organization in Nowhere is a gap that cannot be argued away and denies it the status of a utopia'.[40] For Abensour, this absence is the central point of the text and the saving grace of the genre: 'The power of Morris's utopia stems from there being no ideal or plan for the moral education of humanity and, furthermore, from the impossibility of there being one'.[41]

For Abensour, the antitheses of openness are closure, didacticism and repression. This is consistent with his later writing on 'persistent utopia' and on democracy and the state. 'Eternal utopia' is a figment contructed by anti-utopians who claim, in order to invalidate the possibility of alterity, that utopia is always a myth of unrealizable harmony. 'Persistent utopia', in contrast, which Abensour derives from Bloch and Emmanuel Levinas, is a genuinely utopian recurrent gesture towards exit, towards an open not yet.[42] His discussions of insurgent democracy, or democracy against the state, are similarly suspicious of institutions themselves: if anti-statist democratic action may give rise to institutional forms, their only legitimate character is 'greater plasticity, more openness to events, and a stronger disposition to welcome the new'.[43] Such an institution, he suggests, occupies a temporal caesura where it must constantly oscillate between the poles of 'relapse into inherited condition' and 'the hold of a form to come, that is in the making'.[44]

It is this emphasis on openness that leads Abensour to contrast Morrissian utopia with 'those utopias that are an imaginary projection of a new mode of social repression of impulses',[45] or written utopia that is 'a closed totality'.[46] The original serial form of *News from Nowhere* is argued to counter this repressive tendency of the written utopia. It revises 'the distinction between author and reader', producing a dialogical and potentially participatory process, and constituting a 'definitive rupture with utopian socialism's monological character'.[47] Serial publication was not innovatory or unique to Morris. But Abensour points here to the potential for a more collective engagement where utopian imagination is embedded in a political or dialogic community. And indeed the circulation of *Commonweal*, where *News from Nowhere* first appeared, was between two and three thousand; most copies were sold at street meetings, including those at pitches where Morris regularly spoke, and Morris read excerpts at meetings of the Hammersmith Socialist Society.[48]

Abensour reads the final section of *News from Nowhere* as the most utopian because it is the most infused with utopian marvelous. This contrasts with Robin Page Arnot's 1934 claim that the most important chapter is 'How the change came about', Morris's description of the revolution and its aftermath.[49] For Abensour, the didactic character of this account decreases its value. Yet this supposes that the prospect of revolution itself was not something capable of mobilizing affective responses in the original audience, many of whom would have recognized its basis in the events of Bloody Sunday in 1887. Zizek argues for the inherently utopian character of the revolutionary moment:

In a proper revolutionary breakthrough, the utopian future is neither simply fully realised in the present nor simply evoked as a distant promise which justifies present violence – it is rather as if, in a unique suspension of temporality, in the short-circuit between the present and the future, we are – as if by Grace – for a brief time allowed to act as if the utopian future is (not yet fully here, but) already at hand, just there to be grabbed.[50]

It is, however, an unnecessary hypothesis that the textual structure and serial publication were conscious strategies on Morris's part. Moreover Abensour lays claim to the definitive and only correct reading of Morris, and does not consider processes of cultural reproduction which are as crucial to literary texts as to musical theatre. All of these run counter to the deconstructive turn in literary criticism, which proposes that there is more in the text than its author consciously intends, and which endorses multiple readings. Abensour is especially critical of readings which treat Morris's hypotheses about the future as posited solutions: the importance of *News from Nowhere* cannot lie in the portrayal of a libertarian socialist utopia, for this reduces it to 'a gem of literary anarchism'. 'One cannot', he says, 'consider Morris's utopia a social-ist parable ... without totally misreading the text'.[51] Such objections assume, as Patrick O'Sullivan says, that Morris did not mean what he said.[52] Political and sociological readings – and their exhaustive critique – remain one of many legitimate ways of reading a text, alongside its capacity to create the subjects and agents who will make and inhabit the institutions of the future. If Morris was the greatest of English social-ists and a fine political writer, the claim for his utopian exceptional-ism needs interrogation. Abensour's re-reading of Morris suggests that conventional readings of other fin de siècle texts may themselves be in need of revision.

Reconsidering Bellamy and Wells

Bellamy's *Looking Backward* is usually read as a rational and materialist Fabian plan, concerned – as Morris suggested – with the machinery of society rather than the life lived within it. It emphasizes material processes of production and distribution and the support of citizens from the cradle to the grave – concerns which continued to resonate in Britain at mid-century with the post-war construction of the welfare state, and which are resurrected with its twenty-first century disman-tling. As late as 1948, a *Daily Herald* review declared: 'A prophet gets reprinted – and he's right so far'.[53] Williams described *Looking Backward* as 'in a significant way a work without desire'.[54] Beaumont's recent contention that desire is identifiable in the processes of shopping and consumption intensifies rather than undercuts the reading of this novel as essentially bourgeois.[55] Moreover, Bellamy's purpose of con-structing a rational society flattens affect and endorses conventional romantic love.

But something quite other can be seen in *Looking Backward*. In 1889, Blavatsky endorsed it as the interim social goal of Theosophy and the basis for social and spiritual renewal:

> The organization of society, depicted by Edward Bellamy, in his magnificent work *Looking Backward*, admirably represents the Theosophical idea of what should be the first great step toward the full realization of universal brotherhood. The state of things he depicts falls short of perfection, because selfishness still exists and operates in the hearts of men. But in the main, selfishness and individualism have been overcome by the feeling of solidarity and mutual brotherhood; and the scheme of life there described reduces the causes tending to create and foster selfishness to a minimum.[56]

Society provides only the optimum conditions for grace, rather than grace itself. This echoes Bellamy's ethical position in his 'The Religion of Solidarity', and the sermon which constitutes the penultimate chapter of *Looking Backward* itself.[57] Theosophists were centrally involved in the global propagation of Bellamy's ideas. They wrote the constitution of the earliest Boston Bellamy Club: 'The principle of the Brotherhood of Humanity is one of the eternal truths that governs the world's progress on lines which distinguish human nature from brute nature'.[58] Later Theosophical writers stressed the ethical element in *Looking Backward* as well as Bellamy's insistence on material equality as the necessary basis of spiritual development: these discussions were influential in Indian politics at least until the 1950s.

A Modern Utopia does not quite conform to the stereotype of a bounded, timeless perfect society either: 'In a modern Utopia there will, indeed, be no perfection; in Utopia there must also be friction, conflicts and waste, but the waste will be enormously less than in this world'.[59] Human beings are not imagined to be perfect or perfectible: Wells refers to 'that inherent moral dross in man that must be reckoned with in any sane Utopia we may design and plan'.[60] This is, in Davis's terms utopia proper, an institutional means of managing human affairs including the potential for conflict, not an Ideal Moral Commonwealth. Moreover utopia is a snapshot in time of a global society always in process. According to Wells, *A Modern Utopia* is modern precisely in this refusal to posit a perfect, static future state, and in the insistence that the good society must be imagined and pursued at a global level.

Form matters here too. *A Modern Utopia* is narrated by the Voice, displaced from the author. His companion, the botanist, is preoccupied with his emotional life, with love and loss; his responses make this imagined world hover between utopia and dystopia. The Voice sees his alter ego in utopia as a wistful image of what might have been: 'My Utopian self is of course my better self ... He is a little taller than I, younger looking and sounder looking; he has missed an illness or so, and there is no scar over his eye. His training has been subtly finer than mine; he has made himself a better face than mine'.[61] The conversation between them is described as telling a story of hurt, loss, damage, failure and humiliation. It exposes the difficulty of the damaged self entering into utopia: 'Here is a world and a glorious world, and it is for me to take hold of it, to have to do with it, here and now, and behold! I can only think that I am burnt and scarred'.[62] The botanist does not want to meet his double, the person he might have been free of the scars of actual living in his own world, insisting that we are those scars, they make us who we are. The friction between the two travellers acknowledges a tension between the larger systemic concern and the individual, human preoccupation with self and relationship. The chapter ends pessimistically: 'We agreed to purge this State and all the people in it of traditions, associations, bias, laws and artificial entanglements, and begin anew; but we have no power to liberate ourselves. Our past, even its accidents, its accidents above all, and ourselves are one'.[63] In the final chapter when 'the bubble bursts', we are reminded that 'a Utopia is a thing of the imagination' – and indeed 'becomes more fragile with every added circumstance, that, like a soap bubble, it is most brilliantly and variously coloured at the very instant of its dissolution'.[64] There is optimism, but there is no blueprint. The contingency of ideas, the limits to imagination, the provisionality of utopian speculation are all explicit:

This infinite world must needs be flattened to get it on one retina. The picture of a solid thing, although it is flattened and simplified, is not necessarily a lie. Surely, surely, in the end, by degrees and steps, something of this sort, some such understanding as this Utopia must come. First here, first there, single men and then groups of men will fall into line – not indeed with my poor faulty hesitating suggestions– but with a great and comprehensive plan wrought out by many minds and in many tongues. It is just because my plan is faulty, because it mis-states so much, and omits so much, that they do not now fall in. It will not be like *my* dream, the world that is coming. My dream is just my own poor dream, the thing sufficient for me. We fail in comprehension, we fail so variously and abundantly. We see as much as it is serviceable for us to see and no further. But the fresh undaunted generations come to take our work beyond our utmost effort, beyond the range of our ideas.[65]

The kinetic element in *A Modern Utopia* was not, as Wells claimed, innovatory, for Morris, Bellamy and Gilman had all assumed that change would continue. *Looking Backward* focuses primarily on the shape of the new society; the transition to it gets little space and social development within utopia even less. But this is not a static or a bounded society. There is a process of the 'betterment of mankind from generation to generation, physically, mentally, morally ... and each generation must now be a step upward'.[66] Bellamy hedges his bets between evolution and education in this process, suggesting that the separation of intimate relationships from economic dependence allows sexual selection free play in the improvement of the race. And if *Looking Backward* is limited to a description of Boston, Bellamy's initial intentions were otherwise; his original plan was for a planetary version set in the thirtieth rather than the twentieth century.

The limits of utopia

Utopists such as Moylan, Jameson and Darko Suvin agree with Abensour that the proper role of utopia is estrangement, calling into question the actually existing state of affairs, rather than constructing a plan for the future. All, of course, see this as the first step towards political change. Estrangement is also intrinsic to sociology: defamiliarizing the familiar, representing the practices of daily life as needing explanation, if not critique. Mass Observation was precisely about the recognition of our own practices as strange, as well as ephemeral. If sociology consistently rejected explicit utopian alternatives as the basis for a critical understanding of ourselves, by the end of the twentieth century this rejection became central to readings of the utopian tradition itself. For Jameson, as for Abensour, the purpose of utopian fiction is no longer to provide an outline of a social system to be interrogated in terms of its structural properties, still less treated as a goal. Utopia is important less for what is imagined than for the act of imagination itself, a process which disrupts the closure of the present: 'Utopia as a form is not the representation of radical alternatives; it is rather simply the imperative to imagine them'.[67]

For Jameson, as for Abensour, this process circles around desire. His 2005 *Archaeologies of the Future* is subtitled *The Desire Called Utopia and*

Other Science Fictions. Thus 'we might think of the new onset of the Utopian process as a kind of desiring to desire, a learning to desire, the invention of the desire called utopia in the first place' – a passage bearing a remarkable similarity to Abensour's.[68] Jameson is concerned to uncover what is under the surface, the unconscious of the text, and therefore to proceed as if 'the ostensible content, the manifest topic or subject matter, always masks a different one of an entirely different nature'.[69] For Jameson, as for Abensour, form is more important than content here, and the function of utopian writing is negation and critique, not building an alternative. Utopia's proper role is not to resolve tensions, but to hold them in mutual opposition. Any apparent resolution in an institutional proposal is necessarily ideological:

> We have come laboriously to the conclusion that all ostensible Utopian content was ideological, and that the proper function of its themes lay in critical negativity, that is their ability to demystify their opposite numbers. The examination of the anti-Utopia, then, of the fear of Utopia, has led us to identify a fundamental source in the very form of Utopia itself, in the formal necessity of Utopian closure. In addition we have been plagued by the perpetual reversion of difference and otherness into the same, and the discovery that our most energetic leaps into radical alternatives were little more than the projections of our own social moment and historical or subjective situation.[70]

One of the consequences of reading utopia as (in Abensour's sense) heuristic rather than systematic, and as exploratory rather than prescriptive, is that it provides an alibi for what otherwise might be seen as the weaknesses, absences and failures of the iconic register of the utopian text – the limitations of, for example, both Morris's and Piercy's treatment of cultural and political pluralism. Jameson (like Abensour) suggests that these failures do not need an alibi. Failure is an inevitable part of the process of trying to think utopia itself rather than a characteristic of particular representations. He argues (like Marx and Morris) that utopia is literally unimaginable. The imaginable always falls short of utopia, so that actual utopian texts 'bring home in local and determinate ways, and with a fullness of concrete detail, our constitutional inability to imagine Utopia itself; and this, not owing to any individual failure of imagination but as the result of the systemic, cultural and ideological closure of which we are all in one way or another prisoners'.[71] Utopias enable us to explore the structural limits of what is thinkable, 'in order to get a better sense of what it is about the future that we are unable or unwilling to imagine'.[72] Thus 'the true vocation of the utopian narrative begins to rise to the surface – to confront us with our own incapacity to imagine Utopia'.[73] The function of the utopian text can only be 'to provoke ... to jar the mind into some heightened but unconceptualizable consciousness of its own powers, functions, aims and structural limits'.[74] Tim Clark similarly stresses the importance of failure as a crucial feature of modernism (rather than postmodernism) in art, a movement which he sees as intrinsically utopian, claiming that 'the courting of failure and indescribability is one main key' to 'the visual culture of the last two hundred years'.[75] His reasons are perhaps similar to Jameson's: 'It is only in discovering the system [of representation]'s antinomies and blank spots – discovering them in practice I mean – that the first improvised forms of contrary imagining come to light'.[76] For Jameson, referring back to Louis Marin, utopia is always 'organised ... around a blind spot or a vanishing point', a point of disappearance.[77]

Abensour contends that the very openness of *News from Nowhere* underpins its capacity to cathect and educate desire, and sees this as distinctive. Jameson, who reads Morris with surprisingly flat-footed literalism,[78] suggests that utopian literature often fails to connect at the level of affect. He criticizes the 'timeless placidity' of life in utopia, arguing that 'the reproach of boredom ... is in reality one of the deepest fears motivating political anti-Utopianism'.[79] This accusation is always the disguised expression of something else: it 'can ... clearly be seen to be so much propaganda for the excitement of market competition'.[80] Nevertheless, Jameson proposes that libidinal investment in utopia is difficult because it is impossible to imagine ourselves radically otherwise: the prospect of annihilation of one's actually existing self evokes existential terror.

Again, many utopias are sensitive to the difficulties here. Abensour suggests that the caesura between past and future properly occupied by insurgent democracy requires (or induces) a discordance at the level of individual and collective subject rather than the Blochian concordance of *Heimat*. The sense of displacement of self – a manifestation of unease – pervades the experience of William Guest in Nowhere. He is encumbered by his old self and is ominously told: 'You will find it a happy world to live in; you will be happy there – for a while'.[81] John Goode argues that in Morris's text 'the gap between present and future becomes a nightmare of one's own non-existence'.[82] The botanist refuses to meet his utopian other. *Looking Backward* portrays West lost in the new Boston and later returned to the old Boston which is no longer tolerable. Both episodes register terror at the disjunction between self, time and place, threatening the very integrity of that self. In *Woman on the Edge of Time*, Connie, the visitor to utopian Mattapoisett, projects this disjunction on to her relationship with her daughter, who would be lost to her in the new world, but simultaneously embraces that loss as a price worth paying:

> Suddenly she assented with all her soul to Angelina in Mattapoisett, to Angelina hidden forever one hundred fifty years in the future, even if she should never see her again.... She will be strong there, well fed, well housed, well taught, she will grow up much better and stronger and smarter than I.... She will be strange, but she will be glad and strong, and she will not be afraid. She will have enough. She will have pride. She will love her own brown skin and be loved for her strength and her work.[83]

Such difficulties should not be overstated. We live with a measure of unease in our own world. Our children are always partly lost to us by generational and other differences of experience. We encourage them to imagine themselves differently from the start, asking what they want to be when they grow up, or promising possibilities 'when you're bigger'. Empathy is built on the capacity to imagine oneself, literally, other-wise; acute difficulty in doing this is regarded as a disability. Sociologist Anthony Giddens described the stories we tell ourselves about who we are, who we were, and who we might become as narratives of self. He too linked this to late modernity, in which the self becomes a reflexive project and identity is constantly under revision. Such stories include 'downsizing', trading fast-paced urban living and visible material consumption for an imagined higher quality of social relationships. They may be delusionary, entailing forms of rural life that require high levels of capital available only to the rich, and not necessarily implying smaller ecological footprints; but they do envision an alternative set of desires and satisfactions. These narratives are not always liberatory. There is overwhelming cultural pressure to monitor and control our bodies through diet and exercise: imagining the perfect honed and healthy – and especially not obese – self points to downsizing of persons rather than lifestyles. Health and longevity become an individual responsibility, and physical imperfection, illness and death itself marks of failure. Managerial texts offer technologies of self prescribing conformity to models of personal behaviour and promising financial and social success: they are perhaps the only dreams the powerful wish us to have, offering as they do a more comfortable fit between our disciplined selves and the demands and satisfactions generated by the world we currently inhabit. Imagining ourselves otherwise is thus imposed on us and extracted from us. Structural as well as ideological processes are at work here. Richard Sennett argues that character, in the sense of a coherent and consistent developmental narrative of self depends crucially on the possibility of stable employment.[84] If this is true at an individual level, the possibility and nature of collective narratives also depends on structural and institutional processes, a point Marx made very clear in relation to class consciousness. Envisaging ones desires and capacities somewhat changed is an everyday occurrence. The question of how this is or may be oriented to social transformation is a social and political question, not primarily one of human imaginative capacities.

The novel form itself addresses these issues. The *bildungsroman* focuses on the formation of character and the quest for identity, whose contingency upon circumstances is central, as in Charles Dickens's *Great Expectations*. The figure of the *doppelgänger*, usually the dark side of the self but adopted in a positive mode by Wells, is not confined to the utopian genre. It is there in Fyodor Dostoyevsky's 'The Double', in Robert Louis Stevenson's Jekyll and Hyde, in James Hogg's *The Private Memoirs and Confessions of a Justified Sinner*. Hogg also uses the device of a found narrative, common in utopias and dystopias. The effect of this, or of double or multiple narratives, is to produce cognitive and affective displacement. This displacement or unease becomes the subject and a defining feature of the novel of modernity. Dorothy Richardson's *Pilgrimage* sequence of thirteen novels was written from 1914 onwards, thus predating both James Joyce and Virginia Woolf.[85] *Pilgrimage* is a kind of *bildungsroman,* centred on the protagonist Miriam Henderson's negotiation of identity. But the difficulty of this negotiation rides on the discrepancies between direct experience, available discourse, the capacities of language, and the gendered character of these. Richardson registers abstract reason as dominating male experience of and orientation to the world. Her experimental writing emphasizes experience as embedded in space, place, time and relationship, where objects, settings and changing light take on an active force. Richardson posits a synthesis between reason and reflection as a feminist (or at least distinctly female) experience of the world, whose articulation is travestied by the mere phraseology made available by male dominance of language – or perhaps by language itself.

Beyond the open frontier

Jameson argues without derogation that utopias, like the modernist novel, are increasingly absorbed in an auto-referential exercise of examining 'the possibility of their own production' and 'the interrogation of the dilemmas involved in their own emergence as utopian texts'.[86] Whether this is actually a feature of the texts, of literary theory, or of both, there is a risk of disengaging from the social and political world. Recognizing provisionality, reflexivity, dialogue and an element of inevitable failure may be useful. Overemphasis on openness, process and impossibility is not, and sidestepping the substance of imagined alternatives can go too far. Abensour and Jameson are Marxists, but perhaps over-influenced by understanding that any future we envision will of course not come to pass. David Harvey is also a Marxist, but a geographer whose approach to utopia is less steeped in literary theory and more grounded in political economy, leading him to resist excessive openness or closure.

In *Spaces of Hope*, Harvey differentiates two strands in utopian thought. Utopias of spatial form, dreams or plans for the ideal city or maps of alternative social institutions projected into place are contrasted with utopias of process such as the free market. Harvey argues that there is a contradiction between these strands. Utopias of spatial form have to compromise with the social processes they set out to control; but utopias of process, in their actual realization, 'lose their ideal character, producing results which are in many cases exactly the opposite of those intended', such as 'increasing authoritarianism and inequalities rather than greater democracy and equality'.[87] The opposition is problematic in partially collapsing sociology into geography: social institutions and practices are elided with spatial form in the imagination of an alternative society. Harvey proposes a more dialectical spatio-temporal utopianism. He notes that some utopian writers, including Geddes, Mumford, and Wells, attempt this synthesis, and that this becomes more explicit in Piercy and others of her generation.

Harvey takes issue with writers who want to keep choices about the future endlessly open, or want to keep their own hands clean of prescription. Eternal openness leaves utopia as 'a pure signifier of hope destined never to acquire a material referent'.[88] It is politically evasive. It entails 'a failure to recognize that the materialization of anything requires, at least for a time, closure around a particular set of institutional arrangements and a particular spatial form and that the act of closure is in itself a material statement that carries its own authority in human affairs'.[89] The refusal of closure is a refusal to take responsibility around the question of that authority. Without such closure, we cannot define or discuss where we might want, collectively, to go. Of course we are unable to 'leap outside of the dialectic and imagine that we are not embedded and limited by the institutional worlds and built environments we have already created';[90] by implication, then, our imagined alternatives must be provisional and accompanied by some reflexive awareness. But eternal openness offers no direction home. It leaves us, says Harvey, quoting Roberto Unger, 'torn between dreams that seem unrealizable and prospects that hardly seem to matter'.[91]

Harvey's title, together with his ongoing commitment to social change, reminds us that desire is not enough and returns us to the question of hope. Even Jameson, despite defining utopia as a sub-genre of science fiction, is eventually forced to distinguish between utopia as literary text and the 'thing itself'. Only thus can we rescue transformative political thought or future-oriented sociology from the excesses of postmodern literary and social theory. Critique which disrupts the ideological closure of the present is essential, but it is even more important to disrupt the *structural* closure of the present. The way texts are read, as well as their putative intrinsic character, affects their potential social function. Even critique depends on some degree of plausibility of the utopian alternative. If this is absent, dreaming the world otherwise risks appearing to be compensatory fantasy, mere wishful thinking. Hope requires us to imagine a potential new society and to imagine it as possible. The transformative function of utopia depends on preserving utopian desire, but offering (as Morris does) an argument about the conditions of utopia's (partial) realization and desire's (partial) fulfilment. From here, reading utopian texts against Mills's key questions, as sociology, remains necessary. And indeed such readings do continue. In *Fool's Gold?*, Lucy Sargisson treats twenty-first-century utopian texts as social and political theory whilst demonstrating their conscious deployment of social scientific knowledge: thus Sally Miller Gearhart's 2002 *The Kanshou* requires equal and open communication, described as 'true-talk' and modelled on Habermas's ideal speech situation.[92]

Bloch's concrete utopia or the vision Morris sought to keep before the eyes of the working classes require that we read utopias literally and take them seriously in that mode, although they certainly do not require that we only read them in this mode. Without a certain element of closure, specificity, commitment and literalism about what would actually be entailed in practice, serious criticism is impossible. If utopia is constrained both by possible imagination and imagined possibility, the political task is to push outwards the limits of both. The imagination and critique of utopian alternatives as speculative sociologies of the future generates forms of knowledge, of social systems that are at least theoretically possible and of tendencies in the real that might make them potentially really possible. We are embedded in conditions which resist both contrary imagination and oppositional action. Both the anti-utopian present and our understanding of contingency mean our attempts at the imaginary reconstitution of society must be provisional, reflexive and dialogic and, as Wells said, subject to exhaustive criticism. But the conditions under which we live, which are not of our own choosing, require us to create radically altered means of livelihood, ways of life and structures of feeling. Only a form of utopian thought and of reading utopia that engages with the actual institutional structure of the present and the potential institutional structure of the future can help us here, and this demands an understanding of utopia as method rather than as goal.

7
The Return of the Repressed

The repression of active engagement with alternative possible futures has given way in recent decades to wider consideration of utopia in sociology and social and political theory. These discussions have, however, been ambiguous. They feature repeated demands for 'realistic utopias'. Some overtly positive discussions of utopia privilege particular models of the real and place severe limits on utopia's alterity in ways that are anti-utopian in effect. Some writers who resist or oppose the terminology of utopia are more supportive of radical social transformation and affirmative of the potential role of the social imaginary. In most cases the institutional specificity and the holism implied by the Imaginary Reconstitution of Society are lacking. Science is still invoked as a brake on utopian thinking. There has also, of course, been a deluge of writing about the environmental crisis which has a future orientation and implicit utopian as well as dystopian themes. Some theoretical writing about the future, while not directly addressing utopia, helps to demonstrate the usefulness of taking a standpoint outside actually existing conditions.

The economic crisis provoked Michael D. Higgins, sociologist, poet and President of the Republic of Ireland, to assert that '[i]t has been one of the weaknesses of the Left that it has not drawn on the richness of its own utopian inheritance'.[1] Higgins, who over a decade ago referred to utopia as a necessary country, argues for a new politics of solidarity. He insists that '[w]e need a discourse which will envisage the alternative, inclusive society and the new social economics. This is what Ernst Bloch called "anticipatory illumination". It is not only about the right to survive, it is about the right to flourish'.[2] Higgins follows Bloch in his insistence on grounded hope and in affirming the need for future alternatives. Higgins was not the only sociologist showing a renewed interest in utopia, which was manifested in a range of books and articles.[3] Among them was Erik Olin

Wright's 2010 *Envisioning Real Utopias*, emerging from the Real Utopias project at the University of Wisconsin, generating the theme of the 2012 American Sociological Association Conference and appearing to mark a major rapprochement between sociology and utopia.

Utopia qualified

This rapprochement is, however, tentative and qualified, indicating the distance still to be bridged between social theory and utopia rather than their integration. There is no evidence of a shared theoretical canon or conceptual framework; discussions proceed with little or no engagement either with utopian literature or utopian commentary. There is a constant anxiety about the utopian mode, leading to disavowals of its imputed negative features. Even its strongest advocates are mildly defensive: Chamsy el-Ojeili, who construes social theory as an 'intertwining of scientific, utopian and ideological activities', distances it from utopia as an 'unrealistic idea of perfection' and 'a future imagined as harmonious, transparent and universally happy'.[4] David Harvey, whose *The Enigma of Capital* is an exemplary intertwining of Bloch's cold stream of analysis and warm stream of humanistic passion for an alternative to capitalism, declares, 'Of course this is utopian! But so what! We cannot afford not to be'.[5] Most are intensely ambivalent. The reservations circle around familiar themes, especially utopia's alleged totalizing or totalitarian tendencies and the questions of realism and possibility. Thus Immanuel Wallerstein rejects utopianism in favour of 'utopistics' or possible, 'realistic' futures, and his reasons are conventional:

> The real problem, with all utopias ... is not only that they have existed nowhere heretofore but that they seem to me, and to many others, dreams of heaven that could never exist on earth. ... And utopias can be used, have been used, as justifications for terrible wrongs. The last thing we really need is still more utopian visions.[6]

The most frequent qualification is that utopia should be, or in particular cases is, 'realistic' or 'feasible'. This recurs across disciplines and outside the academy in relation to both cognitive models and prefigurative practices. Habermas calls for a realistic utopia based on human rights; Barenboim calls the West-Eastern Divan Orchestra a realistic utopia.[7] The relation between realism and utopia may be considered a tension or a contradiction: the idea of realistic utopia troubles both concepts, surfaces the politics of perceived possibility, and interrogates the relationship between present and future.

Mannheim argued that both utopia, defined as an idea which transforms the world in its own image, and ideology, which sustains the
status quo, are non-congruous with reality, adding absurdly that 'only
a state of mind that has been fully sociologically clarified operates with
situationally congruous ideas and motives'.[8] He distinguished absolute from relative utopias; the latter seem 'to be unrealizable only from
the point of view of a given social order which is already in existence',
whose dominant groups have a vested interest in declaring utopian and
unrealistic the social and political aspirations of subordinate classes.[9]
The boundary between utopia and the possible is by no means obvious and always contestable. As Bloch put it, 'possibility has had a bad
press', and '[t]here is a very clear interest that has prevented the world
being changed into the possible'.[10] Discussion of potential possibility
is silenced by the limits of public discourse or already invalidated as
utopian. Yet only that which seems impossible is remotely adequate to
the extremity of the condition of the world. Hence the resonance of the
1968 slogan, 'Be Realistic: Demand the Impossible'.

Qualifying utopia as realistic sets limits on its legitimacy, potentially
confining it to a conservative reading of the present or binding imagination too closely to what can be imagined as possible rather than what
can possibly be imagined. What remains may be only, in Mannheim's
terms, a form of ideology.[11] But the collapse of utopia into the real is not
necessary: the real may be understood as latency and tendency rather
than the fully existent. For Daniel Singer, the utopian term requires an
'attempt to change society, and not just to mend it'. Realism requires
that utopian aspiration is based in existing potentialities. But society
does 'contain the elements of its *potential* transformation' and the possibility of radical change is therefore real. Singer quotes Walt Whitman:
we are at a moment of suspension when society 'is for a while between
things ended and things begun'.[12]

The standpoint of the future

The complex politics of resolving 'realistic utopia' in an anti-utopian
or transformative direction are explored below principally through the
work of Richard Rorty, Roberto Unger and Erik Olin Wright. However,
the countervailing pulls towards what actually exists and towards a
better future are illuminated by a parallel discussion that does not engage
directly with utopia. Barbara Adam is a sociologist interested primarily
in time, social theory and ecology. *Future Matters*, written in 2007 with
Chris Groves, develops a distinction between present futures and future
presents. Present futures are imagined, planned and projected in and for

the present: the future appears from the standpoint of the present. Future presents are both imagined and produced by actions in the present, but the standpoint is the imagined future. Adam and Groves argue that 'the divergent standpoints involved affect not just our action but our ethical potential: responsibility for the future requires that we are able to take the standpoint of the future present and have the capacity to move knowledgeably between the two approaches'.[13] Rather than being 'an empty "not-yet" subject to our will and design',[14] the future is open, albeit already latent in our practices in ways both visible and invisible to us. Our actions in the present may mortgage or foreclose the future: thus '[c]ontemporary contexts where past and present futures are already in progress require that we grasp *as real* latent processes that set future presents in motion'.[15] We are embedded in processes of future-making that are at least partially opaque to us, and continually 'constructing our own futures through imagination and action'.[16] The argument about latency, process and becoming and the role of human action is close to Bloch – who is not mentioned, despite the recurrence of the term 'not-yet' in *Future Matters*. However, Adam and Groves view the 'not-yet' as a present future, whereas for Bloch it may be a future present.

Adam and Groves stipulate the need to defend an 'ethical vision that places the "good life" at its heart'; to 'make the future tangible, the invisible visible';[17] to embed a future-to-present direction in our social thought; to develop a positive vision of the future. They argue that scientific knowledge of the future is not possible, so that our orientation to the future must be informed by socio-cultural ethics, wisdom, imagination and responsibility, and this is a collective task. Only thus can futurity be redeemed. I waited for utopia, but it did not come. Yet utopian theory, as we have seen in Chapter 6, specifically addresses utopia's double face as projection into the future of current dilemmas and potential future offering a critical perspective on the present. Bammer in particular notes this 'doubled vision', in which the utopian mode has the ability to simultaneously 'project itself forward and from this imaginary place in time look back on its own origins'.[18] Utopia moves always between the standpoint of the present and the standpoint of the future.

Realism and utopia I: Carr and Rawls

Google delivers about a quarter of a million hits for 'realistic utopia' and 'realistic utopianism'. Almost two-thirds of these refer to the political philosopher John Rawls. Rawls distinguishes between 'realistic utopia' and 'utopian realism'. He reads the latter term, which comes from

E. H. Carr's 1939 discussion of international relations as hostile to utopianism: Carr opens with an indictment of utopianism from a realist perspective, contrasting these in terms of ethics and power. However, Carr continues with an equally caustic criticism of realism: 'Consistent realism excludes four things which appear to be essential ingredients of all political thinking; a finite goal, an emotional appeal, a right of moral judgement and a ground for action'. [19] He argues, therefore, that 'any sound political thought must be based on elements of both utopia and reality' – principles which are in constant struggle and which therefore render all utopias necessarily provisional.[20] In *The Law of Peoples*, Rawls proposes a 'realistic utopia', an international order called a Society of Peoples. Its principles extend the theme of justice as fairness set out in his earlier *A Theory of Justice*. His use of the term 'realistic utopia' is more important in the present context than the substance of his prescription or its detailed critique. Rawls argues that Carr's utopian realism presents 'reasonable political opinion as a *compromise* between both realism (power) and utopianism (moral judgment and value)', but that such a compromise is always determined by power; the realistic utopia differs in that it 'sets limits to the reasonable exercise of power'.[21] A realistic utopia is one that 'could and may exist'; it is achievable and consistent with what we know of the laws of nature, including human nature.[22] Rawls recognizes 'that there are questions about how the limits of the practically possible are discerned and what the conditions of our social world in fact are', endorsing speculation despite these limits to our knowledge;[23] thus he echoes Mannheim's point about the problematic boundary between absolute and relative utopias. In general, Rawls argues, '[p]olitical philosophy is realistically utopian when it extends what are ordinarily thought of as the limits of practical possibility'.[24] The Society of Peoples is specified in terms of content as 'a reasonably just constitutional democratic society' or more simply 'a liberal society',[25] which restricts as much as extends the perception of possibility. And although Rawls also argues that the idea of realistic utopia is 'importantly institutional', his argument largely remains at the level of theoretical abstraction (as is the nature of political philosophy). It constantly privileges the political over the economic and the social and thus does not engage fully with societies as institutional systems. And the function of Rawls's utopia is the antithesis of that suggested by writers such as Abensour, Jameson, Suvin or Moylan, who stress the importance of estrangement. For Rawls, the function of realistic utopia is quite the reverse: it 'reconciles us to our social world' by demonstrating that 'a reasonably just constitutional democracy existing as a member of a reasonably just Society of Peoples is *possible'*, providing a long-term political goal.[26]

The tension between realism and utopia occurs in relation to both abstract theory and practical politics, where it is expressed in the opposition between pragmatism and utopia. Karl Popper identified utopia with intellectual and social closure, insisting on the superiority of gradual and piecemeal change. The usual meaning of political pragmatism, more usually contrasted with ideology, is pursuit of 'what works'. It prioritises short-term fixes for problems within the current system; questions of the viability or justice of that system itself, and certainly radical alternatives, are placed outside legitimate political debate. There are, however, different kinds of pragmatism. The tension between realism and utopia can be resolved either in a conservative direction (as is actually the case with Rawls), or one which, as Rawls proposes, extends the perception and indeed the boundary of the possible. These opposite possibilities are illustrated by Richard Rorty and Roberto Unger.

Realism and utopia II: Richard Rorty

Rorty is one of the writers el-Ojeili cites as part of the turn back to utopia in the 1990s. Rorty has been described as 'utopian, hopeful and optimistic without being reckless, unrealistic and undemocratic' – a set of oppositions already suspicious of utopia.[27] He makes strong claims for the necessity of social hope and the importance of utopian speculation; yet he coopts the terminology of utopia to positions that are antagonistic to fundamental change, an anti-utopian position disguised by his explicit commitment to social hope.

Rorty argues that 'historical narrative and utopian speculation are the best sort of background for political deliberation'; that the best kind of historical narrative is that which 'segues into a utopian scenario about how we can get from the present to a better future'; and that the excision of this kind of narrativity from political and social theory results in, and represents, a loss of hope.[28] It is part of the superiority of '[we] moderns' over 'the ancients' that we are able 'to imagine a utopia here on earth', this representing 'a massive shift in the locus of human hope ... from eternity to future time';[29] and '[t]he utopian social hope which sprang up in nineteenth century Europe is still the noblest imaginative creation of which we have record'.[30] The deconstructive turn in social theory cannot 'make obsolete the old-fashioned utopian scenario, the one that leads to a global society of freedom and equal opportunity'.[31] He praises Habermas and John Dewey as examples of 'antiauthoritarian philosophers of human freedom and social justice' who are still 'devoted to ... utopian social hope' and to the kind of philosophy that allows 'the imagination to play upon the possibilities of a utopian future'.[32] Indeed, Rorty comes close to arguing that some form of the utopian impulse is what makes us distinctively human. The 'quest for knowledge' should be demoted 'from the status of end-in-itself to that of one more means towards human happiness', and 'trust, social cooperation and social hope are where our humanity begins and ends'.[33]

Rorty hopes for 'full social justice', glossed in Marx's terms as 'a classless society', a world in which 'the free development of each is the condition for the free development of all'.[34] He hopes that 'some day we shall be willing and able to treat the needs of all human beings with the respect and consideration with which we treat the needs of those closest to us, those whom we love'.[35] He hopes for a 'global egalitarian utopia'.[36] He contrasts this with the reality that one per cent of citizens of the United States own forty per cent of their country's wealth. A national and global overclass is emerging, accompanied by the 'steady immiseration of everyone else'.[37] This was written several years before the 2011 Occupy movement headlined the difference between the one per cent and the ninety nine per cent. This overclass, says Rorty (echoing Wells), has 'less and less at stake in America's future, and more and more invested in an efficient and productive global economy'.[38] The 'brutal struggle between the corporations and the workers', is one in which 'the corporations are winning'.[39] Levels of inequality are morally repugnant, so '[o]ur children need to learn, early on, to see the inequalities between their own fortunes and those of other children as neither the Will of God nor the necessary price for economic efficiency, but as an evitable tragedy'.[40]

In *Achieving Our Country*, Rorty reclaims the romantic utopianism of Whitman and Dewey, crediting them with a transformative vision in which 'America is destined to become the first cooperative commonwealth, the first classless society. This America would be one in which income and wealth are equitably distributed, and in which the government ensures equality of opportunity as well as individual liberty'.[41] Rorty suggests Whitman and Dewey provided a narrative that demanded engagement in the utopian project of achieving that new society. In that secular, this-worldly, project 'utopian America ... replace[d] God as the unconditional object of desire'; 'Dewey wanted Americans to share a civic religion that substituted utopian striving for claims to theological knowledge'.[42] Rorty argues that this involved 'replacing shared knowledge of what is already real with social hope for what might become real', and consequently '[f]orgetting about eternity, and replacing knowledge of the antecedently real with hope for the contingent future'.[43] The contrast between hope and knowledge underlines the importance of contingency: America's self-creation is merely possible, rather than inevitable, with Whitman and Dewey's refusal of 'knowledge', 'making room for pure, joyous, hope'.[44]

Rorty's account of American intellectual history is, as he says of Dewey and Whitman's utopianism, a mythological narrative constructed for a political purpose rather than a representation intended to correspond to a fictitious 'real', and it has the same utopian intent. Rorty's version of pragmatism refuses criteria of truth or falsehood in favour of social efficacy: 'we call beliefs true when the adoption of them makes us better able to achieve happiness'.[45] The purpose is the achievement of a version of 'America' claimed as the essence of the American Constitution. Rorty asserts elsewhere that 'America was founded upon an ethical concept of freedom. It was founded as the land of the freest society, the place where democracy is at its best, where the horizons are open'.[46] He declares wildly that '[m]y native country has world-historical importance only because it cast itself in the role of vanguard of a global egalitarian utopia. It no longer casts itself in that role, and is therefore in danger of losing its soul'.[47]

Barack Obama's 2008 acceptance speech as President-elect of the United States contained the same theme of realizing the American Constitution. It opened: 'If there is anyone out there who still doubts that America is a place where all things are possible; who still wonders if the dream of our founders is alive in our time; who still questions the power of our democracy, tonight is your answer'. It ended with the assertion that 'This is our time ... to reclaim the American Dream'.[48] The echo, of course, is of Martin Luther King's 'I have a dream', similarly projected as the true realization of the Constitution: 'I still have a dream. It is a dream deeply rooted in the American dream. I have a dream that one day this nation will rise up and live out the true meaning of its creed: "We hold these truths to be self-evident, that all men are created equal"'.[49] Again, this is utopian in the sense of embedding a view of a good society and in requiring radical change: those words imply a very different institutional structure. Arguably, King's speech was genuinely utopian and transformative, while Obama's utopian rhetoric was mobilized in support of a reformist agenda. Ironically, by 2012, despite building his original campaign on the hope for a better future, Obama was viewed as utopian only by his opponents, for whom it was a conventional term of abuse.[50] Mitt Romney's 2012 presidential campaign against Obama recycled the Cold War 'socialism equals communism equals fascism'. Bumper stickers included 'Obama is a socialist, Muslim and a dumb ass'; 'the socialist Obamanation of America', on a red ground with a hammer and sickle and image of the Kremlin; 'Comrade Obama', in yellow, with a hammer and sickle, on a red ground. One anti-Obama badge reads 'The Nazis were Socialists too'.

A second element in *Achieving Our Country* systematically undermines its critical, transformative and utopian import. It lays claim to 'good' utopianism but rejects 'bad' utopianism. Rorty distinguishes the good reformist Left from both the bad revolutionary Left and from the bad new intellectual Left that has substituted cultural politics for real politics. Included in the reformist Left are 'all those Americans who, between 1900 and 1964, struggled within the framework of constitutional democracy to protect the weak from the strong' – including people who described themselves as communists and socialists.[51] This broad church incorporates some who would hardly appreciate Rorty's endorsement, such as the anarchist Emma Goldman who was deported from the United States. The Frankfurt School are commended for their imputed 'attempt to modulate Marxism down into plain, social democratic, reformist left politics'.[52] According to Rorty, the social democratic left was replaced – or at least weakened – by 'the people – mostly students – who decided, around 1964, that it was no longer possible to work for social justice within the system'.[53] This is an extraordinary claim given the rise of the civil rights movement at exactly that juncture. The essential point is that 'good' Lefties are not revolutionaries.

Rorty is virulently anti-communist and hostile to Marxism, running these together with fascism in familiar anti-utopian ways. Thus, 'I think of Marxism and fascism just as conspiracies, not as ideas. I don't think they should be given any intellectual dignity'; or, 'I don't believe that Marxism has any more importance than the so-called philosophy of National Socialism. It was just an excuse for the gangsters to rule'.[54] He aligns himself with 'anglophones who never studied [Marx] very hard when they were young and are not inclined to start now',[55] and suggests that in the United States 'nobody cares if you have read Marx – not even Fredric Jameson'.[56] Yet he also claims that 'Marx ... explained the injustices produced by nineteenth-century capitalism better than anyone else'[57] – which would in itself be compelling reason to read Marx, and to apply, as Harvey does, those analyses to contemporary capitalism. At the same time, Rorty describes both the New Testament and the Communist Manifesto as 'inspirational' vehicles of social hope, even if that hope takes the form of 'false prediction'. We should, he says, 'skip lightly past the predictions, and concentrate on the expressions of hope'.[58] But understanding Marx is for Rorty far less important than the mobilizing myth of the American Constitution: Marx has 'nothing in common with the idea of democratic socialism', whose purpose is 'to create institutions which can gradually reduce the subordination of production to profit, do away with poverty, diminish inequality, remove social barriers to educational opportunities, and minimise the threat to democratic liberties from state bureaucracy and the seductions of totalitarianism'.[59] The threat to democratic liberties from economic exploitation and market monopolies passes without comment. His insistence on the 'irrelevance' of Marxism and Communism ignores the role of McCarthyism in excising these trivialities from American politics and culture and severely muting the possible forms of their expression.

Rorty is utopian in promoting an image of the good society, and perhaps also in the derogatory sense of being unrealistic about the means of its realization. But this is an anti-utopian utopianism. The celebration of the American Constitution and hostility to Marxism are braided together to close down the limits of imaginative and practical possibility. Rorty's commitment to the free market is unquestioning, even if 'the free market is not an end in itself. It is just one means among others to further the development of a utopian democratic society'.[60] 'Pragmatism is just a continuation of ... viewing American democracy as the greatest thing ever invented, the source of all good things', and 'ordinary liberal democracy is all the ideology anybody needs'.[61] The central political judgement of *Achieving Our Country* is that 'the Left should get back into the business of piecemeal reform within the framework of a market economy'.[62] There is no room for non-capitalist envisioning: there is, indeed, no alternative; and there is no room for questioning whether non-gradual change may be either necessary, or indeed forced upon us by the contradictions between capitalist accumulation and environmental sustainability. This, then, is not the education of hope or desire, but an exercise in social and ideological control. After three decades of the rise of the neo-liberal utopia/dystopia, social democracy is, as Rorty suggests, itself utopian. However, both social democracy and especially its identification with constitutional perfectionism ensure that the standpoint remains firmly that of the present future, effectively substituting a continuing present for a future of possibilities. Any qualification of utopia as feasible, achievable or realistic needs to be scrutinized for this anti-utopian tendency.

Realism and utopia III: Roberto Unger

In contrast to Rorty, Unger overtly opposes utopianism, but he develops a radical pragmatism that is more open to imagination and experimentation. His 1998 *Democracy Realised* lies closer to Bloch's idea of educated hope. It is a summary statement of Unger's hopes for a gradual transformation of the global *status quo* into a world that is more democratic and more economically just, through a process he describes as democratic experimentalism. Here Unger's arguments are pitched in terms of the institutional structures of society, and a process of change of those economic, social and political structures and processes through step-by-step improvisation and collective learning. The radical potential of pragmatism is made explicit in his later book *The Self Awakened*.

Like Rorty, Unger starts from a market framework, but one in which 'market economies, free civil societies and representative democracies can assume many different institutional forms'.[63] Like Rorty, Unger regards both Marxism and Keynesianism as 'discredited'.[64] Like Rorty, Unger distinguishes between 'the good part of Marxism, the transformative aspirations', and the 'bad part, the historical fatalism'.[65] Like Rorty, Unger is critical of aspirations for revolutionary change. But Unger's argument leads in a different direction. The idea of revolution supposes substituting one indivisible social totality for another. This is an illusion about how change happens that neglects the institutional openness of systems and their room for manouevre and space for improvisation. Unger does share the anti-utopian fear that 'when reality resists the illusion, the would-be revolutionaries may resort to violence, seeking in physical force the means to make good on the hypertrophy of the will'.[66] He is therefore, like Rorty and Rawls, explicitly gradualist and anti-necessitarian. But if change comes from tinkering with the system, it should be 'motivated, sustained and cumulative tinkering'.[67] Unger does not refuse to challenge fundamental aspects of the existing system, but rather aims 'to associate the idea of discontinuous structural change with the practical attitudes of the person who forever asks: What is the next step?'.[68] He makes specific proposals about economic and social reforms, shaped to countries at varying stages of development and occupying different positions in the global economy. His political goal is an alternative to neo-liberalism, that 'requires connected and successive institutional innovations'.[69] Radical pragmatism means recognizing our partial and contingent knowledge and devising ways of changing the institutional order bit by bit so that more experimentation is possible.

In *The Self Awakened,* Unger explicitly distances himself from the political position of American pragmatism, or democratic perfectionism:

> A first hallmark of democratic perfectionism is the belief that a free society has an institutional formula that, once discovered (as it supposedly was by the founders of the American Republic and the framers of the American constitution), needs to be adjusted only in rare moments of national and world crisis and, even then, only to adapt its enduring truths to changed circumstances. This ... amounts to a species of idolatry.[70]

This 'cult of the Constitution' effectively denies the alterability of social life, fetishizing a particular set of institutional arrangements. 'It is a heresy ... that ... diverts and corrupts, through its error in drawing the line between the mutable and the immutable features of our existence' – a heresy, moreover, 'armed, and identified with the power of the United States', which should be resisted.[71]

Unger's pragmatism differs, then, from Rorty's in its political intention. Imagination plays a central role. It is deployed in the practical activity of social improvisation: 'The master tool of democratic experimentalism is institutional innovation, practiced not from on high, with fanciful blueprints and perfectionist designs, but with the materials at hand and in the situation of the moment'.[72] In his own work '[t]he program is not a blueprint. It is a set of connected ideas and proposals, tentative in spirit and adaptable to circumstance. I have chosen to explore this programmatic direction at points both relatively close to present arrangements and relatively distant from them. The direction is what matters'.[73] The problem of blueprints, for Unger, is that they are external to the systems they are intended to change, and he criticizes (especially Anglophone) political philosophy for 'treat[ing] the formulation of normative principles and ideals as an activity separate from, and prior to, the design of institutional arrangements'.[74] This is, as I have suggested earlier, a reflection of its unsociological character, and its weakness as utopian method: the latter is characterized precisely by the instantiation of abstract principles in institutional systems. As Unger says, '[i]nstitutional debates and experiments are not a separate and subsidiary exercise; they represent our most important way of defining and redefining the content of our ideals and interests'.[75]

Unger's suspicion of blueprints does not imply anti-utopianism. As I have argued throughout, utopias are not blueprints. More importantly, Unger does not regard imagining alternatives as unrealistic.

He recognizes that 'utopian' is often a way of invalidating visions of a better world because 'we have lost confidence in our ability to imagine structural change in society'.[76] The importance of a 'visionary' element in sustaining and directing political change is a constant theme:

> The visionary ... intimation of a reordered social world, with its poetic attempt to connect present personal experiences to hidden social possibilities, helps right the scales of risk by enlarging the imaginative terrain on which the debate takes place. As the consequences of reforms for the understanding of interests and ideal become manifest, the boundary shutting the instrumental off from the visionary begins to open. Then history makes more room for imagination.[77]

We need imagination in the short term and in the long term. For Unger, '[t]he practical imagination of institutional alternatives enables us to recognise transformative opportunity and act on it', and this 'requires a larger vision of society and history that can help and inspire its work'. Moreover, imagination has a role in preventing social change occurring in a catastrophic or revolutionary manner: it 'does the work of crisis without crisis'.[78]

Imagining alternatives helps to counter conformity by contradicting the taken-for-granted character of the real. 'The detailed image of an alternative is an insufficient condition, but it may also be a necessary one. The builders of an alternative will need such an image both to resist the gravitational pull of the dominant conceptions and to work out the operational logic of the institutions they establish'.[79] This recalls Morris's observation that although all alternatives are bound by their historical context and the temperament of the writer, they are nonetheless necessary to maintaining the struggle for a better world. Indeed, commentaries on Morris demonstrate other affinities with Unger. For John Goode, the function of the dream form in Morris's writing is neither to posit a goal nor to provide an escapist fantasy, but 'to insist on a whole structure of values and perspectives which must emerge in the conscious mind in order to assert the inner truth of that actuality, and give man the knowledge of his own participation in the historical process which dissolves that actuality'.[80]

For Unger, as for Jameson, changing the world demands a changed subjectivity. But rather than seeing this as a fatal restriction on utopian imagination and possibility, Unger suggests that the change in us must happen slowly and with our consent. It involves 'the intimation of a different world, in which we would become (slightly) different people, with (slightly) revised understandings of our interests and ideals'.[81] This aspect of Unger's argument, which develops a utopian ontology, is discussed further in Chapter 9 below. The situated process of transformation of ourselves in the world leads to a 'remaking of our understanding of the actual by the imagination of the possible' and 'requires a large measure of detachment from the now dominant culture'.[82]

It is not unrealistic to imagine alternatives; neither the real nor the possible is limited to the actual. To confuse realism with what currently actually exists is, says Unger, to accept surrogate standards; rather, 'we must be visionaries to become realists'.[83] What is taken as real and what is possible are defined by both imagination and by praxis. 'Ideas exercise their decisive power upon the demarcation between the actual and the possible when they begin to animate the available forms of social action'.[84] We customarily think in terms of possible futures and their pursuit following from the definition of reality and possibility, but we need to think in the opposite direction – from future to present rather than present to future, from the possible to the real as well as from the real to the possible. Reality and possibility are interconnected, for '[t]o understand a state of affairs is to grasp its possible transformations: what it could become under different conditions or as the result of different events'.[85] Unger rejects the language of a horizon of possibilities in so far as this implies a series of 'spectral' possibilities or a fixed series of alternatives suspended in the future waiting to be actualized; this serves to limit the openness of the future by failing to understand that action *creates* possibility, both imaginatively and institutionally. And while we customarily assume that causal processes and relationships are immutable, time and change 'go all the way down'; even these laws may be subject to change, indicating a greater possibility of openness.[86] Unger's suspicion about horizon seems to joust with the ghost of Bloch, although their positions are similar. For Bloch, the concept of horizon does not imply an array of fixed alternatives; he also takes a processual view and similarly includes future possibility within the real. Zizek goes further, suggesting that the facticity of the real contains the detritus of unrealized past possibilities as well as the elements of potential alternative futures.

For both Unger and Rorty, the future is claimed as an arena of hope rather than knowledge. But whereas Rorty's attachment to the American Constitution spells institutional closure and the rejection of utopian alterity, for Unger the future is open, and through democratic experimentalism may be made more so. This offers a more hopeful accommodation between pragmatism and utopia. It does not mean that anything is possible, but that step-by-step changes of ourselves and our world could lead to a transformation of social structures and of the capacities and capabilities of those who inhabit, produce and reproduce them. Thus, '[w]e act as if a certain conception were possible in the hope of making it possible. However, such hopes are justified only so long as the self-fulfilling prophecy they embody tells a story we can begin to live out in the here and now'.[87] The point, says Unger, is not to rescue pragmatism, but to 'raise up our humanity'.[88] Echoing the darkness of the lived moment, he draws attention to the fine line between abstract utopia or hoping for the unattainable, and imagining, hoping for, and claiming too little, and to the impossibility of being certain that we will draw that line in the right place:

> We lack the metric with which to measure the proximity of our programs to our circumstances. We must walk, in relative darkness, the narrow path between wishful thinking and the denial of the pragmatic, prophetic residue in our understanding of transformative possibility. We lack the metric, and always will.[89]

Real utopias: Erik Olin Wright

The tension between pragmatism and utopia also informs the US sociologist Wright's 2010 *Envisioning Real Utopias*, perhaps the most significant example of sociology's return to utopia. Wright presents this as the outcome of 'a dialogic process', developed through over fifty talks in eighteen countries, web postings, teaching and discussion within Wisconsin's Real Utopias Project from which it emerged.[90] He describes it as emancipatory social science: 'the word *emancipatory* identifies a central moral purpose in the production of knowledge – the elimination of oppression and the creation of the conditions for human flourishing. And the word *social* implies the belief that human emancipation depends upon the transformation of the social world, not just the inner life of persons'.[91] Critique of the present must be combined with exploring institutionally specific alternatives that are desirable, viable and achievable. This appears to be utopia as method deployed to explore possible alternative futures; yet adherence to particular conceptions of reality and science undercut the utopian claim. For Wright, real means 'actually existing', a position very different from that of other utopian writers. Part of Bammer's project is to 'counter the notion of the utopian as unreal with the proposition that utopia is powerfully real';[92] for Bloch and Unger, the real includes that which is not yet. For Paolo

Friere, '[r]eality as it is thought does not correspond to the reality being lived objectively, but rather to the reality in which the alienated man imagines himself to be'.[93]

Wright's tripartite argument begins with diagnosis and critique, moving through possible alternatives to processes of transformation. Both in terms of critique and reconstruction, Wright argues for institutional specificity. Critique requires that we show that suffering, harm and inequality are not inevitable but caused by social structures and institutions. Any proposed alternative must be couched at the same level. Most utopian social theory and normative political philosophy fail here, because typically (as I have argued in relation to Rawls) the emphasis is 'on the enunciation of abstract principles rather than actual institutional designs'.[94]

In substance, Wright offers a stringent critique of capitalism. It embeds class relations that perpetuate unnecessary human suffering and blocks the conditions for human flourishing. It limits individual autonomy and violates 'liberal egalitarian principles of social justice'. It is inefficient, biased towards consumerism and environmentally destructive. It corrodes community and limits democracy. It fuels militarism and imperialism. These claims are made from a particular normative standpoint, but also as social *science*:

> The starting point for building an emancipatory social science is identifying the ways in which existing social institutions and social structures systematically impose harms on people. It is not enough to show that people are suffering or that there are enormous inequalities in the extent to which people may live flourishing lives. A scientific emancipatory theory must show that the explanation for such suffering and inequality lies in specific properties of institutions and social structures. The first task of emancipatory social science, therefore, is the diagnosis and critique of the causal processes that generate these harms.[95]

The second part of the book begins with an extended exposition and discussion of the historical trajectory beyond capitalism predicted by Marx. The following chapters on the 'socialist compass' and 'real utopias' are the 'utopian' core of the book, proceeding from more general claims to institutional examples. Wright's normative starting point is a commitment to broadly equal access to the necessary material and social means for human flourishing, 'necessary' implying equality of opportunity rather than substantive equality. Political justice requires broadly equal access to participation in decision-making. These indicate some version of socialism, defined as 'an economic structure within which the means of production are socially owned and the allocation and use of resources for different social purposes is accomplished through the exercise of "social power"'.[96] The contrast between socialism and capitalism which is dominated by markets and private ownership is expected. But socialism is also distinguished from state ownership of the means of production, or 'statism'. Social power is rooted in civil society, and the direction set by the socialist compass entails extending the power of civil society over the state, over economic power, and over economic activity. Wright adopts a fashionable preference for 'civil society' and localism, an antipathy to the state widespread across the political spectrum. The socialist compass operates with a narrow view of the economy; it neglects economic activity outside the formal labour market, gender and the environment. My purpose, however, is not the exposition and exhaustive critique of Wright's utopia, but an exploration of his utopian method.

The rehabilitation of utopia turns out to be limited. Wright does not refer to utopian literature, those exercises in speculative sociology that present alternative ways of being, nor to theoretical commentary on utopia and utopianism, and even his discussion of utopian socialism is based on a single secondary source, Martin Buber's *Paths in Utopia*. It is not clear what is intended by the phrase 'utopian social theory', even as this is criticized for its abstraction. The 'real utopias' that Wright outlines entail the 'fundamental redesign of different arenas of social institutions' and not 'general, abstract formulations of grand designs'.[97] They are actually-existing institutional, or prefigurative, practices. In Wright's sense, the West-Eastern Divan Orchestra is a real, rather than (merely) a realistic utopia. His own examples include participatory city budgeting, unconditional basic income, workers' cooperatives (including those at Mondragon) and Wikipedia.

This appeal to 'real utopias' is deeply ambivalent about the utopian mode, which is assumed to be fundamentally unrealistic:

> Utopias are fantasies, morally inspired designs for social life unconstrained by realistic considerations of human psychology and social feasibility. Realists eschew such fantasies. What we need are hard-nosed proposals for pragmatically improving our institutions. Instead of indulging in utopian dreams we must accommodate to practical realities.[98]

The Real Utopias Project 'embraces' this 'tension between dreams and practice'.[99] Utopias may act as regulative ideals, and even if unachievable may contribute to political mobilization. But they are dangerous, for 'vague utopian fantasies may lead us astray, encouraging us to embark on trips that have no real destinations at all, or, worse still, which lead us to some unforeseen abyss'.[100] Out of this need for visions of an alternative social order and the constraints of present conditions arises the need for 'Real Utopias':

> What we need, then, is 'real utopias': utopian ideals that are grounded in the real potentials of humanity, utopian destinations that have accessible waystations, utopian designs of institutions that can inform our practical tasks of navigating a world of imperfect conditions for social change.[101]

Wright endorses the role of the social imaginary in constructing possibility: 'what is possible pragmatically is not fixed independently of our imaginations, but is itself shaped by our visions'.[102] The term 'utopian' continues to serve as a derogatory indicator of impossibility: Pure communism is ... a utopian fantasy, since a complex society could not function without some sort of authoritative means of making and enforcing binding rules'. Michael Albert is criticized for a proposal 'more like a utopian vision ... than ... a viable design for a real utopian alternative to capitalism'.[103]

Real utopias, or examples of redesigned institutions, are necessarily partial rather than systemic. Wright is not the only commentator to prefer partial rather than holistic utopian proposals, although his reasons are different. Bammer, as we saw in Chapter 6, contends from a feminist perspective that partial utopias resist the conservatism inherent in closure. Wayne Hudson, in *The Reform of Utopia*, argues in postmodern vein for partial rather than holistic utopian thinking.[104] Jeffrey Alexander, ostensibly favouring 'robust utopias', endorses these as partial, fragmentary, and largely directed towards the reform of (aspects of) civil society rather than the constitution of a radically other social order. Alexander's account reprises the fear of totality as totalizing and incipiently totalitarian. Wright refuses speculative holism, even though such systemic thinking is embedded in his critique. He thus rules out, in relation to the future, one of the great virtues of the utopian (and sociological) approach, namely the ability to explore how different spheres interact at the institutional level. This creates difficulties with his argument. He is, as we have seen, anti-statist, notwithstanding his comments on 'pure communism', and yet it is difficult to see how basic income can work on any substantial scale without state-level distributive mechanisms. Appealing to civil society is, as Harvey points out, quite as problematic as any modernist or statist planning; the real question is how to connect political activities and institutions across social and geographical scales.

The usefulness of 'real utopias' as institutional models for an alternative future depends on how we read such prefigurative practices, including whether and how we imagine them scaled up. Alternative practices are not necessarily oppositional, and may neither intend nor be susceptible to generalization. Davina Cooper reads spaces and practices including public nudity, a venue for casual lesbian and trans sex, and Summerhill School as forms of everyday utopias. They provide spaces for being otherwise, but Cooper's analysis concerns their epistemological rather than their practical critical function. Viewing them through the lenses of equality, care and property respectively interrogates these concepts, which necessarily oscillate between ideational meanings and actualizations, opening up utopian possibility.[105] Lucy Sargisson sees intentional communities as spaces for being otherwise, the focus often as much or more on self-transformation rather than on modelling a large-scale social alternative, although that may also be an aspiration.[106] When Barenboim describes the West-Eastern Divan as a realistic utopia, he is not suggesting that orchestras should be the basic unit of social organization, although the Sistema projects imply there should be far more of them; the orchestra is a real space for making music and remaking selves, but a metaphor rather than a model for the good society.

There are prefigurative practices which intend expansion to the whole. Owen envisaged communities coalescing into a cooperative commonwealth and replacing capitalist relations. The Spanish village of Marinaleda in Andalusia, described by Dan Hancox in *Utopia and the Valley of Tears*, is similarly intended as the model for a transformed Spain. Marinaleda's mayor, Juan Manuel Sánchez Gordillo, says:

> We're trying to put in place now what we want for the future. But we don't want to wait till tomorrow, we want to do it today. If we start to do it today, then it becomes possible, and it becomes an example to show others, that there are other ways to do politics, other ways to do economics, another way to live together – a different society.[107]

He adds: 'Utopias aren't chimeras, they are the most noble dreams that people have. Dreams that through struggle, can and must be turned into reality'.[108] Hancox visited Marinaleda amid the crippling austerity and unemployment of Spain's economic crisis and the protests of the *indignados*. As part of these protests, which have included flash performances of flamenco dance in Spanish banks, in August 2012, Gordillo (who thinks banks should disappear) led supermarket raids for food to distribute to the destitute. Marinaleda, a self-styled 'utopia towards peace', has proved remarkably resilient in the face of the crisis partly because of its distinctive mechanisms of housing construction and ownership. It is an anarcho-communist agricultural village developed over thirty years on expropriated land, deliberately choosing labour-intensive crops to create jobs which have been sustained when employment elsewhere has collapsed. Hancox is careful not to assume that Marinaleda conforms to the way in which it is projected in the social imaginary, and indeed notes the complexity of admiration and suspicion that surrounds it.

Wright privileges real utopias because he thinks they give a better guide to future options than imagined totalities. There is clear intent to scale up. But this immediately brings imagination into play. Does this mean a multiplication of Marinaledas? That would ignore Marinaleda's place in a wider society within which its products are transported and marketed, and where construction materials, for example are imported and financed by the Andalusian government. Scaling up means diversification, imagining a wider and more complex economy and society – and one in which it may be rather less viable than in a village of 3000 people to simply abolish the police force. The tradition of Spanish anarchism within which Marinaleda emerged is, like Wright, anti-statist. Yet Marinaleda's viability depends on inaction by the state: Hancox notes the oddity of tolerance for the original and ongoing seizure of land. Spain has a history of popular revolt, but also a history of brutal repression by state or insurgent nationalist forces. It seems highly unlikely that a *general* expropriation of property of this kind would go unchallenged. As Gordillo says, 'Power uses violence when something of theirs is touched that they don't want touched'.[109]

The partial institutional form of real utopias cannot be generalized other than within an imagined totality. Real utopias are always only 'blueprints of possibility'.[110] Gordillo's dream is 'that the natural resources and the riches the worker produces will come back to him, instead of being usurped by a few. ... The dream of equality; the dream that housing should belong to everyone, because you are a person and not a piece of merchandise to be speculated with'.[111] That, first in Marinaleda, then Andalusia, then the world, but not as repetition: that was then, this is now. Hancox ends with a statement of faith that the Spanish people 'will create something new, because their history and public culture have equipped them to do so – and more darkly, because they have no alternative',[112] 'because on top of everything the numbers of hungry people keep growing'.[113]

Real utopias thus only inform alternative futures when imagined as part of a wider whole. But Wright's reason for caution here is our inadequate knowledge: potential utopian function is limited through the qualification of realism, but also through privileging science over imagination. For Wright, emancipatory social science seeks to 'generate scientific knowledge' which will enable a reduction in human suffering and oppression. 'To call this a form of social *science*', he says, 'recognizes the importance of systematic scientific knowledge about how the world works'.[114] Real utopias must be both viable and achievable, and we just don't 'know' enough about the project or process of transformation. For Wright, as for Unger, possibilities are created rather than fixed: 'the conscious strategies of actors ... *transform the conditions of their own actions*'.[115] But 'if we take seriously emancipatory social science as a form of *science*, not just philosophical critique ... the discovery of such possibilities depends upon the progress of knowledge'.[116] Moreover, 'our capacity to generate scientifically credible knowledge about social conditions beyond the near future is very limited', so that our struggles and strategies always outstrip our 'knowledge', in this sense: there is always a gap between 'the time-horizons of scientific theory and the time-horizons of transformative struggles'.[117] This is more than a claim that our practice in the world is always risky, that we cannot escape the darkness of the lived moment even through the light of anticipatory illumination. Rather than turning to imagination as a resource as Unger or Adam and Groves do, Wright's caution becomes an argument against utopia. Its restrictive and delegitimizing effect is exemplified in his critique of Albert's 'parecon' model of a potential participatory economy:

I do not think we have enough grasp of the issues to know how a complex economic system organized through decentralized planning councils without any markets would actually function, or even whether such a structure would be even minimally viable. What we have observed and can study are specific workplaces in which democratic-participatory principles are rigorously in place, as well as a variety of more macro-settings where meaningful forms of participatory councils have operated (as in the participatory budget in Porto Alegre). But these limited settings hardly constitute an empirical basis for making confident claims about how an economic system built on these principles would or could function. This of course does not imply the converse – that we know enough now to be sure that parecon as envisaged by Michael Albert is impossible – but admitting that parecon might be possible (because of our ignorance on a range of problems) is insufficient grounds upon which to propose a transformative project that confidently rejects any role for markets in a democratic egalitarian society.[118]

Albert's model, like all utopias, may properly be subjected to exhaustive critique. But Wright's mode of argument blocks off the Imaginary Reconstitution of Society when it cannot lay claim to legitimacy in existing accepted 'scientific' knowledge. It also fails to recognize what is generated through the holistic modelling of alternative institutions – the utopian method – as knowledge, despite the fact that much scientific knowledge depends on modelling possible scenarios. 'Scientific' knowledge, or the lack of it, becomes a criterion for limiting the utopian hypothesis, binding 'real' or 'viable' utopias closely to the present, and reproducing the opposition between science and utopia that has haunted sociology since its inception.

John Urry's 2011 *Climate Change and Society*, a rare sociological engagement with debates about possible futures in the light of environmental crisis, takes a more holistic approach than Wright and one more favourable to the state. He proposes a reorientation of sociology to address the resource base as well as the social structure of societies, and a reconstitution of society as 'resource capitalism', embedding a different relationship between society and nature in which nature would not be subject to short-term calculations of profit. His four alternative scenarios for the future are Corbusier (perpetual consumerism), Schumacher (local sustainability), Hobbesian (regional warlordism) and Digital (networked low carbon). The last is Urry's preferred version of what he calls resource capitalism. The implied level of regulation suggests a social organization scarcely identifiable as capitalism, which is driven by capital accumulation and expansion in a way a society that conserves its resources cannot be. Retaining the term seems either contradictory or an attempt not to frighten the capitalist horses who are at the same time the horsemen of the apocalypse. But these are attempts at 'whole society' global futures, albeit outlined in a couple of pages each. Urry insists on the importance of alternative imaginaries, and on social reflexivity and the imagination of alternative futures. The exigencies of the present mean, he says, that 'we will all be forced to become futurologists whether we like it or not'. Again, this is a kind of utopian method, although Urry refuses the term in favour of scenario-building. While partially conceding the knowledge-generating capacities of utopianism, he rejects it because of its normativity and because 'utopian thinking has not been well regarded in social science'; this, of course, like sociology's neglect of resources, reflects more on social science than on utopia.[119] But Urry distances himself from utopia to maintain his credentials as a social scientist, and in so doing again reproduces the false antithesis between sociology and utopia.

Thus the utopian impulse in sociology warily, self-questioningly, and setting its own limits, reasserts itself. We need to push forward to a less cautious and more imaginative engagement with possible futures, in which utopia is understood as a creative form of sociology, building on the strengths of the discipline which include its focus on institutions, its systemic holism, its attention to subjects and agents as well as structures and processes. Above all, we need to understand utopia as a method rather than a goal, and therefore as a process which is necessarily provisional, reflexive and dialogic. It is always suspended between the present and the future, always under revision, at the meeting point of the darkness of the lived moment and the flickering light of a better world, for the moment accessible only through an act of imagination.

Part III

8
Utopia as Archaeology

We turn now to setting out the Imaginary Reconstitution of Society as a method. This is not the invention of a method, but the identification of how the utopian mode works as speculative sociology. Indeed, my argument is that this is how most explicitly utopian proposals from the fin de siècle on are intended, as provisional and reflexive models of possible futures open to criticism and debate; and where this is not how they are intended, it is nevertheless how they should best be treated. Readings that interrogate the unconscious of the text, or explore the formal means by which the utopian marvelous or the quality of grace is conveyed, are also important, for these bear on their capacity to address what it means to be human, and this is a fundamental element of utopia as method.

Utopia as method has three modes. The first is an archaeological mode, piecing together the images of the good society that are embedded in political programmes and social and economic policies. The second is an ontological mode which addresses the question of what kind of *people* particular societies develop and encourage. What is understood as human flourishing, what capabilities are valued, encouraged and genuinely enabled, or blocked and suppressed, by specific existing or potential social arrangements: we are concerned here with the historical and social determination of human nature. This was identified by Mills as a central constitutive question for sociology. The third is an architectural mode – that is, the imagination of potential alternative scenarios for the future, acknowledging the assumptions about and consequences for the people who might inhabit them. These in turn must be subject to archaeological critique, addressing the silences and inconsistencies all such images must contain, as well as the political steps forward that they imply. These are not, then, three different methods, but three aspects of the same method subject to shifting emphases, which form the subject matter of these next three chapters.

The premise of utopia as archaeology is that most political positions contain implicit images of the good society and views of how people are and should be, the latter often elided in statements about human nature. The utopias underlying political claims and policy initiatives are rarely owned, especially by governments which lay claim to a pragmatic approach, ostensibly rejecting 'ideology' in favour of 'what works'. Utopia (or ideology) is the imputed flaw of others. Their visions of the good society – in McEwan's terms, Christ's kingdom on earth, the workers' paradise, the ideal Islamic state – are designated utopian (and dangerous).[1] Western democracy is, as noted in Chapter 1, less often acknowledged as utopian.

Archaeology undertakes excavations and reconstructions of both artefacts or cultures, based on a mixture of evidence, deduction and imagination, representing as whole something of which only shards and fragments remain. Where images of the good society are buried and denied, they are rendered partial and fragmentary. Utopia as archaeology entails the imaginary reconstitution of the models of the good society underpinning policy, politics and culture, exposing them to scrutiny and critique. Wendell Bell and James Mau endorse the 'effort to tease out the implicit images of the future in studies that do not purport to be studies of the future';[2] substitute 'the good society' for 'the future', and we have utopia as archaeology.

Complete description is not possible; all accounts of past, existing or potentially existing societies are partial. Even relatively developed utopias have significant silences, and the deconstructive methods of late twentieth-century theory underline the importance of identifying and interrogating these. The utopian method in archaeological mode entails identifying these silences and interpolating the absent but implied elements – filling in, where possible, what is missing, or simply making evident the blank spaces. It overlaps the ontological mode in so far as it interrogates implicit models of persons. Nor is the boundary between utopia as archaeology and as architecture absolute: at what point does reconstruction become rebuilding? If the purpose of the Imaginary Reconstitution of Society in all modes is to expose utopia to judgment, this critical process is not necessarily hostile. It can be undertaken either in the spirit of unmasking or in the spirit of restitution – in Ricoeur's terms, a hermeneutic of suspicion or a hermeneutic of faith. As Harvey says, 'Critical reflection on our imaginaries entails ... both confronting the hidden utopianism and resurrecting it in order to act as conscious architects of our fates rather than as "helpless puppets" of the institutional and imaginative worlds we inhabit'.[3]

Utopia as archaeology sits comfortably with a sociological approach. I have used it for over three decades to examine aspects of policy and politics and explore their contradictions, unspoken conditions and proposed social formations, particularly in relation to the conflicting neo-liberal and neo-conservative utopias of the New Right and the meritocratic utopia of New Labour.[4] It is a powerful mode of critique of explicitly political positions. But the purpose of utopia as method is to make explicit embedded ideas of the good society and bring them to democratic debate, and there are utopian tropes (or, in Mumford's terms, *idola*) in contemporary culture that have cross-party appeal. They are contested, if at all, only at the margins. Here, then, the archaeological mode is demonstrated in relation to three of these, all of which are widely assumed to be good things and the foundation of a good society: meritocracy, civil society and economic growth. These are not three distinct utopias; for meritocracy and growth are integrally related, together with some versions of 'community' and civil society.

Meritocracy I: Michael Young

In 1957, Michael Young, a British sociologist and author of the 1945 Labour Party manifesto, wrote *The Rise of the Meritocracy*. The manuscript was turned down by eleven publishers, demonstrating the marginality of the utopian form to sociology, although once republished by Penguin the book sold several thousand copies and was translated into seven languages.[5] Unusually for a sociologist, Young used the utopian method as a mode of social and political critique, demonstrating how creative play of this kind generates knowledge. He explored the institutional forms, conditions and consequences of a society in which position is based on merit and where 'intelligence and effort together make up merit'.[6]

The sociological context included the argument by two American sociologists, Kingsley Davis and Wilbert Moore, that inequality was universal, necessary and positively functional. Differences of prestige and economic reward attract scarce talent to the most functionally important positions in society: 'social inequality is ... an unconsciously evolved device by which societies insure that the most important positions are conscientiously filled by the most qualified persons'.[7] Critiques pointed to the lack of equality of opportunity and social mobility and the consequent waste of talent.[8] In Britain, the political context of

Young's intervention was an increasing acceptance of inequality, noted by Peter Townsend in 1959:

> During the last ten years the general image of the Labour Party as presented to the public seems to have undergone a subtle but significant change. The party now seems to be characterised by a diminished attachment to moral and social principle ... Among the reasons for this shift in political character a future historian might well pick out for special attention the fading of interest in the subject of inequality. The main political parties and trade unions, together with economists and sociologists, appear to have called a truce over inequality.[9]

This was the beginning of Labour's lengthy transition from commitment to greater equality to espousing equality of opportunity, finally completed by Tony Blair's New Labour in the 1990s which was overtly committed to building a meritocracy, a society in which talent and work are the criteria for economic and social reward. The Blair and Brown governments were scarcely successful in this, but the apparent reasonableness of the aspiration indicates that it is deeply entrenched in contemporary culture, including among sociologists. Thus Halsey says 'Michael Young was content to leave his readers with a now famous formula: $IQ + E = M$, where IQ is measured intelligence, E is effort, and M is merit. Sociologically this is a good frame. Unfortunately, none of these variables could be measured in ways from which policy could be unequivocally inferred'.[10]

Young, however, objected to Blair's positive use of the term meritocracy, for his book is a dystopian satire, not a utopian proposal for a better society, and a savage attack on the idea that such a society is a possible or desirable option.[11] It suggests that such a society would be seriously flawed and contain the seeds of its own downfall. The narrative form reflects this. The main body of the text is an insider's image of the society narrated by a sociologist and member of the elite, describing the development of the meritocratic society and emergent social unrest: thus '[t]he purpose of this essay is to discuss some of the historical causes of the grievances that erupted in the May risings. My theme is that, whether or not these were explicitly organized by the Populists, they were certainly organized by history'. This critical account of tensions and flaws includes a self-mocking warning about blindness that derives from particular social positions and interests, limiting the explanatory and predictive powers of sociology. The narrator says: 'One belief is implicit throughout: there are no revolutions, only the slow accretions of a ceaseless change that reproduces the past while transforming it'.[12] The framing exposes this as hubris: the 'editor' tells us that the author was killed in further unrest at Peterloo and could not correct his account before publication. The device of the found manuscript renders this a critical dystopia rather than giving it anti-utopian force – that is, it argues that *this* version of the good society is not as good or as viable as it seems, not that the project of creating a better society itself leads to failure or disaster. It represents sociological accounts of the past and present, let alone the future, as utopian constructs which must always be understood as provisional and which require reflexive attention to the position from which we make them.

The narrator records a historical shift from promoting equality to promoting equality of opportunity, the 'equality of opportunity to be unequal'.[13] The gap in standards of living between different classes is extreme, but not based on inequality in pay. Nominally, all draw the same basic allowance (known as the Equal). But the professional classes are deemed to need better conditions to make their proper and superior contribution to society: peace, quiet, larger houses to accommodate necessary books and pictures, even domestic servants to avoid their wasting time on such trivia as shopping and housework. These privileged conditions are funded through a system of expenses or payments in kind by employers – rather like an extension of politicians' expenses.

Meritocracy promotes upward mobility through talent and application. This depends on the identification of scarce talent, appropriate stratified education and allocation to occupations, as well as on cultivating appropriate motivation and avoiding poverty of aspiration. And '[t]he social ladder was so long – the gap between the styles of life of upper and lower classes so wide – that promising children had to begin their climb through the schools at the earliest age possible'.[14] Scientific advance was pushing back the point of accurate assessment from three-year-olds to unborn babies. In Young's dystopia, the educational ladder was a social ladder for individuals; half a century later, William Nicholson's dystopia *The Wind Singer*, portrayed a society based on tests applied to individual members from the age of two, where poor results resulted in the whole family being downgraded.

The trouble is that meritocracy also implies downward mobility. Young suggests that privileged groups would inevitably seek to subvert this and preserve the position of their less gifted offspring. Social mobility and intelligenic marriages mean that talent is redistributed across the class system, so heredity and merit converge. But the correlation between the intelligence of children and parents is not perfect. A market developed with 'stupid babies from elite homes being sent, sometimes with princely dowries, in exchange for clever ones from the lower classes', together with cases of outright theft of bright children from the poor.[15] Above all, the equation of relative deprivation with failure generates complacency in the successful and social resentment and unrest among the unsuccessful. Attitudes harden. The elite, knowing themselves superior rather than simply lucky, become 'so impressed with their own importance as to lose sympathy with the people whom they govern'.[16] The lower classes know they are genuinely inferior, a knowledge reinforced by the continual possibility of retest. For men a 'mythos of muscularity' is partial compensation, but the sense of indignity fuels social conflict. This account of the psychosocial consequences of purportedly or actually meritocratic systems restated Melvyn Tumin's critique of Davis and Moore: they produce an unequal distribution of self-esteem, motivation and sense of membership, and foster hostility, suspicion and distrust. Young's narrator expects this resentment to remain an inarticulate rumbling rather than a serious threat, because any able, natural leaders have risen out of the lower classes. This is a vain hope.

Women lead the opposition, partly in protest at state formalization of cross-class adoption, but partly because of their (intrinsic) nature. Young uses the generic masculine and the position of women is ambiguous. They are educated on the basis of talent, and work in the professions; however, they raise their own children rather than leaving this to dim (mainly female) domestic servants. Gendered roles give them a more rounded view of worth: 'Were we to evaluate people, not only according to their intelligence and their education, their occupation and their power, but according to their kindliness and their courage, their sympathy and generosity, there could be no classes'.[17] They propose a new meaning of equality of opportunity, 'for all people, irrespective of their "intelligence", to develop the virtues and talents with which they are endowed, all their capacities for appreciating the beauty and depth of the human experience, all their potential for living to the full' – an approach with requires common and comprehensive education, rather than a selective and segregated system.[18] The narrating sociologist both understands and misunderstands this: 'Women have always been judged more by what they *are* than by what they *do* ... more for their warmth of heart, their vivacity and their charm than for their worldly success. It is therefore understandable that they should wish to stress their own virtues, only regrettable that in this the quality have joined with women of no more than ordinary ability'.[19] The cross-class commonality of women has not been eliminated by the institutions of meritocracy, providing the means of articulating the resentment of the dispossessed in social protest, revolutionary or otherwise.

Meritocracy II: Will Hutton

We do not, of course, live in a meritocracy. From the mid-1970s there was a global trend of rising inequality, with an increasing share of income and wealth going to profits and a decreasing share going to wages, and a dramatic rise in the share taken by the top one per cent. By 2010 the UK was experiencing levels of inequality unparalleled for the best part of a century, accompanied by rampant inequalities of opportunity and a decline in social mobility. The professions were increasingly dominated by the small minority educated in independent schools. The greatest change was in journalism, skewing public discourse further towards the perspective of the rich. Socio-economic inequalities were compounded by those of ethnicity, gender and disability. Early assessment revealed an increasing gap in educational attainment of poor and rich children from the age of three, irrespective of initial ability. Young predicted that public schools would die out as the state provided as good or better education. In reality, they continue to play a key role in the reproduction of class inequalities in modern Britain. Such stark differences in opportunity are a problem from a meritocratic perspective, partly because they waste allegedly scarce talent, but more importantly because they undermine the legitimacy of inequality itself. For there is a pervasive view that inequality is good, that high rewards are justifiable as long as they are the result of 'success' rather than 'failure', and the playing field (if it has not been sold off) is reasonably level.

The persistence of meritocracy as aspiration is exemplified by Will Hutton's discussion of fairness in his 2010 *Them and Us*. This reflects the dominant discourse about economic crisis and austerity, assuming the need for severe cuts in public spending alongside some rises in taxation. Hutton's goal is a world in which people get what they deserve and deserve what they get, embodying a deeply ingrained cultural assumption that the closer we can get to such a paradise of equal opportunities the better. Unlike Young, he sees this as an 'achievable utopia', and because achievable, superior to any 'unattainable utopian vision' of right or left.[20] Hutton opposes the neo-liberal utopia of untrammelled free markets, and, like Rorty, is hostile to a mythologized Left including communism, socialism, trade unionism and Marxism. Thus 'the trade unions' capture of the state ended in the breakdown of social democracy', and '[m]ost contemporary theorists of social science or justice would run a mile from being dubbed Marxist – with its connotations of authoritarianism, command economics and economic failure' (Harvey? Wright? Unger? Jameson?). Even Rawls is placed within the 'long shadow' of Marx, sharing the imputed belief that 'human nature is entirely a product of social condition'.[21]

Hutton's conceptual model is a tripartite one of economy, state and society. His Keynesian economics endorses state intervention to maintain economic growth and moderate market outcomes, including detailed proposals for regulating the financial sector. He criticizes excessive rewards, excessive inequality and the illusion of meritocracy, observing that the middle and upper classes 'are becoming increasingly adept at ensuring that their children possess the capabilities and qualifications to populate the upper echelons of economy and society' and endorsing the justice of downward as well as upward mobility. [22] He deplores the economic cost of inadequate upward mobility and notes the presence of greater uncertainty, insecurity and anxiety. But for Hutton, these are not intrinsic to capitalism or meritocracy: 'a properly run, competitive, open capitalism is a means for people to receive [the] just and proportional deserts' that are the essence of fairness.[23] Not for Hutton the prayer, 'Oh God, remember what thou hast wrought in us and not what we deserve', that places our shared humanity above a calculus of merit that might find us all wanting, nor Hamlet's similar recognition '[u]se every man after his desert, and who should 'scape whipping?'.[24]

Hutton sees equality as the antithesis of fairness, and as outdated and unpopular: the egalitarian beliefs of 'the left ... clash with deeply held notions of fairness'.[25] The left are also stupid, believing equality to be self-evidently the basis of the good society and that 'the better-off will willingly accept whatever transfer is needed to achieve it *and* will give up bourgeois ideas that desert should be proportional to effort and contribution'.[26] Hutton departs from Young's equation, for talent, like social circumstance, is simply a matter of luck. Fairness means justice and proportionality, requiring that rewards should be commensurate with effort, or more precisely with the effectiveness of that effort. This, he asserts, is a key part of 'our' culture, but also a universal disposition of human nature, 'hard-wired' and 'part of our DNA'. Proportionality justifies inequality: 'big rewards are justifiable if they are in proportion to big effort, because big effort grows the economic pie for everyone',[27] and those who 'accept greater responsibility and greater demands, and who respond by utilizing greater discretionary effort, skill and emotional resources, should be rewarded proportionally more than others'.[28] There are, then, both deserving and undeserving rich – a view widely shared, including by some relative egalitarians. Stewart Lansley, unlike Hutton, argues that inequality stifles investment and growth and emphasizes that 'executive compensation is only weakly correlated with a company's success'. He too argues that some of the rich 'deserve their hard-earned places' because 'through a mixture of exceptional skill, effort and risk-taking, [they] have contributed to increasing the size of the cake by creating new wealth and in ways which benefit others as well as themselves'. The undeserving rich (most of the super-rich) are those 'who rig the system to enrich themselves by unfairly grabbing a larger size of the cake at the expense of everybody else'.[29]

For Hutton, rewards *should* flow to diligent, sustained and successful effort with socially valued outcomes. As he acknowledges, the actual distribution of the social product bears no relation to effort or social utility. The New Economics Foundation estimated that low paid jobs such as childcare, hospital cleaning and waste recycling generate between seven and twelve pounds in social value for every pound spent on wages; conversely, city bankers, advertising executives and tax accountants destroy seven, eleven and forty-seven pounds worth of social value respectively for every pound that they create.[30] Hutton also argues, citing Hobhouse, that individual productivity always depends on social institutions, justifying taxation as a return to the collective, in the form of the state, of its due share. Hobhouse suggested that a maximum of twenty per cent could be attributed to individual factors, but Hutton does not suggest restoring top marginal tax rates to their 1970s level of eighty per cent. He understands that pay is determined by market forces embedded in complex systems of social assumptions and power, but he does not explain how the assessment of social value is to be ideologically or institutionally wrested from market control, or recognize a fundamental contradiction between the capitalist market as a distributive mechanism and fairness construed as desert.

The distinction between deserving and undeserving rich is, of course, a reflection of an older separation of the deserving and undeserving poor. Hutton adopts the prevalent hardening of attitudes here. He argues that needs-based claims for redistribution from rich to poor are based on the false belief that 'inequality is not driven by personal capacities, choices and values'.[31] Welfare on this model is unaffordable, but his principal objection is moral. Fairness means 'proportional rewards and punishments for our actions, for which we should take responsibility'.[32] Just desert means that we should hold 'people to account for the degree to which they try, deserve our support or play the system'.[33] It implies blame and punishment: 'Virtue, effort and contribution should and will be rewarded; malevolence, fecklessness and idleness must be punished'.[34] The principle of desert is reconstituted on the basis of contribution rather than misfortune. 'How much beyond the bare minimum for survival should benefits be pitched if the poor have made no contribution towards them?'[35] Contribution is narrowly interpreted as payment of taxes and national insurance, confining it to paid work and the formal economy. He suggests a significant rise in unemployment benefit for the first year for those who have previously been employed; without a contributions record, people should (it seems) not qualify for benefits at all. Other forms of social contribution are trivialized as lifestyle choice: 'is society obliged to help someone who "needs" to play video games, change the shape of their nose or stay at home to care for a sick relative?' And why should women be supported to stay at home to raise children, if they aren't wealthy enough to afford it?[36]

Meritocratic ideas of fairness make social mobility central. Official documents proclaim that '[i]n a fair society what counts is not the school you went to or the jobs your parents did, but your ability and your ambition'.[37] 'A fair society is an open society. A society in which everyone is free to flourish and rise. Where birth is never destiny'; and 'fairness is 'about social mobility'.[38] The political focus is on upward rather than downward mobility, partly because this is a more attractive selling point. But it is also consonant with supply-side explanations of unemployment, inequality and poverty, which imply that a properly skilled workforce can all move up, rather than with recognizing the occupational structure as demand-led. The generation who benefited from the post-war expansion of university education experienced a simultaneous expansion of professional jobs, reinforcing the illusion of a one-way escalator. More recently, labour markets have become increasingly polarized between relatively secure and higher paying jobs and lower paid and less secure jobs. The hollowing out of jobs requiring middle-level skills and earning middle-level pay has been disguised by describing white-collar and service-sector jobs and workers as middle class. Downward mobility from these middle positions both within and across generations, together with deteriorating pay and conditions for many workers, has resulted not from a meritocratic redistribution of talent, but from the restructuring of economies and increasing insecurity of work and wages.[39]

Young's imaginary society was relatively secure: citizens were guaranteed a minimum acceptable standard of living, and later the 'Equal'. In contemporary society, insecurity spreads across the whole society apart from the really rich: most of those in professional occupations are only a redundancy notice away from poverty. It creates fear of falling, the subject of many Dickens novels. As Richard Wilkinson and Kate Pickett have shown, social gradients in health (for children and adults) are linked to the widening disparity in incomes, while inequality itself has a negative impact on health and wellbeing, and on mortality rates, across the whole social spectrum. Even the well-off die younger in unequal societies.[40] The cultural presumption favouring meritocracy endorses equal opportunities rather than equality. Equalities legislation prohibits discrimination against individuals on the basis of defined characteristics including gender, age, race, religion and sexual orientation. It is designed to promote fair competition in a radically unequal system, not to reduce economic inequality. Walter Benn Michaels suggests that the consequent focus on diversity and identity politics actually reinforces inequality, disguising the fundamental differences of class that are untouched by it. The pursuit of equal opportunities and its associated meritocratic dream is not a diminished version of equality, but its antithesis.[41]

The rhetoric of meritocracy far outstrips the reality, but Young's prediction of arrogance above and resentment below has been realized. Owen Jones documents the rising hatred and demonization of the working classes. Austerity and welfare reform have been accompanied by vilification of the poor. The rich hate the poor, as do those for whom the poor constitute a reminder of the fate from which they seek to distance themselves. There is plenty of resentment, born of disregard and dispossession. Lone mothers and benefit claimants have been demonized in the tabloid press. Disabled people are officially subjected to demeaning and ludicrous fitness-for-work tests, increasingly regarded as benefit scroungers and at risk of verbal and physical assault. Public sector workers are pilloried as leeches on the wealth-creating 'tax-payers'. Only rarely is resentment directed at the rich, leading one senior politician to echo Bellamy by declaring, '[b]ring back the guillotine ... for bankers'.[42] There is occasional objection to the millions extracted from the public purse through profits from government contracts, although it redounds more upon government 'wasting tax payers' money' than on the profiteers.

Immigrants and ethnic minorities, whether Irish, Jewish, Roma, New Commonwealth or East European, have been recurrent targets of resentment; racism has sometimes been rearticulated as cultural difference, most recently in hostility to Muslims. Where Young saw resentment as the product of meritocracy, Hutton reads it as caused by its targets. Thus 'the fear of immigration is rooted in the reality that immigration has indeed increased'.[43] Immigration causes 'natural and immediate resentment' because 'too many immigrants have access to free prescriptions, medical care, schooling and housing before they have made adequate contributions. It is unfair. The sense of injustice enters the bloodstream'.[44] Hutton ignores differences between immigrants and asylum-seekers and the specific eligibility conditions for different benefits and services as well as the economic contribution of migrants.

Resentment deflected in this way onto different segments of the working class fuels the possibility of fascism rather than that of a better and more humane society.

What kind of people, and what kinds of relations between them, are implied in the meritocratic model? It is intrinsically individualistic and competitive, so that is how people must be induced to be, although Young suggests maintaining the necessary levels of motivation may be problematic. Worth is a matter of productive capacity, and people are (literally) valued only in relation to this single aspect. The rebellion is centred on the demand for a wider view of human capacity and human potential. For Young, the reduction of human beings to competitive automata is dealt with as it was in much sociology of the time, by the assumption that women, by nature, nurture or both, are the repository of affect, leaving men to unalloyed instrumentality and competitiveness. The utopian trope of community or civil society supplements that of meritocracy, positing a social sphere governed by a different set of values.

Civil society

Civil society is now deployed as a new utopia constituting, as el-Ojeili says, a 'sphere of plurality, civic freedoms, civility, and co-operation … opposed to despotism, corruption, exclusionary nationalism, totalitarian desires for moral unity, and other bad stuff'.[45] This utopia is one of spontaneous social self-organization independent of market and state and presented as morally superior to both, a position implied by Wright. Abensour endorses insurgent democracy against the state, and thus a repoliticization of civil society, and is himself strongly anti-statist. Yet he recognizes that the place civil society plays in the social imaginary is, to say the very least, ambiguous. It is 'implicitly made up of a confused blend of anti-totalitarianism from the East, of anti-statism, of misunderstood liberalism', and is thus 'an anti-political machine feeding more or less on the belief that politics is necessarily to do with evil'. Its invocation in a society of 'domination and exploitation' plays 'the role of a simulacrum of liberty'.[46]

Social solidarity derives from voluntary effort and cooperation and non-material rewards. There is a long history of both right and left-wing libertarianism. It may incorporate economic organization, such as anarchism, syndicalism, left communism and support for cooperatives and co-partnerships, or it may, as in conservative forms of communitarianism, treat society as separate from or quasi-independent of the economy.[47] If civil society is understood as institutions that derive neither from market nor state but from voluntary effort, there is no disputing its importance to the fabric and quality of social life. Self-organization permeates the social history of production, distribution, education, leisure and social support. Historically, working-class self-organization includes dissenting religion, trade unions, friendly societies, cooperatives, allotments, brass bands, cycling clubs. In some cases, notably in the Settlement Movement and institutions such as Toynbee Hall, these were supported by middle class philanthropic efforts and were intended– sometimes quite successfully – to soften the effects of the market and improve working people's quality of life.

Sometimes the aspiration has been to replace market and state with an alternative economy and society. That, of course, is the fundamental position of anarchism, whose attitude to the state is best encapsulated in the slogan 'whoever you vote for, the government gets in'. It was the intention of the utopian socialism of Owen and Fourier, carried into the cooperative movement's dream of a cooperative commonwealth, often depicted in political iconography as the sun rising over the horizon. It was the intention, too, of the kibbutz movement in Israel, settlements, like Marinaleda, based initially on agriculture. Buber has argued that these attempts to rebuild society from the bottom up were at least no more utopian, in the sense of unrealistic, than the aspiration to make socialism through the capture of the state. For others, local initiatives – Unger's next steps – are prefigurative practices or interstitial utopias: spaces where a better life can be built even in the face of the dominance of market and state. Ernst Schumacher's insistence that small is beautiful, originally an orientation to development, has informed many examples of democratic experimentalism. In the context of ecological crisis, it indicates not so much antipathy but a curious mixture of hope for and fear of the collapse of both market and state, and the wish to build local resilience against the coming downfall of civilization as we know it.

New Labour's 1990s espousal of 'community' as the balancing factor to the free market has been taken much further in the context of post-crisis austerity economics. In Europe, national states now appear impotent. As Wolfgang Streeck argues, European states have been forced to act as debt collectors for international capital; resistance by democratically elected governments has simply been overruled. Both European institutions and the International Monetary Fund are implicated here. Of course the need for austerity is a fiction: there is plenty of money; the problem is who owns it. The crisis of low growth and high personal and national debt is driven, as in the 1920s, by inequality. Far from stimulating economic growth, concentration of wealth reduced productive investment, while the falling income share accruing to labour meant that living standards could only be sustained by rising levels of personal debt – hence the easy availability and promotion of credit. Globally and nationally, the rich have never had it so good. The implementation of Branford's 1921 proposal for a sabbatical year for the money power would quickly eliminate national deficits.[48]

For the Right, the celebration of civil society accompanies a refusal of state responsibility for moderating market outcomes. The 'crisis' has been used as a shock doctrine, an opportunity and justification for the pursuit of a neo-liberal utopian project of permanently shrinking the public sector. Savage cuts in public spending at both national and local levels resulted in rising unemployment, pay freezes and job losses across public and private sectors, reductions in public services and falling living standards. In Britain, voluntary activity was promoted as a replacement for withdrawn services from local libraries to social care, accompanied by rhetoric about localism, handing back power wrested from people by the state, and the 'big society'.

The resultant utopia of civil society against both state and market (but especially against the state) echoes that of the 1920s distributist movement. It can be found across the political spectrum, for example in Phillip Blond's Red Toryism and Maurice Glasman's Blue Labour. Economic liberalism (Branford's money power) produces a grossly unequal distribution of assets. This combines with social liberalism to produce a lethal combination of neo-liberal market and oppressive state.[49] Distributists favour spreading assets more widely, though not generally by the collective re-appropriation of private wealth. Blond proposes asset transfer from the state, and especially the local state, to community groups. The state is portrayed as an impediment to an expanded voluntary sector and local decision making.

Such arguments ignore the post-code lotteries that result from the absence of national standards and the injustice inherent in arbitrary and unaccountable decision making by charitable bodies. There is no guarantor other than the state of equal treatment in terms of benefits, services and the administration of justice. The inadequacy of voluntary activity is exemplified in the rising dependence on food banks which supply emergency rations, nutritionally inadequate for extended use, to those who acquire vouchers from local authorities, doctors or religious organizations: by abrogating responsibility, the state turns its citizens into supplicants at the mercy of arbitrary decisions. In 2013, local authorities in the United Kingdom were effectively forced to refer desperately needy people to food banks rather than offering crisis loans – loans which had previously been centrally administered, but which were devolved with reduced funding that was not ring-fenced.

Replacing state provision with voluntary work in 'civil society' affects women disproportionately. The growth of the public sector expanded paid work for women in roles including teaching, nursing, health visiting and other forms of caring, professionalizing previously unpaid work in ways Gilman would surely have approved. Dismantling the welfare state increases female unemployment and pushes women's work back into the non-market sector, where it is no longer paid or acknowledged as work. The utopia of local voluntary provision ignores the geographic variation in material and cultural resources, and therefore the possibility of absorbing the additional work. And if the state and the local state are not always easily called to democratic account, they remain more potentially accountable than self-styled community groups whose representative character is always questionable. If meritocracy places individuals in mutual competition, these modes of inadequate social protection place them in the position of supplicants, drastically undermining personal autonomy and citizenship. Unsurprisingly, state benefits are simultaneously re-described as a privilege rather than a right.

El-Ojeili sounds a cautionary note about the problematic character of this utopia, and the lack of interrogation, or deliberate obfuscation, of the interpenetration of state, economy and civil society: 'This new optimistic usage of "civil society" downplays any connection to the pursuit of self-interest, to economics, and it also tends to bracket or efface the connections between state and civil society'.[50] As we saw in Chapter 7, the relationship between 'independent' Marinaleda and the state is decidedly ambiguous. More generally, the state provides the legal context for the market through contested regulatory frameworks and property laws. State, market and legal codes affect what kind of voluntary associations can flourish in civil society. In Britain, the development of friendly societies and cooperatives was facilitated by the 1852 legal extension of limited liability achieved by the Christian Socialist movement. The 1906 Trades Disputes Act overturned the 1901 Taff Vale judgment and prevented employers suing unions for losses during a strike; this was fundamental to trade union activity for most of the twentieth century, although legal changes after 1979 deliberately and systematically restricted trade union rights. Self-organization requires material as well as legal conditions to thrive. Trade union membership was facilitated by large work places, those very mines, shipyards and factories that were closed during the Thatcher era. The cooperative movement, besides supplying cheap, unadulterated food, was the cultural heart of the labour movement and the base for the Cooperative Women's Guild. Such movements always attracted the better-off working class more than the acutely poor; they depend on relatively stable work and relatively stable local or work-based communities. But although social and economic policies have eroded the material conditions of working class self-organization, resilience and sociality, contemporary society nevertheless remains run through with different kinds of self-help, charitable and voluntary organizations, as well as the growth of social networking and internet campaigns.

In some areas, many such organizations are faith-based. This raises additional questions about the appropriate boundaries between voluntary organizations and the state, and the religious and the secular, which cannot be resolved by simple anti-statism. A situation where religious groups are the dominant organizations and vehicles of social belonging and identity is itself the product of policies of the national and local state, as Kenan Malik has demonstrated.[51] Forms of multiculturalism that envision society as a community of communities reinforce that process of identification, passing over the lack of homogeneity within designated communities, those (such as secular humanists) who identify with none, and the class, ethnic, religious and political hybridity of many people's backgrounds. My own 'roots' are Lithuanian-Latvian-Irish Jewish, working-class, communist and atheist on one side; on the other, Scottish bourgeoisie and Anglican English gentry, communist, agnostic, and latterly socialist and green.

Economic growth

The third utopian trope dominating the global political agenda is that of economic growth. Growth is the core of Hutton's vision of an innovative economy. It is the exit from crisis anticipated by Europe, the United States, and the IMF. It is the principal measure of economic health: we are daily reminded that growth is good, low growth alarming, no growth or negative growth catastrophic. The pursuit of growth has a wider reach even than meritocracy or civil society. It is the driving force of capitalism.

The function of economic growth is partly ideological. It obscures rising inequality, disguising the divergent shares of the social product going to profits and to wages as the rake-off by the very rich increases both absolutely and relatively. As long as most people's real incomes are holding steady or going up, even if sustained by normalized high levels of debt, these inequalities are felt as a daily insult in affluent societies only by marginal groups excluded from rising living standards. Once growth stalls and austerity economics causes living standards to drop in real terms, inequality becomes visible and contested. People protest, as in Greece, Spain, and the global Occupy movement in 2011 and 2012.

Measures of 'growth' or 'shrinkage' in the economy are based on changes in GDP. GDP measures activity in the market sector of 'the economy' (itself an abstraction from the totality of social practices). It includes all such activity whether it contributes to human welfare, detracts from it (such as the tobacco industry) or is simply necessary to counter the negative consequences of other practices (such as cleaning up after environmental disasters). It measures the flow of market activity, not the accumulated stock of wealth. The same activity may count or not, depending on whether it is part of the formal market sector. Looking after your own children at home does not count; paid childcare does. Growing vegetables on a small-holding counts; growing them for personal consumption does not. Globally, much of women's work falls outside the market and is not counted. Much more is undervalued because women are frequently paid less for their labour, and GDP values goods, services and labour at their market price. Clearly, GDP does not represent a measure of socially useful activity either at an individual or a collective level. It does not measure what matters.

There are serious questions about whether continuing growth in GDP is compatible with ecological limits. Sustainability requires us to think beyond the economic or conventionally sociological and include those environmental questions sidelined from sociology along with Geddes. One of the appeals of localism, as part of the utopia of civil society, is that it recognizes people's attachment to and identification with specific places. The super-rich are paradoxically both more and less invested in place than ordinary people. Two-thirds of the United Kingdom's 60 million acres is owned by one third of one per cent of the population, while land-banking in developed and developing economies is a major investment activity. But, as Wells predicted, the elite has become nomadic and less tied to place and nation. The Russian billionaire Roman Abramovich reportedly said, 'I live on a plane'.[52] However, most of us live on a planet, earth. Climate change, global warming, resource consumption and depletion, and the changing habitability of geographic regions challenge continued economic growth. Ecological footprints estimate the area of the earth needed to sustain the lifestyles of humanity, nations or individuals, including the area of forest needed to absorb carbon dioxide emissions, more narrowly calculated as carbon footprints. London has an ecological footprint 125 times its size, roughly equivalent to the entire productive land area of Britain. If everyone in the world used resources at this rate, we would need three planets rather than one. If everyone used resources at the rate of the United States, we would need at least five planets. We have just the one.

Economic crisis has sidelined the ecological crisis. While governments now affirm the need for sustainable growth, the meaning of this has shifted from ecological to economic sustainability. Economists define sustainable growth as 'a measure of how much a firm can grow without borrowing more money'.[53] At the national level, it is 'noninflationary, stable growth in the economy with full employment'.[54] Sustainable growth in this sense is quite different from sustainable development, which means meeting the needs of the present without compromising the ability of future generations to meet theirs. Ecological footprints imply a collective reduction in consumption, and redistribution away from those who currently have plenty to enable others to survive. They suggests that a return to business as usual in the form of a global average three per cent compound growth is simply impossible. This underpins arguments such as Tim Jackson's *Prosperity Without Growth*. Yet most governments treat sustainable development and economic growth as entirely congruent.

We should examine the best, rather than the weakest, case for this claim, which is set out by Nicholas Stern in his 2009 *Blueprint for a Safer Planet*, subtitled 'how to manage climate change and create a new era of progress and prosperity'. This demands very substantial changes in how we live, but nevertheless treats growth and sustainable development as interdependent rather than opposed. Stern documents the need to radically reduce greenhouse gas emissions and the potentially catastrophic consequences of not doing so. High-carbon growth is effectively impossible. Its costs are so high that business as usual is an anti-growth strategy which will lead to 'immense dislocation and loss of life'.[55] Low-carbon growth, on the other hand, can solve the twin problems of global poverty and global warming. It means reducing European carbon dioxide emissions to (not by) one fifth of their current level, no small task. Switching to low-carbon growth will cost about two per cent of GDP each year in the short term, but will deliver a world better than we have now rather than a future of deprivation:

> The low-carbon world we must and can create will be much more attractive than business as usual. Not only will growth be sustained, it will be cleaner, safer, quieter and more biodiverse. We understand many of the necessary technologies and will create more; and we can design the economic, political and social structures that can take us

there. We require clarity of analysis, commitment to action and collaboration. ... Without strong growth it will be extremely difficult for the poor people of the world to lift themselves out of poverty and we should not respond to climate change by damaging their prospects.[56]

This is a utopian method. It proposes where we should aspire to be in 2050 and asks what policies and structures need to be in place to get there: 'we can then work back to think about the transition from now to then'.[57] Stern accepts that this involves ethical judgements and remarks on the tendency of economists, like other social scientists, to try to evade these. He uses the term blueprint but observes that this does not imply 'a world planner who can identify with full information and wisdom where emission cuts should take place and make sure they happen according to plan'.[58] This is not a 'full programme of reform' but rather a 'clear sense of direction'.[59]

There are four ways of reducing carbon emissions: using energy more efficiently; stopping deforestation; making more use of existing low-carbon technologies such as wind-power and low-emission cars and improved public transport; and developing new technologies. Stern also proposes adapting infrastructure, including buildings, irrigation systems and transport systems, and regulating the expansion of cities and improving their design. Sustainable development requires diversification and flexibility, and therefore the development of human capital, an economist's term for fostering people's capabilities and skills. This is wide-ranging change. However, Stern regards climate change as caused by market failure. The negative consequences of human activity have not historically been priced so the polluter pays. The solution therefore is to correct the market through negotiated global and national emissions targets and trading, and through pricing and taxation.

Global agreement will only be possible on the basis of international redistribution. Developed countries will have to increase aid and accept more stringent emission caps, both because they can afford it, and because historically they have caused most of the problem. Emissions targets and energy rights must be looked at in conjunction with wider question of resources to buy food, shelter and other goods: 'any notions of equality and justice in the allocation of emission rights should be embedded in a broad view of income distribution, responsibilities for supporting economic development, responsibilities for past emissions and the damages they have done, and the different kind of instruments for influencing world income that are available'.[60] Equity must be considered both now and between present and future generations.

Stern's argument is principally about the necessary institutional basis of such an international agreement. There is consequently little attention to the national level and to inequalities within countries – although Stern does say that it is 'now a matter of great urgency to provide an analysis of what low-carbon growth looks like for each country'.[61] Probing the silences in utopian proposals is part of the exhaustive critique demanded by Wells and by utopia as archaeology. If international redistribution must come through governments, Stern suggests that at the national level most of the necessary two per cent of GDP 'would come directly from private consumption and investment rather than passing through public budgets'.[62] The behaviour of individuals, firms and communities should be changed through a process of incentivizing (pricing), education, nudging and some regulation. There is passing mention of the fact that pricing carbon emissions will raise the costs of heating and travel, and 'this will affect poorer people most'. Even if '[l]ow-income groups can be protected ... through the tax and transfer system',[63] tax and transfer is also deemed to have a negative effect on work incentives.

The social element is the least developed; few questions are raised about ways of living. Limits to growth other than climate change, such as water and other resource shortages, are neglected. Walmart is praised for its carbon-reduction policies; its less commendable anti-union employment policies pass unremarked. Stern applauds supermarkets that offer customers the possibility of paying extra at check-out to offset the carbon footprint of their shopping; he does not suggest supermarkets should be responsible for this nor comment on the wider social consequences of their domination of the retail sector. There is little interrogation of what Raymond Williams described as means of livelihood and ways of life, accompanied by particular structures of feeling. Stern does not probe our overall systems of production, consumption and distribution or the desires and wants embedded in them, or present the need for change as involving the education of desire.

The silence about inequality within nations may be understandable in relation to the wider argument, but it matters. Just as Stewart Lansley has shown that inequality is an impediment to growth, George Monbiot has consistently argued that it contributes to the problem of global warming. The sybaritic lifestyles of the super rich include yachts such as the aptly-named WallyPower 118, which is kitted out in teak and mahogany and consumes 3400 litres of fuel per hour at a speed of 60 knots, doing untold damage to the biosphere.[64] This is not exactly conspicuous consumption, for it is invisible to most people and thus not the usual target of exhortations to live more lightly upon the planet. But addressing inequality and overconsumption is a necessary element in reducing environmental impact. But even the idea of low-carbon growth, shared by Stern and Hutton, is very conventional. If both register the need to limit climate change and agree that human capital, health and education need to be included in assessments of development, neither questions the focus on market activity as the measure of the size and health of the economy. Above all, neither addresses the nature of capitalism itself – its need for constant expansion, constant capital accumulation, constant new markets and its consequent drive towards ever greater consumption of everything that can be commodified, priced, sold.

William Morris railed against a system of production for profit that can place no value on the beauty of the earth, which is destroyed by so-called economic progress. His frustration is as relevant today as in 1894: 'What shall I say concerning its mastery of and its waste of mechanical power, its commonwealth so poor, its enemies of the commonwealth so rich, its stupendous organization – for the misery of life! Its contempt for simple pleasures which everyone could enjoy but for its folly? Its eyeless vulgarity which has destroyed art, the one certain solace of labour?' And is 'it all to end in a counting house on the top of a cinder heap?'[65] The cinder heap can only be avoided if we change what the counting house counts: we need to measure what matters.

A critique of GDP can be mounted from the perspective of other measures of social and economic performance. Accepting that three per cent compound growth in GDP is a chimera does not have to mean 'no growth'. Rather, it means rethinking what we understand by wealth, productivity and growth; reassessing what constitutes positive social activity; considering quality of life rather than quantity of production and consumption. This affects what kinds of measures of what kinds of social goods we deem appropriate, whether they are generated in formal market settings or elsewhere. Alternative measures are better than no measures in illustrating the weaknesses of GDP. For example, the Index of Sustainable Economic Welfare and the Measure of Domestic Progress (which succeeded it) include unpaid work and the negative social and environmental impacts of growth and inequality. They suggest that GDP growth and social progress diverged dramatically after 1976 – the date when inequality in the UK was at its historic lowest, and the point when global income shares started to move in favour of profits. The New Economics Foundation's Happy Planet Index (HPI) combines indicators of happy and healthy lives with ecological impacts into a single scale. It also shows negative correlation with GDP growth. International comparisons show that five of the highest scores are in South America.

Costa Rica wins, its ascendancy attributed to several factors: it has rich natural resources; the army was abolished in 1949, liberating public funds for social expenditure; a sensible work-life balance facilitates strong social networks; there is relatively equal treatment of women and strong political participation.

The HPI is almost as problematic as GDP. Health is represented by life expectancy, ecological impact by ecological footprint, while happiness is measured by a simple question about life satisfaction. We must be careful here. Expressed rates of life satisfaction, decoupled from indicators of objective wellbeing, are highly susceptible to differing expectations. The 2009 Stiglitz-Sen Report mainstreams the focus on the wellbeing and happiness of populations rather than on GDP, so United Nations Human Development Indicators now include aggregate measures of human capital, health status and educational participation.[66] Focusing on national aggregates runs a serious risk of diverting attention from distributive questions, since material inequalities within countries, class inequalities in life expectancy and, as importantly, healthy life expectancy, are not addressed. The danger is that questions of distributive justice are sidelined, so that the reorientation of the economy to need rather than profit is obstructed rather than enabled.

And indeed the authors of the HPI are well aware that the question of happiness is much more complex than life satisfaction, although they still overemphasize subjective rather than objective wellbeing:

> For us, being 'happy' is more than just having a smile on your face – we use the term *subjective well-being* to capture its complexity. Aside from feeling 'good', it also incorporates a sense of individual vitality, opportunities to undertake meaningful, engaging activities which confer feelings of competence and autonomy, and the possession of a stock of inner resources that helps one cope when things go wrong. Well-being is also about feelings of relatedness to other people – both in terms of close relationships with friends and family, and belonging to a wider community.[67]

Moving further in the direction of an ecologically sustainable future takes us into the realm of utopia as architecture. But any proposal for a better world necessarily entails claims about what is good for people and makes them happy, or claims about possibilities for human beings as they are and as they might be. We turn next, therefore, to utopia as ontology.

9
Utopia as Ontology

In Chapter 5, I argued that sociologists have subjected themselves to a triple repression: of the future, of normativity and of what it means to be human. New students are frequently inducted into sociology through an interrogation of the idea of human nature, emphasizing that what we understand as 'human nature' is what seems to be normal among the human beings we encounter, but that this is historically and socially determined and variable. Thus the skills, habits, tastes, beliefs and social practices of human beings in the bronze age differed markedly from our own, as did the customary ways of being of pre-conquest indigenous peoples in the Americas, Australia and Africa. Hence Mills's question of '[w]hat varieties of men and women now prevail in this society and in this period? ... In what ways are they selected and formed, liberated and repressed, made sensitive and blunted?'.[1] Hence also Marx's reluctance to specify in detail the institutions of a future good society because we cannot predict the needs and wants of future generations. The insistence on the social formation of persons, of personality or of character predates Marx: Owen's doctrine of circumstances argued that any character, from the best to the worst, could be given to individuals and communities by appropriate social arrangements. It has been an important building block of sociology itself, notably in Durkheim's insistence on the social construction of morality. It remains an important bulwark against the more reductionist arguments of sociobiology, evolutionary psychology and neuroscience. But this does not mean there is no such thing as human nature, nor that it is infinitely malleable. As Marvin Harris said, 'a culture-bearing species whose physiology was based on silicon instead of carbon and that had three sexes instead of two, weighed a thousand pounds a specimen, and preferred to eat sand rather than meat [or vegetables] would acquire certain habits unlikely to be encountered in any Homo sapiens society'.[2] One of feminism's many contributions to sociology has been the reminder that we are embodied animals. As Norman Geras has shown, there is a concept of human nature in Marx, beyond the fact of its necessary historical determination.[3] But it is characteristic of human nature to require completion through culture – which is to make a statement about that nature itself.

These arguments impinge on the relation between sociology and utopia because human nature is often used against the utopian modality itself. A frequent objection to utopia is that it demands perfection of its inhabitants, which is inconsistent with the necessarily flawed nature of real human beings. As we have seen, this feeds into the claim that utopia is dangerous: attempts to impose it will mean forcing fallible humans into the procrustean bed of an externally imposed system, resulting in totalitarian repression and violence. John Carey, for example, wrote in 1999 that:

> The aim of all utopias, to a greater or lesser extent, is to eliminate real people. Even if it is not a conscious aim, it is an inevitable result of their good intentions. In a utopia real people cannot exist, for the very obvious reason that real people are what constitute the world we know, and it is that world that every utopia is designed to replace. Though this fact is obvious, it is one that many writers are reluctant to acknowledge. For if real people cannot live in utopias, then the utopian effort to design an ideal commonwealth in which human beings can lead happier lives is evidently imperilled.[4]

Carey then cites Tommaso Campanella's *City of the Sun* in which selfishness is unknown, Louis-Sebastien Mercier's *The Year 2440* in which citizens voluntarily pay more tax than they need, and Bellamy's *Looking Backward* in which the shame attaching to deceit is so great that criminals would rather accept punishment than lie to save themselves. Carey reflects that '[i]t is clear that if these are human beings, then the people we have been living among all our lives belong to some other species'. He goes on to cite Soviet Communism as a vision which 'fits precisely ... (and ... disastrously) into a utopian mould', referring to Lenin's claim that the 'higher' phase of Communism will involve transformed human subjects – leading, in Carey's view, to cruel and unnecessary punishments and murder.[5] Where utopia is concerned, the Cold War is still with us. Carey's argument can be countered in its details: if those we live among display selfishness, there is also a great deal of selfless and cooperative behaviour observable in most societies; in the more affluent countries in the world, there is considerable charitable giving over and above enforced taxation, as well as the donation of time in volunteering, and indeed, there are people for whom and circumstances in which lying is felt to be worse than punishment, as dramatized for example in the film about German resistance to Nazism, *Sophie Scholl: The Final Days*. But the general argument from sociology is stronger, and here sociology and utopia again coincide in the belief that we might, in other circumstances, be otherwise.

I would go further. The ontological mode of the Imaginary Reconstitution of Society, of utopia as method, is necessary for two reasons. First, any discussion of the good society must contain, at least implicitly, a claim for a way of being that is posited as better than our current experience. It entails both imagining ourselves otherwise and a judgement about what constitutes human flourishing. Wilhelm Hennis has argued that Max Weber's sociology has been persistently misunderstood: its central question is 'how human beings are *formed*, or shaped or impressed by the world they find themselves in', and Weber also contended that 'every order of social relations could be evaluated by reference to the type of humanity associated with it'.[6] The archaeological mode of utopia as method properly includes the ontological, in excavating the assumptions about human nature and human flourishing that are embedded in political positions and institutional proposals, as well as in overtly utopian literature. Utopians always have an account of human nature, and they vary considerably. The second reason is the need for utopia not just to account for, but to speak to, the level of affect. The education of desire implies that utopias take their force from releasing a potential self from some of the 'wounds and scars … [from] living here, down here, below'.[7] These questions return us to the early chapters of the book – the existential quest figured there in terms of grace.

We could begin where the previous chapter ended, with happiness. The desire for a better way of being usually implies greater happiness, though sometimes only by way of greater virtue. Hence utopia generally intends to produce more happiness or human flourishing through changes in social arrangements. It depends, of course, what is meant by this. Many contemporary discussions draw heavily on Aristotle, as does the field of virtue ethics. For Aristotle, humans achieve happiness through reason and virtue, through exercise of their capacities and the development of their potential. It is an active rather than a passive view of flourishing, in which individuals must be free to make decisions about both ends and means, in living a life that they have reason to value. The view of happiness here is very different from some usages in popular or public discourse. Flourishing differs from mere hedonism, the pursuit of short-term pleasure. In Huxley's *Brave New World*, for example, the dystopian society creates people who are cheerful and kept that way by the mood-altering drug soma. The critical voice claims the right to be unhappy, as a condition of freedom: this is a claim for existential depth, for the importance of loss and longing, and for flourishing. Huxley's later novel *Island* approaches those questions directly; it is in large part an existential utopia concerned directly with the conditions for enlightenment and grace, and their simultaneous fragility and persistence within global capitalism. Drugs are used here, but only as occasional supplement to the learned discipline of meditation.

In Britain, happiness has recently become an overt concern of public policy. In part this is because of the evidence of widespread unhappiness and depression in children and adults and increasing resort to drugs. Short courses of Cognitive Behavioural Therapy (CBT) have been proposed to teach people to think differently about themselves in the world, as a cheaper and possibly more effective solution. This presumes that misery is not the rational human response to social circumstances and is an individual rather than a social pathology. And, as in *Brave New World*, the valued mode of being in our own society is extraversion and relentless positivity.[8] As ever, when something becomes an object of policy, measurement follows. This is often banal, relying, as we have seen, on subjective reports of life satisfaction which cannot account for differing expectations and senses of entitlement, still less touch on the deeper question of flourishing. Conveniently and unsurprisingly, such indicators show that above a certain level, happiness does not depend on income and is related to the quality of social relationships, encouraging the fiction that material factors and inequality are unimportant. Similar problems arise with the concept of wellbeing. This is potentially closer to the idea of flourishing, and more susceptible to objective indicators including health and mental health, although measures again tend to restrict its scope and depth.

Human flourishing, happiness and wellbeing all entail both a view of what human beings are (that is, a view of human nature) and a normative claim about what is good for them. So too do arguments about human needs. Indeed, one of the most frequently cited theories of human need also sees self-actualization as a central and highly valued element in what it means to be human. However, Abraham Maslow views needs as a hierarchy, in which this is the highest level. The lower levels must be met first: physiological needs, the need for safety and security; the need for love and belonging; the need for self-esteem and the respect of others (in that order). Like all theories that try to distinguish between basic needs, other needs, wants and desires, this is problematic because it abstracts needs and their individual owners from their social context. Just as Bloch argues that lack is articulated in terms of what would meet it, William Leiss argues that needs are always experienced as needs for specific objects and processes which carry social and symbolic meanings. Thus:

> there is no aspect of our physiological requirements (the famous basic needs for food, shelter, and so forth) that has not always been firmly embedded in a rich tapestry of symbolic mediations. Likewise what are called the higher needs – love, esteem, the pursuit of knowledge and spiritual perfection – also arise within a holistic interpretation of needs and are not separated from the material aspects of existence.[9]

Rooting a utopian ontology in need does not avoid evaluation. Leiss argues for a wholesale reorientation of need away from commodification and the market, just as Marcuse calls for a new reality principle free from the introjected distortions of capitalist domination. The utopian method posits a new matrix of needs, satisfactions and symbolic meanings. The education of desire implies such a transformation. Yet Abensour's view of the education of desire does not involve a given end: it remains open. Utopia as method requires that we posit this new matrix from both an individual and an institutional point of view – an unequivocally normative move.

How can we approach the question of utopian ontology without evading the question of human nature and human flourishing yet while preserving the sense of their historical determination, in a way that enables us to develop an argument about the institutional parameters of a better society? In *Why Things Matter to People*, Andrew Sayer argues 'for a robustly critical social science that explains and evaluates social life from the standpoint of human flourishing' in which emotions are understood as part of reason rather than in conflict with it. He says, as I have argued above, that the critical element of social science always implies normative judgement based in a conception of human flourishing, but this is usually a 'hidden or repressed premise'.[10] Sayer suggests that '[a]s sentient beings, capable of flourishing and suffering', we are 'particularly vulnerable to how others treat us' and that 'our view of the world is substantially evaluative'.[11] Wellbeing is an objective condition.

It is also relational: we exist not as discrete individuals but necessarily embedded from the outset in relations with others. And if '[j]ust what constitutes a good life as a whole is surely elusive, ... that doesn't prevent us from being able to distinguish better from worse experiences and situations, and thus some of the elements of the good life'. Indeed, 'as needy beings we can distinguish at least roughly between flourishing and suffering, or more specifically between hunger and sufficiency, disrespect and respect, hostility and friendliness, boredom and stimulation, and so on'.[12]

In his earlier *The Moral Significance of Class*, Sayer argued that class relations essentially involve humiliation. In *Why Things Matter to People*, he makes dignity central. So did Bloch, especially in *Natural Law and Human Dignity* and the reiterated figure of the upright gait, an image of embodied dignity. So too does Habermas in 'The Concept of Human Dignity and the Realistic Utopia of Human Rights'. There is international sanction for this: Article 1 of the Universal Declaration of Human Rights, adopted by the United Nations in 1948, begins: 'All human beings are born free and equal in dignity and rights'. This is itself a performative and a utopian statement. We begin, then, on the fourth level of Maslow's hierarchy.

Although he does not present it as such, Sayer's argument is also deeply utopian. He addresses, as I do here, the existential before the institutional. He construes the human situation as one of necessary suspension between present and future. Thus 'this is where we live – between the actual and the possible, between present flourishing or suffering and future possible flourishing or suffering';[13] 'We live between the positive and the normative, on the slippery slope of lack, able to climb up it, and indeed extend it upwards by constructing new forms of flourishing and protection'.[14] This gives rise to a processual ontology, one of becoming, both at an individual and a social level: 'We live between what is and what could or should be; ethical ideas themselves are related both to the kinds of beings we (think we) are and the kinds of beings we (think we) should become through our actions'.[15] Similarly, Bloch wrote '[t]he emotion of hope goes out of itself, makes people broad instead of confining them ... The work of this emotion requires people who throw themselves into what is becoming, to which they themselves belong'.[16] The process of becoming is both individually driven and socially constrained. Sayer quotes C. S. Lewis: 'We seek an enlargement of our being. We want to be more than ourselves', and argues that this urge and capacity are part of what it means to be human: 'This capacity for *becoming* – for developing in a host of different ways, and for acquiring new skills and dispositions – is a striking feature of human nature'.[17] Drawing on Margaret Archer, he observes that adverse circumstances can jeopardise any and all of our human properties, which therefore exist only as potentialities: 'We should therefore think in terms of human becoming rather than human being as a given state, where becoming is contingent, path-dependent and open-ended rather than towards any particular goal'.[18]

Sayer's processual ontology avoids closure but does not evade specificity. This is a needs-based conception of social being, albeit one where needs are explicitly registered in terms of lack, wants and desires. As he says, it is evident that individuals' capacities, needs, desires do not all pull in the same directions or form a harmonious whole. In a Blochian manner, he sees lack as entailing a drive to meet that lack. Thus '[c]onditions like hunger and longing simultaneously involve deficiency and a drive to remedy it';[19] and '[c]oncern, desire, longing and sense of lack do not merely passively register a difference between two states, one that is given and one that does not exist, but involve an impulse, drive or pressure to move towards the latter. They are thus world-guided in responding to the difference and action-guided in seeking to resolve it'.[20] A properly sociological understanding of what is must include these dimensions of 'lack and becoming, suffering and flourishing', and thus must include 'an orientation to future possible states'.[21]

It is also a needs-based understanding of *social* being, which brings its own attendant vulnerabilities. Sue Gerhardt has shown how the very physical structure of the infant brain as well as its habitual functioning develops through interaction with an engaged care-giver.[22] Social relations are constitutive of who we are, and our very survival depends on attachments and commitments. But the 'capacity for developing attachments and commitments that come to figure prominently in our wellbeing makes us highly vulnerable should they be lost'.[23] Concepts of human agency, he suggests, emphasize our capabilities. As human beings, though, we are not only capable, but vulnerable, dependent and needy and 'our vulnerability is as important as our capacities'.[24] Consequently, the condition of humanity is one of shared incompleteness, which, together with our unavoidable vulnerability has consequences for how we think about care. Sayer argues that '[t]he ability to care does not rest on a rational calculation of self-interest, but is a common natural social disposition' and that '[b]eing able to receive and give care is therefore central to human social being and not – as so much philosophy and social science has assumed – a matter of marginal interest'.[25]

It is worth pausing on Sayer's words, clearly chosen with great care. Amartya Sen's emphasis on the development of capabilities as the proper goal of justice and development is here not contradicted but modified. The words vulnerable, dependent, needy are usually critical or at best patronizing. The now frequent use of the terms 'vulnerable adults', 'vulnerable children', 'vulnerable elderly' and so on suggest not just that some people are more vulnerable than others (in unspecified ways) but that there might be such a being as an invulnerable person. Dependency, too, has negative connotations especially in relation to those receiving state benefits. To describe an individual as needy is a usually a criticism of their orientation to others. Sayer reminds us that this is the human condition, of each and all of us, alone and together, and a language which demeans that makes us less than human while asking us to be, more than, or at least other than, human.

For Sayer, how we understand dignity is predicated on this fundamental human condition of vulnerability, of both others and ourselves. Thus '[t]o treat someone in a dignified way is not to ignore their vulnerability and dependence on others, *but rather to treat them in a way which discreetly acknowledges that vulnerability without taking advantage of it, and to trust them not to use their autonomy in a way which would take advantage of our own vulnerability'.*[26] An extreme opposite is the behaviour we call evil, which Sayer describes as 'a means by which the perpetrator attempts to remove his own vulnerability by shifting it onto the victim, and feels empowered in doing so, at least briefly'.[27]

This has institutional implications. For Sayer, the problem of disrespect and unequal dignity is not primarily one of individual interpersonal behaviour to be remedied by exhortations to behave better, but a question of social structures – implying the need for a different social order and hence for utopia as architecture. Thus '[t]he moral problems of unequal dignity are primarily the product not of disrespect or undignified behaviour within free-floating, ephemeral, interpersonal social relations, but of social structures that make people's lives objectively unequal within their society'.[28] Sayer rejects piecemeal change: 'the idea that the good can be reached simply by removing "bads," step by step, without having any conception of the good and how it could be realized in feasible alternative forms of social organization, is naïve in the extreme'.[29] But again the sociologist hesitates: 'Manifestly superior and feasible successor systems or practices are needed before it becomes rational to remove what we have at present, even if we know that existing arrangements are problematic'.[30] Nevertheless, some features are clear, in particular a much greater equality of condition that calls into question capitalism itself. Sayer argues that the structures of inequality and injustice intrinsic to capitalism are necessarily inimical to dignity and to the development of human capacities: 'Capitalist relations of production and dynamics produce structural injustices in which many are consigned to lives of exploitation and domination, and are unable to realise their potential' and '[w]here inequalities are structural features of societies then people cannot stand in dignified relations to one another'.[31] The modes of utopia as ontology (the nature of persons), as archaeology (of capitalism) and as architecture (of a better society) are indivisible.

Sayer's account overlaps with Roberto Unger's. Both develop a processual ontology of becoming. Both cast this in relational terms. Both relate the question of human capacities and their development to existing social institutions and the need for change. Sayer casts this in terms of dignity, Unger in terms of grace. As we have seen in Chapter 7, Unger proposes a particular form of utopian method, rooted in social practice and entailing both institutional and existential transformation. *Democracy Realized* sets out his hopes for a gradual move from the global neo-liberal *status quo* to a world that is more democratic and more economically just. The economic, social and political structures of society are open to transformation through improvisation and collective learning. Hope and imagination are central to short-term creative action, and to a longer term sense of direction and 'a larger vision of society and history that can help inform and inspire its work'.[32] In this active process improvisation creates possibility, both objectively and through the capacities of human beings to change themselves and their circumstances. The practice of democratic experimentalism opens up new possibilities for the social future and simultaneously enables (and constrains) changes in people as subjects and agents. *The Self Awakened* develops these claims in what amounts to a utopian ontology with central themes of grace, transcendence and connection – building also on Unger's much earlier work, *Passion: An Essay in Personality*, which asserts that it is possible to develop an account of identity that is neither trivial nor context-bound.

Unger rejects the term ontology as well as the term utopia. But this is a refusal of a *timeless* ontology. Just as Geras has shown that there is a concept of human nature in Marx despite its historicization, so too Unger is concerned with a non-essentialized ontology. If '[t]he legitimate successor to ontology is a history of nature, historicizing the laws of nature as well as the kinds of things that arise in the course of this history', the whole argument of *The Self Awakened* is about what it means and could potentially mean to be human, and the implications of this for creating a world adequate to human flourishing. The project is to rebuild the world, but in order, and in the process, 'to raise up our humanity'.[33]

Unger's tone is often passionate and messianic. Like Tillich, he asserts the tragedy of our human condition but also the possibilities for grace and connection born out of mortality and vulnerability. The question of what we are to do, here, now, is always in mind, alongside the more distant vision of a better society where the disjunction between longing and circumstance will be reduced:

> The single idea that resounds on every page of [*The Self Awakened*] is the idea of the infinity of the human spirit, in the individual as well as humanity. It is a view of the wonderful and terrible disproportion of that spirit to everything that would contain and diminish it, of its awakening to its own nature through its confrontation with the reality of constraint and the prospect of death, of its terror before the indifference and vastness of nature around it, of its discovery that what it most shares with the whole of the universe is its ruination by time, of its subsequent recognition that time is the core of reality if anything is, of its enslavement to orders of society and culture that belittle it, of its need to create a world, a human world, in which it can be and become itself even if to do so it must nevertheless rebel against every dogma, every custom, and every empire, and of its power to realize this seemingly impossible and paradoxical program by identifying, in each intellectual and political situation, the next steps.[34]

Like Sayer, Unger sees human beings as essentially capacity-bearing beings, and as possessed of an innate context-transcending capacity, just as Sayer argues that we seek always to live beyond ourselves. For Unger, it is an emergent property of the human mind to create the infinite out of the finite; one innate characteristic of the mind is its non-mechanical character, its capacity to outrun and subvert the given, in short, to imagine. While we are always and everywhere constrained and constructed by historical circumstances, these circumstances vary in the extent to which they permit and enable human agency, and they never shape us fully. There is always 'a residue of unused capability for action, association, passion, and insight worth having'.[35] People are, then, always more than Carey's 'real people', because '[we] never completely surrender'[36] – a position implicit also in Boltanski's concept of unease. Transcendence is the capacity to imagine ourselves beyond and to act upon, rather than simply react to, the external structures around us. 'Spirit' renders people potentially more 'god-like' because less suborned, more creative, freer. Unger translates spirit as 'the resistant and transcending faculties of the agent'.[37] Our godlikeness lies therefore in a 'quality of context-transforming spirit'.[38] This is, then, a wholly secular argument, although I will come back to the implications of Unger's use of quasi-theological language.

Like Sayer, Unger regards our situation and our being as inherently social. Connection, like transcendence, recurs in both *Passion* and *The Self Awakened*, and the echoes between earlier and later work are precise: 'We ask of one another more than any person can give another: not just respect, admiration or love, but some reliable sign that there is a place for us in the world' reiterates earlier claims that '[t]here is no end to what people want of one another'; people 'want a sign that there is a place for them in the world', and '[w]e seek in others more than an opportunity to live out our sense of longing and jeopardy; we seek an answer to the enigma of our existence or a way to forget this enigma altogether'.[39]

Unger describes *Passion* as 'a speculative and prescriptive view of personality from the standpoint of a single but pervasive aspect of our experience; our desire to be accepted by one another and to become, though this acceptance, freer to reinvent ourselves'.[40] It opens with '[t]he world is real and dense and dark' recalling Bloch's repeated references to the darkness of the lived moment.[41] Unger characterizes the human condition in terms of unlimited mutual need and unlimited mutual fear – our need of acceptance, love and connection with the other, and our fear of the vulnerability this need imposes, leading to a tension between longing and jeopardy. From this issues a quest 'for the basic freedom that includes an assurance of being at home in the world', an echo of Bloch's *Heimat*.[42]

For Unger the reshaping and overhauling of the given facts include the facts of self and character. Specifically, the flexible potential of self, as someone who could act, experience and be otherwise, must resist and overcome the ossification of character, the accretion of habits and dispositions limited by specific historical circumstances. For Bloch, '[w]e have in us what we could become'.[43] For Unger, the basic features of selfhood are 'embodiment, contextuality and the grasping for the supracontextual'.[44] And flexibility. Unger valorizes a flexible self, in which you 'experience yourself as an identity that is never wholly contained by a character and that grows to greater self-knowledge and self-possession by the willed acts of vulnerability or the accepted accidents of fortune that put a character under pressure'.[45] Dispositions limited by circumstance. Resistance, will, acceptance. These issues are also addressed by Richard Sennett, whose early work (with Jonathan Cobb) on the hidden injuries of class again registers the centrality of humiliation. In *The Corrosion of Character, The Craftsman*, and *Together*, Sennett returns to these themes, arguing that flexible capitalism undermines the conditions for the development of what we culturally understand as character by removing stability and craftsmanship from the organization of work. The flexible self demanded by market forces appears more as a disposition limited by circumstance. But *Together* posits interpersonal and social cooperation as a form of craft skill. It may be a capacity, but it is one whose development into a capability may be blocked by adverse circumstances and always requires practice. He would agree with Unger that freedom from rigidity and from compulsion enable better interpersonal relations, and that they underpin political action. As Unger puts it:

> The readiness to experiment with different kinds of encounters, and with their distinctive styles of vulnerability, is akin to central features of the practical, transformative political imagination: its refusal to take any established set of alliances and antagonisms for granted, its effort to mobilize people in ways that are not predefined by the existing order, and its capacity to make these essays in mobilization the means for building new varieties of collaboration and community in the practical affairs of society.[46]

Passion is not contrasted with reason: it refers to 'the whole range of interpersonal encounters in which people do not treat one another as means to one another's ends'.[47] The ability to imagine ourselves otherwise and the possibility of being otherwise entail remaining open to our vulnerability and jeopardy in encounters with others. The goal of 'patient and hopeful availability', or 'moral perfection', is a combination of ardour and gentleness.[48] Gentleness, or sympathy, involves a particular orientation to the other: 'It is to see and to treat the other as a person always precariously and incongruously caught in finite and conditional worlds and situations, character and body, and thus entangled in circumstances disproportionate to the context-transcending capacities of the self'.[49] The integration of this with ardour, with engagement in life, prevents the treatment of the other as a means to an end.

This echoes the central thesis of Martin Buber's contrast between two orientations to the world, the I-it and the I-Thou. The former is an instrumental relationship, in which objects, processes and persons are manipulated or viewed as means to our own ends. The latter is the meeting with another in a connection for its own sake. Theologically, the I-Thou is also a meeting with a transcendent 'Thou', but it valorizes a particular kind of connection in interpersonal relations. It is a position echoed by the Christian communitarian John Macmurray, who argued that not only is human life essentially social, but the distinguishing human characteristic is intentionality. We are therefore most distinctively human not as 'I' but as 'you and I' in a mutual relationship of recognition of the other who is not treated as a means to an end. Only in such a pure relationship, which assumes agency, responsibility and choice on the part of self and other, is a genuine meeting of persons possible. Macmurray deploys both dignity and equality here, arguing that a good society must be organized and judged in terms of meeting the actual and substantive needs of its members, including these interpersonal needs. He went on to say that 'a capitalist society does not organize its social activity in this way', but values individuals in terms of their contribution to social organization.[50] Morris said that 'fellowship is life, and lack of fellowship is death'; and said that in hell, or modern society which amounts to much the same thing, we will cry on our fellows to help us but 'shall find that therein is no help because there is no fellowship, but every man for himself'.[51] Macmurray argues (as Morris did) that material equality is the necessary condition of personal relationships tending to the I-Thou. Buber too points in a similar direction in *Paths in Utopia*, in large part a defence of 'utopian' socialism but also an affirmation of the kibbutz movement.[52]

For Buber, the I-Thou is possible because we understand ourselves to be in the same predicament as the other. For Levinas, the other, as well as the transcendent Other, is radically unknowable, and a relationship conceived as one of communion or sympathy wrongly reduces this radical otherness to sameness. The ethical relation to the other stems from insurmountable difference and is not reciprocal. It entails a responsibility for the other which cannot be demanded in return, which is unconditional – a sort of ethic of grace. In explicitly disconnecting reciprocity and responsibility Levinas's position contrasts markedly with the familiar political rhetoric of rights and responsibilities. The distinction between other and Other is critical, for the Other is both a transcendent and a utopian concept. As Colin Davis put it, 'the Other is not another self, but is constituted by alterity'; and 'Desire is desire for the absolutely Other'.[53] There is a 'darkness in which the Other is never fully seen, known or possessed';[54] it is a mystery and an enigma. Davis concludes 'in Levinas's account of the history of philosophy, the Other is ultimately restored to the Same; but the residual sense that, despite such appropriation, the Other ... has not yet been fully grasped, ensures the survival of alterity and its continuing resistance to the authority of the Same'.[55] This resonates with the tension between utopia and its object of critique, and the failure of the former to break free from the conditions of its production. One might say utopia is always ultimately revealed as a reflection of the present; but the residual sense that, despite this, utopia has not yet been fully grasped, ensures the survival of alterity and its continuing resistance to the authority of the present.

Unger stresses that our knowledge of the other is 'inescapably and radically incomplete',[56] which may place his account of moral perfection closer to Levinas than to Buber. But like Adam Phillips and Barbara Taylor in *On Kindness*, Unger holds that we are driven to others not from duty but by our own need. Love and kindness are an expression of our inherent sociality, not of altruism.[57] Our dealings with one another in the world depend on faith, which is again open to 'a purely secular interpretation'.[58] The encounter with another entails emotional and/ or cognitive risk in going beyond what can be rationally justified. One can be sure neither of the veracity of some cognitive beliefs nor that one's vulnerability, especially in loving another, will not be exploited or betrayed. Faith and grace are linked. Acts of grace entail refraining from attacking another's exposed or heightened vulnerability – a definition of grace that is almost identical with Sayer's definition of dignity. This echoes some vernacular uses of the terms grace, gracious and graciousness, which include the practice of passing over or covering for the weaknesses or social lapses of others rather than exposing or confronting them, thus collaborating in a mutual process of saving face. And Unger goes on to comment that it is in the absence of such grace that another, implicitly non-secular, grace would be needed or appealed to.[59] For grace is often absent from our dealings with one another; and Unger addresses 'negative' emotional states and orientations of hatred, vanity, pride, envy, jealousy, pride, lust as well as compulsion and addiction – all viewed as responses to the primary predicament of unlimited need and unlimited fear in relation to the other. 'Spiritual corruption' means turning occasions of vulnerability into 'devices of dependency, withdrawal, and self-delusion'.[60] This is congruent with, if not identical to, Sayer's 'evil'. But hope, love (both sexual and asexual) and faith are also possible responses to and outcomes of our common predicament. Hope and its 'anticipatory power' are described in Blochian terms: 'hope differs from mere expectation. ... It is a predisposition to action rather than merely a foretaste of pleasure. It instantiates a conceived future rather than merely looking to it'.[61]

The object of Unger's project is always a transformation of social relations and personal experience in the material world:

> The hope held out by the thesis that we can change our relation to our contexts will remain hollow unless we can change this relation in biographical as well as historical time, independent of the fate of all collective projects of transformation. It will be hollow as well unless that change will give us other people and the world itself more fully. That the hope is not hollow in any such sense represents part of the thesis implicit in the idea of futurity: to live for the future is to live in the present as a being not fully determined by the present settings of organized life and thought and therefore more capable of openness to the other person, to the surprising experience, and to the entire phenomenal world of time and change. It is in this way that we can embrace the joy of life in the moment as both a revelation and a prophecy rather than discounting it as a trick that nature plays on spirit the better to reconcile us to our haplessness and our ignorance.[62]

For Unger, actual relations with real persons in the here and now are more important than abstract relations with groups or in possible future scenarios. Nevertheless, nothing 'excuses us from the need to imagine an alternative human world and to imagine it in a way that enables us to act in the present as if this alternative had already begun to emerge and its anticipated norms had already begun to bind us'.[63] There are institutional conditions and consequences, as one would expect given that the personal and political are so deeply intertwined. Flexibility of self depends upon material welfare. The development of individual and collective capabilities and capacities also has a material basis, calling for 'a set of capacity-ensuring rights and resources' that 'must find their counterpart in practices and institutions that keep society open to alternative futures and inspire in politics and culture a contest of visions'.[64] It is, says Unger, perfectly possible to 'devise institutions and practices that, by diminishing the distance between the ordinary moves by which we reproduce them and the extraordinary moves by which we change them, make us greater, freer and more human'.[65] There are implications too for the politics of identity, especially Unger's valorizing of prophetic identity. He means that human identities need to be more strongly articulated in terms of what people individually and collectively might become, rather than in terms of where they come from: we should 'call on prophecy more than upon memory'.[66] It is a position shared by Philip Pullman, who makes a similar point about the dangers of fixing a sense of self in terms of religious 'identity', which is only one aspect of our origins and complex, shifting being in the world.[67] It is reiterated by Edward Said, describing a 'sense that identity is a set of currents, flowing currents, rather than a fixed place or a stable set of objects'.[68] In particular, Unger suggests that we should educate our children to be prophets, through the development of their capacities, which – like all education – entails hope, transformation and a move beyond what now is and what we now are. It is a matter of capacities and of imagination: as Adam and Groves put it, '[t]he continual reaching beyond what we *are* to explore what we *might* become is the motor that generates the narrative structure of our lives'.[69]

Pullman's polarization between where we come from and what we might be can be overdrawn. Tradition is constructed. It is a manifestation of collective memory, which, as Susan Sontag says, is always a stipulation of what is important. But there are different ways of remembering, with different implications for future possibilities. Bloch works with a distinction between anamnesis and anagnoresis. *Anamnesis* is 'simple' recall, perceived by Bloch as intrinsically conservative. *Anagnorisis* is a process of recognition, where the gap between past and present is not collapsed. As Vincent Geoghegan puts it:

> In *anagnorisis* memory traces are reactivated in the present, but there is never simple correspondence between the past and the present, because of all the intervening novelty. The power of the past resides in its complicated relationship of similarity/dissimilarity to the present. The tension thus created helps shape the new. The experience therefore is creatively shocking.[70]

The construction and use of memory can be seen in the art of Jeremy Deller and in the way political demonstrations, especially commemorative demonstrations, operate existentially. Deller choreographs public performance as art. His work includes the re-enactment in 2001 of the Battle of Orgreave, a seminal event of the 1984 Miners' Strike. Film of the re-enactment and a supporting installation about the history of the dispute were included in Deller's 2012 Hayward Gallery exhibition. Intentionally or not, it exemplifies how events that are excised from public discourse as politics can re-enter as art. This reaches an audience that would never otherwise encounter the infamous 'Ridley document', in which even before the 1979 election, the incoming Conservative government planned to break the miners' union. The Hayward exhibition title Joy in People (itself a wonderfully utopian concept) derives from a glorious banner made for another event, *Procession*, which was a parade through Manchester in 2009 co-created by Deller and diverse local groups. Another banner illustrates the shifting of identity between class and ethnicity noted by Malik. 'Our Ancestors were at Peterloo' invokes the occasion in 1819 when cavalry charged a peaceful demonstration in Manchester, killing eighteen people and severely injuring several hundred. Is this, I wondered, oddly exclusionary in a multi-ethnic society where many people's ancestors certainly weren't at Peterloo? Does it imply the kind of Englishness Patrick Wright questions in *On Living in an Old Country*? No, countered my companion. It is about our class ancestors, placing ourselves in that tradition and enacting class solidarity as a possibility for the future. It is independent of biological and ethnic ancestry. My misreading prompted his rueful recall of being once mistaken for a racist when wearing a T-shirt depicting Stonehenge above the legend 'Once upon a time this land was ours' that was intended as a statement of solidarity with new age travellers violently evicted at the 1985 Battle of the Beanfield. Ambiguity and changes of meaning in cultural reproduction are ineradicable.

'Procession' is part of a coincidence of art and politics that has been described as 'Life as Form'.[71] Demonstrations perform a utopian transformation of identity even when not conceived as art. Participation is ostensibly instrumental, aimed at exerting political pressure, but they are also, and perhaps primarily, expressive and solidaristic, transforming 'not in my name' into 'not in our name'. Visual display plays an important role here. Banners and placards transform massed individuals into identifiable groups, taking part as collective representatives of political, religious, ethnic, local and other institutional groups, and declaring common objectives. They illustrate both the diverse social locations and identifications of participants and their common orientation to collective change. They simultaneously place us in different traditions and open up possibilities for a common future. And people often take their children, their very presence a statement of that future orientation.

The mobilization of tradition can work here as *anagnorisis*, the element of shock that is the currency of situationist art achieved in different ways. On one demonstration against public sector cuts, the William Morris Society marched with a facsimile of the banner of the Hammersmith Socialist League that Morris himself would have carried.

This was not a nostalgic gesture to an antiquarian interest, but a statement of the continuity of struggle, of repetition that is not repetition. It provoked different responses, including a baffled 'I've never heard of you', as well as the historically informed 'you haven't existed for a hundred years', and the recognition that 'you must be the William Morris Society'. But sometimes the correspondence between past and present does its own work, as in the seventy-fifth anniversary rally of the Battle of Cable Street a few months later. The official placards made the link between 1936 and 2011 through the historic slogan 'they shall not pass', directed now at countering new expressions of hatred and resentment. Banners commemorating the International Brigades who fought in the Spanish Civil War were carried alongside banners from trade union and community groups from London's contemporary East End, including the trenchant statements from the RMT: 'No to racism and fascism'. The banners are a means which people identify themselves with their own specific traditions and loyalties, while the procession forges a new solidarity. It suspends precisely the differences those banners signify, creating, temporarily, a situation of fellowship, of meeting, of grace, and pointing it towards the possibility and necessity of re-formed selves and a reformed future.

Given the similarities between Sayer's focus on dignity and Unger's elaboration of grace, we should consider what is gained or lost by the adoption of theological terms. Some have read *The Self Awakened* as a post-secular, rather than an unequivocally secular, argument. The danger, then, is potential misunderstanding and the risk of being ignored and dismissed. Sayer's book avoids such pitfalls, while still challenging deep-rooted assumptions in the social sciences by insisting that reason and emotion, as well as science and normativity, are indivisible. But something is gained with the language of transcendence and grace, an existential depth perhaps best clarified through Bloch's discussions of religion in *The Principle of Hope* and *Atheism in Christianity*.

There may be a historical as well as a conceptual resonance here. Bloch's work profoundly influenced liberation theology in South America in the 1960s and 70s; Unger was born in Brazil in 1947, lived there throughout the 1960s, and left for graduate studies at Harvard in 1969. The utopian strands in this context are many and varied, not least the building of the new capital city of Brasília in the 1950s, designed by the modernist architect Oscar Niemeyer. The architecture itself may be seen to embody the Christian-Marxist dialogue, for Niemeyer also designed the spectacular new cathedral with its stained glass roof of blue, green and white. There are also echoes in Unger's work of the radical educationalist and utopian Friere, who in turn acknowledges Marx, Fromm and Marcuse as influences. Where Unger seeks to raise up our humanity, Friere makes central the 'ontological and historical vocation of becoming more fully human'.[72] Friere also uses the language of 'transcendence' to denote 'the capacity of human consciousness to surpass the limitations of the objective configuration'.[73] His pedagogic programme is both utopian and a method. It is founded on the basic assumption that humans have an ontological vocation to be subjects that act upon and transform the world, and in so doing move 'towards ever new possibilities of fuller and richer life individually and collectively'.[74] In this respect, Friere's position is itself close to that of Bloch.

For Bloch, the world is essentially unfinished, and the future must be brought into being by human agency: our participation in this process is inescapable. The world is intrinsically and necessarily in process of becoming. The path of development is indeterminate and contains multiple possibilities that are not set against the real, but are part of it. The anticipation or forward-dawning of a world transformed, of possibility on the horizon, attests to a utopian process. Bloch's key concept of the 'not-yet' encompasses both absence and anticipation, and is characteristic not only of the external world but of the human condition. The idea of a self-transforming humanity is therefore central. In the later parts of *The Principle of Hope*, Bloch discusses religion as a repository of utopian imagination, and the questions of alienation of and reclamation by the self are pivotal. Bloch's arguments echo Marx's assertion that religion is not simply the opium of the people, but the heart of a heartless world and the spirit of spiritless conditions. He insists that the necessary move to atheism is one which reclaims the essentially human characteristics that have been projected onto God and Christ because they cannot be expressed or encountered in the constraints of the world as it is. In *Atheism in Christianity*, he quotes Marx:

Religion is the fantastic realization of human nature, inasmuch as human nature has no true reality ... Religious misery is at once the *expression* of man's real misery and the *protest* against it. Religion is the sigh of the oppressed creature, the heart of a heartless world, the soul of soulless conditions. It is the opium of the people. The suppression of religion as man's illusory happiness is the demand for their real happiness ... The criticism of religion has plucked the imaginary flowers from their chains, not so that man may wear a dreary unimaginative chain, but so that he may throw off the chain and pluck the living flowers ... The critique of religion ends with the doctrine that the highest being for mankind is man: with the categorical imperative, therefore, to overthrow every state of affairs in which man is degraded, enslaved, abandoned and despised in his very being.[75]

Reclamation of our alienated capacities restores human agency, brings the Kingdom of Heaven within historical time and opens the future to a process which is a double exodus into human and social transfiguration. Transcendence is not removal from or beyond the world, but its immanent and imminent transformation. The ontology involved here is an 'ontology of Not-yet-being', just as the cosmology is one of the not-yet-become. It entails, in Bloch's terms, transcending without transcendence – which maps on to how Unger understands transcendence.[76] Theistic language recurs throughout Unger's work, in references to 'godlike power and freedom', the 'godlike powers of ordinary humanity', the 'divinization of the person', the 'divinization of humanity', the 'path of divinization'.[77] It makes sense in a secular argument only as the reclamation posited by Bloch. We make ourselves more godlike as we become the people that we are not yet: for that full humanity is something which has been alienated from us. What both Unger and Bloch figure here is a view of humanity that has moral and existential depth, that is construed in terms of becoming and that remains open to possibility at the level of the individual and the social.

This might explain, but does not in itself justify, the linguistic strategy. What is at issue here is the evacuation of existential depth from secular culture as a result of such alienation, leaving no adequate secular language to replace metaphors of faith, grace, spirit and transcendence. The language itself is a vehicle of the education of desire. Contemporary discourse polarizes religion and secularism as belief versus unbelief, with the terms unbelief and atheism mere negations with no positive signification. Dominant forms of atheism, notably those of Richard Dawkins and Christopher Hitchens, involve a reductionist and mechanistic position, and take religious fundamentalism as their target, extended to characterize religion in general. Bloch refers to reductionist scientism as 'stupid materialism', and quotes Lenin: 'Intelligent idealism is closer to intelligent materialism than stupid materialism is'.[78] Bloch's own dialectical materialism has 'the notice above its door: No mechanists allowed'.[79] The dominant discourse is one in which fundamentalist religion and strident atheism based on bad science stand opposed. As Karen Armstrong argues in *The Case for God*, bad science meets bad religion. Such a polarized discourse leaves little space for the potentially positive content of secular humanism.

Unger complains that where spiritual intensity is not alienated into religion it is sequestered into the field of art, emptying philosophy and social science and the politics of our being in the world of these questions: 'the human spirit as portrayed in the humanities – escapes from the stifling structure of everyday life. Having escaped it, it then floats above, disembodied, unwilling and unable to infuse and reanimate the spiritless world of routine and repetition'.[80] Hitchens approves this sequestration, appealing to 'the study of art and literature, both for its own sake and the eternal ethical questions with which it deals'.[81] He refers to Ian McEwan's 'ability to elucidate the numinous without conceding anything to the supernatural'.[82] Sayer makes little reference to the aesthetic sphere, although an aside about Flamenco recalls duende, pointing to the overlap between readings of dignity and of grace: 'There is an improbable conjunction of dignity or self-command in bearing and movement with catharsis, particularly in the singing – the sheer intensity of each commanding respect'.[83]

The treatment of the transcendent human spirit in art, music, literature and responses to (evolved) nature is precisely the subject of Steiner's *Real Presences*, and of *The Sunrise of Wonder*, an autobiographical anthology arranged as letters to his grandchildren by Michael Mayne, one-time Dean of Westminster. Mayne articulates the spirit infusing these often secular passages in a Christian religious direction, suggesting that wonder is the fundamental religious category. But this is not a necessary move. Susan McManus identifies wonder as the fundamental utopian category. Phillippa Bennett, writing about the atheist and Marxist Morris, argues that it is the fundamental human category. She notes, as does Mayne, Gradgrind's hostility to wonder in Dickens's *Hard Times*. Bennett suggests:

[W]onder is best defined less as a *response* than an *attitude* towards the world. To wonder is not so much the ability to experience the occasional spontaneous epiphany as the willingness to be perceptive and receptive to the opportunities for wonder that present themselves to us on a daily basis. And, just as importantly, it is the willingness to allow those opportunities and experiences to affect, and perhaps even transform us – to allow them to challenge our preconceptions and renew our vision. To do so, is to recognize the most fundamental and radical aspect of wonder – its revolutionary potential.[84]

Bennett suggests that the whole of Morris's work is driven by the desire to reclaim wonder, just as Bloch and Unger seek to return sequestered spirit to the social world in unalienated form. Perhaps this contest over the ownership of wonder reveals that it is possible, if difficult, to articulate existential depth in secular terms. One can, I think, similarly contest the ownership of grace. And if dignity, as articulated by Sayer, is a foundational concept of social justice and the condition for grace, grace itself reaches further towards the more utopian existential quest for connection and *Heimat*.

There are, of course, many other possible and actual normative accounts of human ontology. Utopian accounts are always contested, and should be so. The central point of the ontological mode is that the utopian method necessarily involves claims about who we are and who we might and should be. These claims, like the institutional parameters of the good society, need to be made explicit through the archaeological mode and developed in terms of their implications for the architectural mode. A commitment to dignity and grace is here a preliminary to considering what is necessary to make them more of a reality and less of an aspiration. And the approach taken by both Sayer and Unger suggests that the utopian project is not imperilled by our incapacity to change and become otherwise, but impelled by our capacity, need and desire to do so.

10
Utopia as Architecture

Utopia as architecture is its culturally most familiar mode: imagining a reconstructed world and describing its social institutions. This is the terrain of utopian fiction. It is also the mode anti-utopians like best, keeping the possibility of living differently safely bound between book covers. As we have seen in Part I, the expression of utopian desire cannot be confined in this way but leaks into every aspect of human culture. Utopia as architecture incorporates the ontological mode, positing inhabitants who feel and want, as well as behave, differently from ourselves. Therein lies the education of desire. The balance between institutional and ontological concerns varies. This final chapter addresses the social forms demanded by the principles of dignity and grace outlined in Chapter 9, keeping in view the self-creating and institution-creating capacities of human beings.

Negation and criticism are much easier. Sociologists are comfortable with the cognitive operations involved in unmasking embedded assumptions, so utopia as archaeology sits easily with social theory as critique. Utopia as ontology or architecture is more troubling. The ontological mode crosses the boundary of the split selves demanded by reason and by the academy: grace appears in sociology neither as object nor orientation. Utopia as architecture is a form of critique, but it negates through the conjuring of alternatives that are also positive proposals. A long stanza of the medieval poem 'The Land of Cokagyne' lists the absences from that paradise: quarrelling, anger, death; lack of food or cloth; serpent, wolf or fox, flea, fly or louse, worm or snail; night, thunder, sleet, hail, storm, rain or wind.[1] Utopia offers more than this. It is an attempt to figure (and figure out) the absent presence. It demands speculation, judgment and suspension of disbelief on the part of both writer and reader. But that suspension is temporary, confined to the architectural moment of utopia as method. It is followed always by the archaeological moment that interrogates the inconsistencies and silences of its architectural counterpart. Utopia as architecture is both less and more than a model or blueprint. Less, in being a provisional hypothesis about how society might be, offered as part of a dialogue, neither intending nor constituting a forecast, recognizing itself as in part a present future. More, in inviting both writer and reader to imagine themselves, as well as the world, otherwise. Institutionally, archaeological and architectural modes move between critique and reconstitution, mirroring the existential oscillation between loss or sorrow and restitution that lie at the root of utopian desire. This combination of existential and institutional aspects is difficult because it breaches disciplinary boundaries. As knowledge rendered imaginatively, the utopian mode deserves more respect than it often gets. It is hard to keep the simultaneous focus on the machinery of society and the life lived within it. But we must try.

The task is to imagine alternative ways of life that would be ecologically and socially sustainable and enable deeper and wider human happiness than is now possible. Higgins argues that '[it] is one of the defining differences between the politics of the Right and the Left that the Left believes in the possibility of creating a truly human society with the economy viewed as instrumental to that end' and that 'the Left can be expected to argue for the defence and enhancement of the public world and the citizen's role within it'.[2] The 'creation of a real and meaningful citizenship' thus requires the defence of the public realm, against the claims and power of private property and personal and corporate greed.[3] Higgins points to the importance of climate change and to the extent and consequences of inequality at every level. He concludes that:

> In the short term it is necessary to stress again that standing as an alternative to the abstract entity of the markets is a form of society built on the principle of solidarity. This in the short term ... means establishing a floor of citizenship below which no citizen would be allowed to fall. ... In a republic, the right to shelter, food security, education, a good environment, and freedom from fear and insecurity from childhood to old age, must be the benchmarks.[4]

Higgins's stricture about the relationship between economy and society implies that we should begin from the kind of society we want and proceed to the kind of economic relations that will sustain and support it, rather than the other way round. What, then, needs to change? Well, just about everything. I sketch here some principles and some institutional conditions: human flourishing; equality of condition; sustainability; rethinking what counts as production and wealth; quality of work; revaluing care; recognizing unpaid work; a regulative and enabling democratic state; and a guaranteed basic income and universal child benefit, both as a goal and as a transitional strategy. I explore something of what these changes might enable, individually and in our relationships with each other.

Human flourishing

All utopian proposals embed a view of human flourishing. In Chapter 9, I have argued for an ontology of becoming that is integrally intertwined with institutional change. This sense of growth and change is widely accepted in relation to children: the United Nations Convention on the Rights of the Child asserts their rights to economic and social security and the 'development of the child's personality, talents and mental and physical abilities to their fullest potential'.[5] It implies prophetic identity, helping children imagine and become their chosen best selves. Life is short: the development of some multifarious possibilities inevitably means the sacrifice of others. But this is a much broader aspiration than meritocratic advantage, prompting the question of when, or indeed if, holistic development should be abandoned and subordinated to market demands. Why should this human right hold only for the first fifth of a generous life expectancy? A processual ontology suggests this should also apply to adults. And it is hard to see how such rights can be put into practice for children without being extended to their parents. A decent society is one which enables people to develop their capacities.

Capacities are not quite the same as the capabilities promoted by Amartya Sen as a necessary element in personal and social development. Education always reflects the values of the social context in defining which talents and abilities are recognized and socially valued, and thus the practical evaluation of worth. In Sen's work, the framework of the market is taken for granted or explicitly endorsed. Valued capabilities thus remain defined by the market. But when we ask our children what they want to be when they grow up, we should not mean only what slot they hope to fill. That way, becoming becomes adaptation. The development of human capacities must be freed from the obsession with marketable skills and reoriented to pleasurable and useful human creativity. In relation to children, this requires a different kind of education, one that builds on their curiosity rather than fomenting anxiety with recurrent testing. They need more access to drama and music, both of which are also forms of social education. The critique of meritocracy suggests that children will only have equal opportunities for creative self-development from a position of material equality. But also at issue is the adult world they inhabit and anticipate. The ideological and material value placed on adult roles casts a long shadow: the development of children's capacities itself and their sense of what is worthwhile are determined by wider social evaluations and structures.

From dignity to equality

Higgins's immediate demand for an acceptable minimum standard of living and quality of life has far-reaching consequences. It is, perhaps, a version of democracy realized. If the idea of a social floor is essential to dignity, some arguments push further towards equality, as Higgins would do in the medium to long term. Sayer and Habermas both argue that dignity implies material equality as the basis of social equality. Social class sets up a contest for dignity. Redistribution and recognition, often treated as alternative priorities, are necessarily interlinked. These two positions leave us suspended between a vision of society based on minimum guaranteed incomes and good public services, and full equality. Both imply a radical reduction in inequalities within and between nation states and the abolition of structural positions of deprivation into which the poor are currently more likely to be delivered.

The more radical demand for equality as the basis of dignity demands something that cannot be delivered by the market. This is what Morris thinks of as equality of condition, a better term than equality of outcome which can be wilfully misread as the imposition of uniformity. For Morris, equality of condition is the basis rather than the antithesis of difference. Diversity necessarily arises because people have different and unequal capacities, dispositions and desires; developing these will produce more, not less, variety. But Morris insisted that 'whatever inequality I admit among people, I claim this equality that everybody should have full enough food, clothes, and housing, and full enough leisure, pleasure and education; and that everybody should have a certainty of these necessaries'.[6] For Morris, as for Higgins, security and freedom from fear of want are paramount.

Morris did not construe equality as Bellamy or Young did, and we most commonly do, as a universal monetary allowance allocated by the state. He opposed unequal distribution on the basis of work or social contribution because it involves a calculus of worth that views individuals only from the point of view of their productivity. If they are viewed as full human beings, merit and desert cannot be the basis for distributive equity. But equal distribution also constitutes a form of rationing that does not acknowledge the uniqueness of persons or variable need. Morris contrasts the distribution of food within a prison and a family. In a prison, he says, portions are weighed and measured; in a family, people eat different amounts, but all have what they want and need because enough has been provided. His example is naïve about the informal processes of allocating food within families: social convention and actual practice may favour men over women, children over adults, or adults over children; women usually get the short straw, illustrated by Margaret Forster's title *Have the Men had Enough?*. Morris is wrong, however, principally because enough has *not* usually been provided. Affluence allows some of us to accept the principle of collective provision free at the point of need in relation to access to clean water, education and healthcare, and to defend this vociferously when it is under attack. Some will use more than others. In Britain, it is only very recently that we have been encouraged to resent some people making more use of health services, blaming ill-health on behaviour and lifestyle, and attributing relative good health to moral superiority rather than good fortune. There is no logical reason why open access should not apply equally to food, energy and transport in a future where '[w]e shall no longer be harried and driven by the fear of starvation'.[7] Morris's most utopian leap is this abolition of calculus and rationing, and the imagination of a society in which 'the free development of each is the condition of the free development of all'.[8] The absence of a social machinery of rationed distribution in *News from Nowhere* then appears as a deliberate act of negation, not of social institutions per se, but of those specific processes.

If this utopia outstrips what most of us can imagine as realistic, feasible or achievable, we should recognize it as a genuinely utopian contradiction of our taken for granted values and expectations. Two things follow. First, while we cannot measure happiness, love or grace, or put a price on the beauty of the earth, alternative conceptualizations of human worth and social progress are plainly possible. If we measure anything, indicators should reflect this scale of values. Second, if abolishing rationing is beyond our imaginative and institutional reach, we can aspire to distributive equality, knowing it to be a compromise and a diminished form of a greater good. That means equalizing cash incomes and providing a wide range of goods and services free at the point of use.

Basic income

The lesser demand of a social floor might be met institutionally through the device of a basic income guarantee alongside improved public services. Basic income is a universal, unconditional payment to all citizens, extending to all the principle of universal child benefit or a minimum income for pensioners. The financial crisis draws into sharp focus the need to find some less punitive way of supporting working-age populations in an era of rapidly rising unemployment and of reducing the complexity and bureaucratic costs of existing benefit systems. Basic income would remove conditionality and be much cheaper to administer. Relatively low amounts compatible with a capitalist economy have been suggested as a replacement for conventional tax and benefit structures, but the levels implied would not be enough to abolish poverty. My purpose here is not a comprehensive exploration of how different levels of basic income would work, and how far they can be pushed within a capitalist framework, although these are important questions. We can imagine basic income at any level we like, pushing progressively further towards equality. Here, I am assuming a level adequate to prevent relative poverty, in order to explore what this would enable in terms of personal autonomy, dignity and opportunities for grace. It is not just a matter of the dignity of the no-longer-poor, but of all of us. John Donne said we are diminished by the death of another; any sense of solidarity turns the unmet need of others and their humiliation into our own shame.

A basic income guarantee would enable people to do nothing. That is not a drawback, but its essential point. It makes basic income a utopian device, rather than just another social policy proposal. Doing nothing is culturally stigmatized, for idleness is the antithesis of the capitalist compulsion to labour. In *The Economic Horror,* Vivienne Forrester highlighted the paradox of the simultaneous indignities of enforced idleness and compulsion to enslaved labour. In late 2012, escalating unemployment rates in parts of Europe included youth unemployment rates of twenty per cent in the UK and over fifty per cent in Greece and Spain – recalling Fourier's remark nearly 200 years ago that '[c]ivilization had not only turned man away from his destiny by making work repulsive; true to its usual penchant for perfecting vice, it had consistently failed to provide enough of its repulsive work'.[9] For if the work that capitalism offers is mostly awful, the consequences of unemployment are worse, both in terms of exclusion from an adequate and legitimate share in the social product and in terms of (increasing) social vilification. Basic income breaks, and denaturalizes, the link between employment and access to the means of life, and endorsing idleness becomes a critical utopian move.

However, 'doing nothing' is here intended also as a positive proposal. Politicians may declare that 'we need to do more and we need to do it faster'. The opposite is true. We need to do less, and we need to do it more slowly.[10] Doing a lot more nothing, including sleeping, would reduce resource consumption, lower stress levels and enable social relations more conducive to dignity and grace; and as Bammer notes, for the protagonists of Monica Wittig's *Les Guérillères*, sleeping can be a form of resistance.[11] Bertrand Russell's 1932 *In Praise of Idleness* proposed something less than its title promised, a working day of four hours made possible by increased productivity of labour. 'Modern methods of production', he said, 'have given us the possibility of ease and security for all' and yet we have chosen, foolishly, to continue to extol the dignity of work. Leisure, whether spent in pursuits seen as high or as popular culture, would, he thought, make us better and kinder people: 'Ordinary men and women, having the opportunity of a happy life, will become more kindly and less persecuting and less inclined to view others with suspicion. ... Good nature is, of all moral qualities, the one that the world needs most, and good nature is the result of ease and security, not of a life of arduous struggle'.[12]

More inclusive social relations can only be enabled, not determined, by economic arrangements. Nevertheless, equality and security, a revaluing of care and a different kind of economy and education would make possible a world where no one lacks the resources of time, energy, education, money or access to services that enable social participation. The effects would be both individual and collective. Abolishing a benefits system that treats claimants as undeserving scroungers and subjects people with disabilities to ludicrous and demeaning assessments would mean an immediate reduction of humiliation and increase in dignity. A utopian argument would go further. Wonder as an orientation to the world, an openness to the utopian marvelous or to grace, presupposes a receptivity in which our being in the world itself, not only in relation to others, is an end in itself. It entails the mode of awareness Buddhists call mindfulness. Marilynne Robinson describes its converse, the destruction of interiority, as *Absence of Mind*. Mindfulness needs stillness and calm rather than frenetic activity and constant stimulation. Both individually and relationally, the capacity to do nothing attentively is a prerequisite for grace.

'Nothing', however, is often not nothing at all. For several years, I asked students taking my utopia course what they would do if their standard of living were guaranteed. Many, though not all, said 'nothing'. This 'nothing' turned out to mean making and listening to music, playing sport, talking with friends, cooking and online networking: 'playing' rather than 'working'. The question of how long they would do nothing for suggested that these pleasures would in many cases eventually turn into or be supplemented by more committed engagement of some kind. 'Play' can, then, also include socially useful activity from a position of freedom; it can be work, but not 'work'. The possibilities of this are diminishing rather than expanding. The 'young old', people who have retired, are in good health, and some of whom have reasonable pensions, are active in many areas of social life. Increases in state pension age erode the presumption that older people are entitled to a minimum standard of living that enables social participation and quality of life, while forcing people (other than the rich) to work longer exacerbates youth unemployment. Pensions are being reconstructed as an unmerited privilege rather than a right, and class inequalities represented as intergenerational conflicts of interest over resources. But if all were entitled to a decent level of income, the current position of the young old could be generalized.

The potential consequences of a basic income guarantee can be seen in already-existing practices, from the mundane to the deliberately prefigurative. People would be free to spend more time with each other; to take care of their children and grandchildren, parents and grandparents; to fix cars and to play sport; to restore canals and steam trains; to cultivate their private or community gardens or allotments; to spend some or all of their time in education, or as artists, musicians, or writers; to devise collective projects; to engage in democratic debate. Katherine Swift gave up regular paid work and spent twenty years making a garden in Shropshire. She gave the world both the garden and her account of its making. *The Morville Hours* is about a garden, and about time itself, the cycle of days, years, lives structured around the Benedictine hours of prayer, both an expression and a vehicle of wonder.

Time and economic security provide the basis for the real revival of civil society that is already a utopian trope, a space that is neither the private world of the family nor the privatized world of market relations. As people free to choose what to do, they – you – we – can extend the existing collective forms of civil society and choose and make new ones, changing ourselves in the process. As Harvey says, 'All manner of small-scale experiments around the world can be found in which [alternative] economic and political forms are being constructed'.[13] Explicitly prefigurative practices include ventures from Transition Towns to the Occupy movements. Occupy began in New York in 2011 as Occupy

Wall Street. It was a protest against corporate greed, against ordinary people, especially the poorest, being expected to bail out the bankers who caused the economic crisis. Tent cities sprang up across the world, under the slogan 'we are the 99 per cent'. The camp outside St Paul's Cathedral in London was forcibly removed at the behest of the City of London Corporation, but not before it had exposed the contradiction between the social gospel of the Anglican Church and its entrenchment in the British establishment, a contradiction resulting in the resignation of Giles Fraser, former Canon Chancellor of St Pauls.

Like Marinaleda, Occupy exists both as reality and representation. Media responses tended to blunt the stark political message of Occupy by representing the movement as wholly countercultural, complaining that part-time participants who continued to go to work, or who went home to look after their kids, were somehow hypocritical. All prefigurative practices are subject to incorporation as merely 'alternative', or subject to delegitimization, and ultimately repression, as wholly 'other'. The 'other' is impossible, acceptable (and thus in its own way incorporated) only as a piece of situationist art: Occupy's placards and banners were instantly collectible as artworks. Alex Hartley's 'Nowhereisland', an unmapped island from Svalbard claimed as independent, with a virtual citizenry of 23,000 people and a consensual online constitution, was towed around the UK as part of the 2012 cultural Olympiad.[14]

To look at Occupy as a prefiguration of the good society might seem paradoxical: surely in utopia, such protest will be unnecessary. The stark injustice that precipitated Occupy may be transcended. But no future society is likely to be free from contested opinions and conflicting interests, so the redundancy of demonstration is not obvious. Material security and freedom from the compulsion to labour increase the viability of participation. Basic income is in this way, as in others, potentially subversive. Whether and in what sense Occupy was or is 'effective' is less important than its creation of temporary autonomous zones and its provision of spaces that keep society open to alternative practices and futures and cultivate the capacity to develop these. Besides the camp, London Occupy created the Bank of Ideas, opened temporarily to the public for 'the non-monetary trade of ideas to help solve the pressing economic, social and environmental problems of our time', and for creative activity, workshops, performance and the exchange of skills.[15] The parallel Free University posed questions at the heart of utopia, both as substance and process: 'How can our human world, the world as we experience it, imbued with consciousness, free will, meaning and value, exist and best flourish, embedded in the physical universe? What is of most value in life? What kind of civilized world should we seek to help create? How do we do it?' [16] It endorsed the playful character of utopia and its probable failure. It complained that universities, as presently constituted, do not further such fundamental enquiry. This venture figured a different kind of education, including adult education open to all those interested, and the material and cultural basis of a more participatory democracy.

Good work

Basic income allows people to do nothing, but we cannot all do nothing all of the time. Removing individual compulsion to labour does not abolish our collective need to provide for ourselves. Socially necessary labour remains, together with human creativity. The negative fantasy of idleness, of benefit recipients 'sat on the sofa all day', and of our incorrigible laziness, is the foundation of and counterweight to compulsory labour. From here springs the worry about lack of work incentives in even the most conditional and punitive of benefit regimes, designed to force people into employment. The actual nature of much work contributes: work, as Durkheim said, is still for most people a punishment and a scourge. Morris had a more optimistic view of who we already are as well as who we might become, arguing that the true incentive to labour is and must be pleasure in the work itself. 'Worthy work ... carries with it the hope of pleasure in rest, the hope of pleasure in our using what it makes, and the hope of pleasure in our daily creative skill.'[17]

Freedom from compulsion implies changes in the meaning, content and structure of work. Gorz argues that:

> It has to be recognised that neither the right to an income, nor full citizenship, nor everyone's sense of identity and self-fulfilment can any longer be centred on and depend on occupying a job. And society has to be changed to take account of this.[18]

This signals not simply a shift in attitudes at a cognitive level, but in modes of identification in which 'work' – in the sense of paid work, or work that you are given to do – can no longer be central to individual life projects.

> But this central problem will only be confronted ... if 'work' ... loses its centrality in everyone's minds, thinking and imagination. And this is what all the established powers and dominant forces are

working to prevent ... The place of work in everyone's imagination and self-image and in his/her vision of a possible future is the central issue in a profoundly political conflict, a struggle for power. Any transformation of society ... requires the capacity to think differently, or quite simply to formulate what everyone is feeling.[19]

Morris's insistence on pleasure in the work itself separates identity only from externally imposed, or alienated, work, not from the exercise of skill. His vision of good work came from Ruskin, who regarded the separation of mental and physical work, and therefore the industrial division of labour, as dehumanizing. Good work involves hand, heart and mind. As Sennett has recently argued, this approach to craftsmanship applies more widely than to traditional handcrafts.[20] Coordination of brain, eye and hand is involved in musicianship, sport, parenting and developing Linux software as well as carpentry or pottery. Craftsmanship requires practice towards proficiency: Sennett suggests ten thousand hours, or three hours a day for ten years. It also entails a distinctive attitude, a commitment to doing the best work possible for its own sake. Morris believed it was possible for people to acquire a range of skills, as he did himself, enabling a reduction in the division of labour and the cultivation of a wider range of individual capabilities. Skill and commitment to quality affect the experience of work, the kind of people we are enabled to become, the relationships we are able to have with each other and the capabilities we bring to participation in civil society.

Capitalism does not encourage craftsmanship. As Sennett says, the acquisition of skill implies its long-term deployment. In the neo-liberal economy, jobs for life are derided as an antiquated and indulgent aspiration. Flexibility of labour means committing time to developing craft skills is a barrier to successful economic participation rather than an investment. Orientation to the quality of the work differs markedly from orientation to one's own saleability. Craftsmanship is antithetical to the neo-liberal requirement of employability through 're-skilling' to the shifting requirements of the market. Work cannot be an expression of an ethically reflexive self; rather, self becomes a mirror of what the market requires.

The character of work and the commodification of workers is inseparable from commodity production. One of the extraordinary irrationalities of modern economic life is the panic induced when people shop less; lack of demand undermines the whole system of capitalist expansion and profit. Yet reducing unnecessary and often unsatisfying consumption is a good thing. As Morris argued, much of what is produced, and therefore consumed, in capitalist society constitutes waste or illth rather than wealth.[21] Wholly unnecessary luxury goods are produced for those with more money than sense, while vast quantities of inferior goods, which no one would buy if they had a real choice, are produced for those who cannot afford anything better. Take a stroll round the luxury goods department of Selfridges in London's Oxford Street, or the designer outlets in the huge Westfield shopping malls at White City or Stratford in London and marvel at the ingenuity, if not the taste, that is invested in parting the rich from their money. Then wander round a branch of Poundland, recalling that some of the staff are on compulsory government work placements and not even paid to spend their days amid such cheap and nasty tat. Or even stand, as I did in February, in John Lewis, that emporium constantly set up as a model for a reformed economy, in front of a display of pink and red Valentine's Day gifts, and wonder whose life could conceivably be the less if none of this stuff existed.

The structure and content of work must change. Sayer suggests that contributory equality is as important as its distributive counterpart. This is not the same as Hutton's contributory principle in relation to eligibility of benefits, but rather concerns the restructuring of work. Equality in terms of what people 'are allowed and expected to *do*' implies 'a society with a division of labour in which high quality work and low quality work were shared rather than segregated into different jobs'.[22] Bad pay and conditions will have to go, along with work that is fundamentally pointless. Why would anyone tolerate them? 'Pay' is relevant if basic income is embedded in a monetized economy where it can be supplemented by earnings taxed at a high (and progressive) level. If Hobhouse is right that eighty per cent of everything we do can be attributed to our social inheritance and context, it is appropriate that the top rate of tax should be eighty per cent, or even that there should be an income ceiling as well as a floor. Full equality, of course, goes beyond this. The point is to create space for the redirection of human energies towards real human needs. But this is possible only in a society in which the distribution of the social product and the organization of work are not effected primarily through the wage relation.

Revaluing care

Restructuring 'jobs' is one thing. But much of the work of maintaining and reproducing human livelihoods takes place outside the market. We should think in terms of what Miriam Glucksmann calls the Total

Social Organisation of Labour.[23] This provides the critical lens inherent in all feminist emphases on the importance and value of unpaid work. It exposes the absurdity of counting childcare as work when it is carried out within the market by a registered child-minder or nursery, but not when it is carried out by a mother who needs to be forced off benefit and into 'work'. It reveals the amount of unpaid work on which we all depend. It shows that 'the economy' does not exist; it is merely an abstraction from social practices looked at from their economic point of view, so that economic activity cannot be morally neutral. This wider perspective denaturalizes market outcomes. It makes it impossible to presume that paid work is inherently more socially valuable than unpaid work, and calls into question the distribution of market rewards, pointing yet again to basic income and equality. It implies construing the whole of the social product as, simply, that, and thus challenging the property rights that support the current inequitable distribution of resources. It implies breaking the link between market profitability and the distribution of the social product – in other words breaking both the wage and the profit relations. It implies the revaluation of care, both financially and in terms of social regard. In 1999, Gorz argued that an unconditional income adequate for a decent existence in the society in question was the only basis for effective validation of, and adequate recompense for, caring, voluntary and non-market activities.

The concept of care often signifies something given or done to children, the frail elderly or working-aged adults with severe disabilities. In this narrow sense, much personal care takes place on an unpaid basis outside the labour market, while such care provided on a paid basis is characterized by low pay and often by poor conditions. This understanding of care, however, implies a distinction between vulnerable recipients of care and others. Sayer and Unger remind us that this is false: we are all vulnerable and in need of care. This wider sense is signalled in social policy by the idea of an ethic of care as an appropriate replacement for the work ethic. Care can also be seen as a craft. To view it thus reveals it as a relational social practice that engages both parties emotionally, cognitively and physically and demands and develops embodied skills. A simple example is the way new parents learn how to lift, hold, nurse and comfort their child and how quickly, for most, this physical and psychical process moves from uncertainty to apparently automatic ease. The child, too, learns how to initiate and cooperate with (and, when they choose, how to resist) this physical and emotional interaction. The same is true of the daily ways we care for those close to us, both children and adults. Care takes time, both to learn and to practise. It is a process quite antithetical to notions of efficiency based on how fast a 'task' can be 'completed'. It implies being with the other, as an end in themselves, for as long as the encounter and any functional content lasts. The deep development of craft in its widest sense is itself embodied knowledge, dispersing real appreciation of what is entailed in making (art or music or software) and in caring throughout a wider population. The time that this requires is also part of the necessary slowing down of our ways of life and the transformation of our means of livelihood.

Care can also be understood as an orientation to others and to ourselves in which, in Pete Seeger's words, we seek to 'bind up this sorry world with hand and heart and mind'.[24] Adam and Groves argue that a perspective of care includes care for the planet and for future generations. It is central to sustainability and intrinsically acknowledges the relationship between present and future. It sensitizes us to a non-reciprocal responsibility for the future – which can be mapped on to Levinas's insistence on our non-reciprocal responsibility for the other. But recognizing care as a craft skill can cut both ways in terms of gender equality. Material security can be the basis on which (mostly) women are pressured into arduous and socially isolated roles as informal carers, in which non-reciprocal responsibility becomes a vehicle of oppression: women have historically had far too much non-reciprocal responsibility for others. Preventing this is a political matter, but revaluing care makes it less likely. Hope resides in the reality that men too benefit from the intimacy developed in relationships of care, and that the capacity for and receptivity to grace is only accidentally gendered.

Towards sustainability

Morris's argument for equality of condition depends on sufficiency, if not abundance. But the existence of limits may also point towards equality, albeit in a form that does require some kind of calculus. Stern assumes that carbon emission reduction and economic growth are compatible. It is safer to assume the opposite: that the ambition of three per cent compound growth is unattainable within ecological limits. The alternative is the development of means of livelihood and ways of life that deliver a good life without either raising the temperature or depleting natural non-renewable resources. As Marcuse said, some manipulated comforts may have to be given up in order that all may have enough. But since 'getting and spending we lay waste our powers', an overall contraction in resource consumption can be part of an improved quality of life. In Morris's terms, this means replacing luxury (for those currently rich) not with austerity or asceticism, but with simplicity and sufficiency for all. Human survival demands that the socially formed matrix of needs, wants and satisfactions is oriented away from material consumption and high carbon emissions. Equity demands that they are oriented away from forms of consumption based on exploitative and unfair trading relations. Human happiness demands that we find ways of engaging with one another that allow less fear, more genuine connection, more love (and, Wells, Fourier and Marcuse would have insisted, better sex).

The questions of sustainability and equality are linked in the idea of 'contraction and convergence'. This principle underpins Stern's approach and international agreements about the progressive reduction of carbon emissions. It derives from Aubrey Meyer, environmental campaigner, founder of the Global Commons Institute and musician. Meyer begins by reflecting that 'both writing and playing music are largely about wholeness and principled distribution of "effort" or practice. Responding to the climate challenge seems much like writing or playing music, where balance on the axes of reason and feeling, time and space, can only come from internal consistency'. Perhaps, he says, 'all life aspires to the condition of music'.[25] For Meyer and Stern, contraction and convergence apply only to national per capita levels of carbon emissions, but the approach can be widened to include other scarce resources and inequalities within nation states. CONVERGE, an international research project dedicated to managing the earth's resources more fairly and effecting a transition to a sustainable future, applies the same principle to the 'sustainability of trade, economics, society, the natural environment, energy, food, governance, wellbeing and consciousness'. CONVERGE seeks processes leading to convergence or contraction, whether they begin with individuals, civil society, economy or state. It involves 'a critical examination of contraction policies in the light of fairness and critical examination of fairness policies in the light of reducing our impact on nature'.[26] Fairness has a quite different political purpose than for Hutton and is closer to Morris's idea of equality of condition. CONVERGE recognizes that equal inputs do not necessarily result in equal outputs: 'fairness, equity, equality and justice reside in the provision of services to each and every one of us – services of habitat, food, community, well-being, energy, materials, governance, trade, and wealth. We can seek fairness not in equal shares or quotas of physical resources but in equal outcomes from the use of differing amounts of materials and energy as appropriate to local context'.[27] This, then, is not a meritocratic interpretation of fairness, but one rooted in our common humanity while seeking to take account of geographical and social difference. Convergence forms a bridge between basic income as an immediate minimal requirement, and the ambition of equality of condition. Basic income is, in that sense, a convergent policy.

Ecological limits point to reduced consumption, and the re-orientation of needs, wants and satisfactions away from resource-intensive and energy-intensive processes. This is not exactly a matter of promoting non-material values and satisfactions. First, the most basic level of material provision is still denied to most of the world's population who are not assured of Higgins's 'right to shelter, food security, education, a good environment, and freedom from fear and insecurity from childhood to old age'. Second, so-called non-material satisfactions cannot be separated from their material and institutional base. Craft workers need tools and materials. Musicians need musical instruments. Both need teachers, and time, and material support during that time. Cash incomes are only part of necessary provision, to be taken in conjunction with the availability of housing, education, healthcare and other public services. This raises the question of scale. If some enterprises might sensibly be organized as small-scale cooperatives, others cannot. We will still need factories, hospitals and schools, transport infrastructure, builders to build them and skilled people to operate them. We will still need water, energy and food supplies. Moves to more localized production will not remove the need for national and global coordination, and thus for national and global institutions.

The state remains necessary. Its collapse, as Urry suggests, would result in enforced localism, possibly dominated by warlordism and certainly making coordination across scales virtually impossible. Among other things, highly specialized healthcare would simply disappear. Basic income as a mechanism of either a social floor or equality, implies an enabling state, one that provides the conditions in which civil society can flourish, by organizing the material frameworks and services on which we all depend. A regulatory state is also essential to curtail wasteful production and consumption or polluting practices. There are many things we will not be able to do: in the absence of technological change, we will have to stop, or at least radically reduce, flying; and looking for a technological fix for this might not be the highest social priority. We will have to slow down. Above all, the state is a necessary vehicle for change. As Harvey says, appropriate social transformation cannot be effected simply from the local level. Whatever action may take place in civil society, 'there is no way that an anti-capitalist social order can be constructed without seizing state power, radically transforming it and reworking the constitutional and institutional framework that currently supports private property, the market system and endless capital accumulation'.[28]

This applies equally at a global level. International inequality continues to grow at an alarming rate. Between 1960 and 1997, the income of the world's richest twenty per cent grew from thirty to seventy-four times that of the poorest twenty per cent.[29] Such inequalities impede economic growth and development whether measured by GDP, or more complex measures of human or sustainable development we might make. They exacerbate the differential impact of climate change. They create migration pressures quite aside from the impact of global warming on the habitability of different parts of the world. Basic income is sometimes referred to as citizen's income, raising questions about who is defined as a citizen and where, and again pointing in the direction of a major redistribution of global resources.

Peter Townsend tentatively considered how the abolition of poverty could be promoted by reconfigured global political institutions. He cited Morris's contrast of a world where 'mastery has turned into fellowship' with the reality that 'while you live you will see all around you people engaged in making others live lives which are not their own'.[30] Echoing Bloch's appeal to warm and cold streams, he argued that '[v]ision is the counterpart of analysis'.[31] Townsend identified the causes of rising international inequality as defective structural adjustment policies, the concentration of hierarchical power, privatization and the shortcomings of targeting and safety nets. He called for a more integrated critique of the processes generating inequality and poverty, and for new social and political institutions constituting an international welfare state. This would include the introduction and legal enforcement of 'measures for international taxation, regulation of transnational corporations and international agencies, reform of representation at the UN, and new guarantees of human rights, including minimal standards of income'.[32] The core principles of equality, sustainability and human flourishing are more challenging on an international scale than within affluent nation states, but the barriers in terms of the dominance of global capital are identical.

Building utopia

'Architecture' in 'utopia as architecture' is, of course, a metaphor, but the actual architecture, the physical infrastructure, matters, too. Sustainable, energy-efficient and affordable housing, schools, hospitals and the availability and physical character of public spaces are all fundamental to material and social wellbeing. Most writing on architecture and utopia, especially that to which architecture students are exposed, treats utopia as a negative signifier, attached to failed modernism.[33] Different styles of architecture appear in utopian fiction as functional and aesthetic questions. The public buildings in Morris and Bellamy's utopias express contrasting views of architectural excellence. For Gilman, the kitchenless house represents the changed position of women and the relation between home and work. Harvey reminds us of the constant rebuilding of cities in the interests of capital. Richard Rogers addresses the relationship between city forms, sustainability and social justice in *Cities for a Small Planet*. Nathaniel Coleman draws on Ricoeur to consider what a utopian architecture might mean in terms that echo Unger's concern with democratic experimentalism. For Coleman, a utopian architecture facilitates social action and interaction that is not pre-determined by planners, architects, or clients. Buildings and spaces are utopian in so far as they are open to changing intentions of people who use them. The pressures against this are extremely strong. Coleman cites Tafuri, who argues that real architecture or flexible architecture open to democratic human purposes is impossible in contemporary capitalism.[34] Capitalist relations, including those between architects and clients, work in the opposite direction, increasingly privatizing space and seeking to control behaviour within it. Contrast the shopping mall, a privatized zone with its own security staff and the right to prohibit photography or exclude people wearing hoodies, with the High Street, a public thoroughfare subject to publicly accountable laws and bye-laws.

If architecture is a metaphor for this mode of utopia as method, some suggest it is a problematic one. Unger proposes that the appropriate image is 'music, not architecture'.[35] Adam and Groves also reject architecture as an appropriate model for approaching the future. Drawing on Plato and Deleuze and Guattari, they argue that architects produce blueprints from the standpoint of present futures, seeking to make plans into reality. The relationship of architecture to the world is one of command. Artisans, in contrast, have embodied skills which involve a sensitivity and response to the material at hand. If we accept that the future is an emergent space, one which is not empty but already real and simply not-yet, we should, she says, see ourselves as sculptors rather than architects. It is the right way to think about the actual making of the future through collective improvisation. But the idea of an architectural blueprint as something to be precisely executed, Coleman suggests, is something relatively new and dependent on computer-driven plans and industrial processes. Historically, buildings would always evolve from drawing to realization: the plan was not the building just as in music the score is not the work.[36] The best architects still embrace the principle of working with the material at hand, in terms of specificities of place, building materials and the lives to be lived within created places. They recognize the need to adapt the original vision in the process of building; and 'plan' to leave these spaces sufficiently flexible for human artisans to sculpt their own collective futures therein. Good architects are also artisans. What Adam and Groves remind us, though, is that utopia as architecture is not the production of a blueprint. It is an imagined future, therefore a present future, which is necessarily provisional and will change in the artisanal making of future presents.

The good society has equality at its core. It demands the public ownership and control of assets currently in private hands. It requires more than that. The way we measure wealth and growth is irrational, and undervalues human activities of care and nurture. The forms of work generated by capitalism do not cultivate craftsmanship in the deepest sense. A radically different form of economy and society oriented to human need rather than profit is the starting point for fuller, freer, more satisfying human relationships. It might be argued that people do not 'want' this, but wants are articulated in particular historical and social circumstances. As Morris put it, 'it must be remembered that civilization has reduced the workman to such a skinny and pitiful existence, that he scarcely knows how to frame a desire for any life much better than that which he now endures perforce'.[37] Morris also says that it 'the province of art to set the true ideal of a full and reasonable life before [people], a life to which the perception and creation of beauty, the enjoyment of real pleasure that is, shall be felt to be as necessary to man as his daily bread'.[38] Art opens us to the possibility of grace, and fosters the desire to build that better life.

On the river

The desire for a better world based on sustainability and equity cannot be fostered by images of austerity and what will be lost, although undoubtedly some things will. All utopias are flawed. The focus must be on what will be gained, something that can be glimpsed in different ways. I find it on the river, where slowing down is gain, not loss. *News from Nowhere* describes the journey up the Thames to Kelmscot, where the story ends. Morris made that journey in reality as well as in utopia, and you can still walk the route along old towing paths and footpaths or follow it by boat. Taking a boat on the Thames, or round the Thames Ring which incorporates the Grand Union Canal and the Oxford Canal as well as the river, is different from walking. You enter into a world governed by different norms and a different sense of time. You depend on a material infrastructure of boats, locks, water hydrants, pump-out stations and waterside hostelries. It is more apparent on the canals than the river that this environment is heavily engineered. Canals have always depended on complex arrangements of feeding water from and to rivers, pumping it uphill, conserving it in side pounds, controlling its flow through locks. Now, you notice the difference between the well-maintained and often mechanized Thames locks and the heavy manual gear of the Grand Union Canal: operating the hundred locks in ninety-seven miles between Brentford and Braunton will improve your core strength faster than pilates. The various houseboat communities living on the waterways doubtless have their own complex structures. But the social relations among boaters in transit prove Russell right. The enforced change of pace produces good nature and collaboration. Navigating locks is an exercise in cooperation. There is no queue-jumping. People wait, chat, set up locks for those who come after, help each other with particularly recalcitrant paddles and gates. Those grounded by a drop in water level, freak winds or simple inexperience are helped. And because there is a great deal of hanging about, especially when the waterways are busy, there is camaraderie that has no purpose beyond itself. The only hierarchy lies in the authority of the lock-keeper if there is one: you do exactly what they say. It is extraordinarily rare for people to break this rule, and when they do it is surprising, disturbing and usually dangerous.

You see the world differently from the water, including the way old towns turn towards the river. Sometimes there is more disgrace than grace. Both Thames and Grand Union Canal are intermittently lined with the degenerate utopia of the regenerated waterside: expensive and hideous flats. But being on the water around the clock – although clocks diminish in importance – offers extraordinary gifts. Days Lock, below Dorchester Abbey in Oxfordshire, is accessible only by boat and footpath. Here I woke at five one day in a summer heat wave and threw open boat hatches. Dawn was just beginning to break. The air was uncannily still, and drifts of pink early morning mist hovered over the water, shrouding river, lock, weir and boats. An hour later, the sun was up and the light pure and clear. But here, on the river, you see more often the patch of blue sky, the gold of the dawn, and even the light in people's eyes. Or at least, you slow down enough to notice them.

Coda: a situated method

All this, it may be protested, is socialism. Indeed. I am a socialist by inheritance and by conviction, as well as a sociologist by profession. The usual response to the protests that 'socialism doesn't work' is that it has never been tried. A more important point is that capitalism doesn't work, which is why the utopian exploration of alternatives is necessary. I have merely sketched some elements an alternative future might incorporate. Inevitably, if this is not wholly ignored, it will be subject to the kind of critique that I have undertaken in Chapter 8. That is the proper nature of the utopian method: from archaeology to architecture and back, exposing contradictions, silences, inadequacies, and interrogating both overt and hidden assumptions about the potentialities and limits of human nature. The central points of my argument are that utopia should be understood as a method, and that as such it should be recognized as intimately related to sociology.

Sociologists are too often marginal to discussions about possible and preferable futures, ceding the ground to engineers, economic forecasters, and evolutionary psychologists, as well as a global capitalist class and politicians with very short-term perspectives. Our very silences shape utopias. The triple repression of normativity, engagement with the future, and human nature that has accompanied the defence of sociology as science needs to be transcended for sociology to take its proper place in imagining and making a better future. Sociology must reclaim utopia, those normative, prescriptive, future-oriented elements that have suffused the discipline from the beginning, but are too often a cause of embarrassment rather than celebration. It needs to be released from a damaging self-censorship, and turn to the vision of a better world that is so often what draws people to the discipline in the first place. If sociologists have no claim to superior imagination or ethical competence, they are no less capable of or responsible for this than anyone else. They should have something to contribute to understanding systemic connections and thus mapping alternatives. If sociology has nothing to offer here, I really don't know quite what it is for.

But sociology must reclaim utopia as method rather than as goal. I am proposing a particular kind of public sociology, one in which both sociology and utopia are revised, or at least read differently. Utopia has been misunderstood as a goal and travestied as totalitarian, but it is best regarded as a method that is both hermeneutic and constitutive. In its hermeneutic mode, it identifies the various and fragmentary expressions of utopian desire. In its constitutive or constructive mode, as the

Imaginary Reconstitution of Society, it is inherently sociological. As speculative sociology, the delineation of potential futures is not prediction or prophecy, nor, precisely, prescription. The imagination of society and ourselves otherwise expands the range of possibilities. Sociology as utopia and utopia as sociology offer multiple, provisional and reflexive accounts of how we might live, suspended between present and future.

Utopianism must be the only form of modelling or scenario-building that is not accepted as contributing to knowledge. But knowledge here must be construed more deeply, as something that involves feelings and desires as well as cognitive statements. Utopia is not simply a thought experiment in the conventional sense, for it necessarily operates at the level of affect as well as intellect. *Contra* Professor Dumbledore, the Mirror of Erised does indeed show us knowledge and truth, precisely because it brings our desires to consciousness and thus into question. Utopia's function as the education of desire makes the ontological mode central to both archaeology and architecture. Utopia as method must address the transformation of needs, wants and satisfactions entailed both in a new society and the transition to it. The process of making and communicating imagined alternative futures must be both affective and cognitive. Moreover, utopia as architecture is a particular kind of scenario-building that not only combines existential and institutional levels, but maintains a double standpoint between present and future. It sustains the tension between these, re-reading the present from the standpoint of the future, transforming it into the history of the future. Present futures are a way of foreclosing or opening future presents, and the utopian mode straddles this tension more effectively than prediction or forecasting.

I am not claiming to invent a method. Rather, my intention is to make explicit a method that is already in use whenever and wherever people individually or collectively consider what the future might bring and how humans might choose to shape it. In naming what is involved in utopia as a method, I mean to encourage and endorse this as a legitimate and useful mode of thought and knowledge-generation. Utopia as method is not and cannot be blueprint. Utopian envisioning is necessarily provisional, reflexive and dialogic. The utopian method allows preferred futures – including the survival of humanity on earth – their proper causal role in the emergent future, rather than leaving this to the potential catastrophe of projected trends. Most policy approaches are both piecemeal and extrapolative, and concerned with damage limitation. This naturalizes the major contours of present society, the structures of global capitalism, the dominance of paid work and the inequalities of the market. The utopian alternative is to think about where we might want to get to and what routes are open to us. But if we know that our hopes for the future are indicative projections of what might be, we know too that these are always coloured by the conditions of its generation. The social imaginary, including its images of potential futures, is always the imaginary generated by a particular society. This is true both in terms of a collective human situation at a given point in time, and of different historical, economic and cultural positionings. Reflexivity is necessary in relation to both these generating conditions, which also underline utopia's essential provisionality. The Imaginary Reconstitution of Society is presented as aspiration, and as a proposition for discussion and negotiation. It is the beginning of a process rather than a statement of closure. The utopian method can be understood as quasi-Brechtian. Jameson argues that in Brecht's theatrical work, techniques of estrangement are used to didactic effect. But Brecht's didacticism is not a closed system; it is never a moral education towards a given end. It involves a call to judgment, or to judgment on a judgment, rather than simply the presentation of a judgment in itself. Such a method demands responsibility from audience as well as presenter.[39]

This underlines the dialogic character of utopian method, reminding us that utopia is a situated method in its operation in the world as well as in the conditions of its production. The method of simultaneously critiquing the present, exploring alternatives, imagining ourselves otherwise and experimenting with prefigurative practices is all around us. It can be seen in environmental NGOs and in the rise of Occupy. Besides embedding prefigurative practices which are simultaneously demonstrative and transformative, Occupy illustrates two further issues about utopia as method. Its international call to 'act locally and globally against ... injustice and to fight for a sustainable economy that puts people and the environment we live in before corporate profits' is undoubtedly utopian, but is institutionally unspecific.[40] Participants were reluctant to make specific proposals for a number of reasons: demands may implicitly endorse existing structures of power; there was no consensus among protestors; the movement had no leaders authorized to speak on behalf of others; the existence of the Occupy movement was more important than producing a manifesto. This last claim mirrors the tensions between process and content, openness and closure, discussed in Chapter 6. Occupy opened up the reality that another world is possible. But, as Harvey says, 'While openings exist towards some alternative social order, no one really knows where or what it is. But just because there is no political force capable of articulating, let alone mounting, such a programme, this is no reason to hold back on outlining alternatives'.[41] The emergence of a truly transformative movement must eventually depend on 'some animating vision of what is to be done and why'.[42]

Occupy illustrates the necessary failure of utopia as method even as an element in its success. For whatever contested images of a better future emerge, they will, if regarded as predictions or as demands, necessarily 'fail' – partly because of the limits of our imagination, partly because of the limits of our power. Even as they fail, they operate as a critique of the present and a reconstitution of the future. Utopia must be continually reinvented as one crucial tool in the making of the future. As Morris said, 'men fight and lose the battle, and the thing that they fought for comes about in spite of their defeat, and when it comes turns out not to be what they meant, and other men have to fight for what they meant under another name'.[43]

The 'thing they fought for' remains elusive and evanescent. Each conjuring of its form is a part – but a necessary part – of a process moving between openness and closure. Marx said that we make our own history, though not under circumstances of our own choosing. Morris said that we must and do make the conditions of our own lives, and that we should be conscious of that, and make them wisely. Bloch said that the hinge in human history is its producer, that we must 'build into the blue and build ourselves into the blue'.[44] We must live in this world as citizens of another. What is required of us is both specific to our distinctive situation, and the same as for every earlier and later generation: Mourn. Hope. Love. Imagine. Organize.

Notes

Preface and Acknowledgements

1. T. Moylan and R. Baccolini (eds) (2007) *Utopia, Method, Vision: The Use Value of Social Dreaming* (Bern: Peter Lang).
2. R. Levitas (2001) 'Against Work: A Utopian Incursion into Social Policy', *Critical Social Policy*, 21(4): 449–65.
3. M. J. Griffin and T. Moylan (eds) (2007) *Exploring the Utopian Impulse* (Bern: Peter Lang).

Introduction

1. H. G. Wells (1906) 'The So-called Science of Sociology', *Sociological Papers*, 3:367.
2. L. T. Sargent (2011) *Utopianism: A Very Short Introduction* (Oxford: Oxford University Press) p. 6.
3. B. Schulz (1998) 'The Republic of Dreams', in B. Schulz *The Collected Works of Bruno Schultz*, ed. J. Ficowski (London: Picador) pp. 266–72.
4. R. Jacoby (2005) *Picture Imperfect: Utopian Thought for an Anti-utopian Age* (New York: Columbia University Press) pp. 113, xiv.
5. G. Kateb (1967) 'Utopia and the Good Life', in F. E. Manuel (ed.) *Utopias and Utopian Thought* (Boston: Beacon Press) p. 239.
6. A. Gorz (1999) *Reclaiming Work: Beyond the Wage-Based Society* (Cambridge: Polity Press) p. 113.
7. E. Bloch (1970) *A Philosophy of the Future* (New York: Herder and Herder) p. 91.

1 From Terror to Grace

1. W. Wordsworth (1809) *The French Revolution As It Appeared To Enthusiasts At Its Commencement*, http://poetry.poetryx.com/poems/726/, accessed 6 April 2011.
2. J. K. Rowling (1997) *Harry Potter and the Philosopher's Stone* (London: Bloomsbury) pp. 152, 157.
3. R. Levitas (1990) *The Concept of Utopia* (Hemel Hempstead: Philip Allan) reissued 2010, 2011 (Bern: Peter Lang).
4. E. P. Thompson (1977) *William Morris: Romantic to Revolutionary* (London: Merlin Press) pp. 790–1. Max Blechman's translation of Abensour (1999) renders this as '[t]he point is not for utopia (unlike the tradition that calls for the "moral education of humanity") to assign "true" or "just" goals to desire but rather to educate desire, to stimulate it, to awaken it – not to assign

it a goal but to open a path for it: ... Desire must be taught to desire, to desire better, to desire more, and above all to desire otherwise'. M. Abensour (1999) 'William Morris: The Politics of Romance', in Max Blechman (ed.) *Revolutionary Romanticism* (San Francisco: City Lights Books) p. 145.

5. E. Bloch (1986) *The Principle of Hope* (London: Basil Blackwell) p. 13.
6. R. Jacoby (2005) *Picture Imperfect: Utopian Thought for an Anti-Utopian Age* (New York: Columbia University Press) p. 35.
7. Bloch, *Principle*, p. 249. See also R. Levitas (1997) 'Educated Hope: Ernst Bloch on Abstract and Concrete Utopia', in Jamie Owen Daniel and Tom Moylan (eds) (1997) *Not Yet: Reconsidering Ernst Bloch* (London, Verso).
8. E. Bloch (1988) *The Utopian Function of Art and Literature* (Cambridge, MA: MIT Press) p. 42.
9. Bloch, *Principle*, p. 1376. The English translation renders *Heimat* as 'homeland'. This never captured the resonance of *Heimat*, and in the context of twenty-first-century US policy, including the Homeland Security Act, the divergence is even greater.
10. F. von Hayek (1946) *The Road to Serfdom* (London: Routledge and Kegan Paul); K. Popper (1945) *The Open Society and Its Enemies* (London: Routledge and Kegan Paul); K. Popper (1986) 'Utopia and Violence', *World Affairs*, 149(1): 3–9; H. Arendt (1951) *The Origins of Totalitarianism* (New York: Harcourt, Brace and Co.); J. Talmon (1970 [1951]) *The Origins of Totalitarian Democracy* (London: Sphere Books); I. Berlin (1990) *The Crooked Timber of Humanity* (London: John Murray); N. Cohn (1993) *The Pursuit of the Millennium: Revolutionary Millenarians and Mystical Anarchists of the Middle Ages* (London: Pimlico) [1957].
11. Jacoby, *Picture Imperfect*, p. 59.
12. Ibid., p. 65.
13. G. Kateb (1963) *Utopia and Its Enemies* (Glencoe, IL: Free Press); K. Taylor and B. Goodwin (2009) *The Politics of Utopia: A Study in Theory and Practice* (Bern: Peter Lang); Jacoby, *Picture Imperfect*; L. T. Sargent (2011) *Utopianism: A Very Short Introduction* (Oxford: Oxford University Press).
14. Jacoby, *Picture Imperfect*, p. 81.
15. Sargent, *Utopianism*, p. 104.
16. Jacoby, *Picture Imperfect*, p. 81. See also R. Jacoby (1999) *The End of Utopia: Politics and Culture in an Age of Apathy* (New York: Basic Books).
17. R. Levitas (2005) 'After the Fall: Reflections on Culture, Freedom and Utopia after 11 September', in *Anglo-Saxonica: Revista do centro de Estudos Anglisticos da Universidade de Lisboa*, Serie II, 23: 299–317. See also R. Levitas (2007), 'Looking for the Blue: The Necessity of Utopia', *Journal of Political Ideologies*, 12(3): 289–306.
18. J. Gray (2007) *Black Mass: Apocalyptic Religion and the Death of Utopia* (London: Allen Lane) p. 123.
19. Gray, *Black Mass*, p. 17.
20. P. Ricoeur (1986) *Lectures on Ideology and Utopia* (New York: Columbia University Press).
21. Gray, *Black Mass*, p. 20.
22. Ibid., p. 20.
23. Ibid., p. 38.
24. Ibid., pp. 26, 16, 15.

25. Ibid., pp. 59, 39, 53.
26. Ibid., p. 39.
27. Ibid., p. 86.
28. J. C. Davis (1981) *Utopia and the Ideal Society* (Cambridge: Cambridge University Press).
29. Gray, *Black Mass*, p. 29.
30. Ibid., p. 197.
31. Ibid., p. 187.
32. Ibid., p. 198.
33. Ibid., p. 21.
34. R. Holloway (2009) *Between the Monster and the Saint: The Divided Spirit of Humanity* (London: Canongate) pp. 133, 136.
35. R. Holloway (2005) *Looking in the Distance: The Human Search for Meaning* (London: Canongate) p. 106.
36. *Catechism of the Catholic Church* (London: Geoffrey Chapman) 1994 pp. 434–6.
37. W. S. Scott (ed.) (1968) *The Trial of Joan of Arc* (London: Folio Society) p. 73. See also G. B. Shaw (1937) 'Saint Joan', in *The Complete Plays of Bernard Shaw* (London: Odhams Press) p. 997; J. Anouilh (1961) *The Lark*, C. Fry (trans.) (London: Methuen) p. 10.
38. T. McDermott (ed.) (1991) *St Thomas Aquinas, Summa Theologiae: A Concise Translation* (London: Methuen) p. 117.
39. P. Tillich (1949) *The Shaking of the Foundations* (Harmondsworth: Penguin) pp. 155, 156. See also P. Tillich (1980) *The Courage To Be* (New Haven, CT: Yale University Press) [1952].
40. Tillich, *Shaking*, p.158.
41. A. Huxley (2009) *The Perennial Philosophy* (New York: HarperCollins) [1945].
42. Tillich, *Shaking*, p. 163.
43. Ibid., p. 164.
44. P. Tillich (1964) *Theology of Culture* (Oxford: Oxford University Press) pp. 7–8.
45. Ibid., pp. 23, 27, 57.
46. M. Mayne (2008) *This Sunrise of Wonder* (London: Darton, Longman and Tod) p. 25.
47. G. Steiner (1969) 'The Hollow Miracle', in *Language and Silence* (Harmondsworth: Penguin) p. 143.
48. G. Steiner (1989) *Real Presences: Is There Anything in What We Say?* (London: Faber and Faber) pp. 143, 180.
49. Steiner, *Real Presences*, pp. 139, 140, 142.
50. Cited in David Drew's introduction to E. Bloch (1985) *Essays in the Philosophy of Music* (Cambridge: Cambridge University Press) p. xl.
51. H. Marcuse (1979) *The Aesthetic Dimension* (London: Macmillan) p. 32–3.
52. Steiner, *Real Presences*, p. 32.
53. P. Tillich (1973) 'Critique and Justification of Utopia', in Frank E. Manuel (ed.) *Utopias and Utopian Thought* (London: Souvenir Press) p. 302.
54. Ibid., p. 299.
55. Ibid., p. 301.
56. Ibid , p. 301.
57. Ibid., p. 307.

2   Riff on Blue

1. H. Carpenter (1998) *Dennis Potter: The Authorized Biography* (London: Faber and Faber) pp. 350–1.
2. E. Bloch (1970) *A Philosophy of the Future* (New York: Herder and Herder) p. 95.
3. Ibid., p. 87.
4. http://209.240.155.221/infocolorsmeanings.html, accessed 25 July 2012.
5. http://www.sensationalcolor.com/color-messages-meanings/color-meaning-symbolism-psychology/psychology-of-color-a-glimpse-into-the-meaning-symbolism-psychology-of-color.html, accessed 25 July 2012.
6. http://www.livingartsoriginals.com/infocolorsmeanings.html, accessed 25 July 2012.
7. http://www.sensationalcolor.com/color-messages-meanings/color-meaning-symbolism-psychology/psychology-of-color-a-glimpse-into-the-meaning-symbolism-psychology-of-color.html, accessed 25 July 2012. Such websites generally do not note that blue can also mean pornographic.
8. J. Balfour-Paul (2006) *Indigo: More than a Colour* (London: Archetype Publications) p. 6.
9. P. Ball (2001) *Bright Earth: The Invention of Colour* (London: Viking) p. xii.
10. J. Gage (2000) *Colour and Meaning* (London: Thames and Hudson) p. 32.
11. www.colourtherapy.net, accessed 25 July 2012.
12. Gage, *Colour and Meaning*, p. 33.
13. J. Gage (1993) *Colour and Culture* (London: Thames and Hudson) p. 204.
14. Gage, *Colour and Meaning*, p. 186.
15. B. Schulz (1998) 'The Republic of Dreams', in B. Schulz *The Collected Works of Bruno Schulz* ed. J. Ficowski (London: Picador) pp. 271–2.
16. Gage records that the Vatican mosaicists worked with 40,000 different colours, of which only 10,752 were classified. The current industry standard colour-matching system of Munsell chips identifies 1500 different colours. These are not named, but identified by a three-part code calibrating hue, chroma or purity and lightness or darkness. Windsor and Newton Artists Oil Colours come in a range of 120 shades. Dulux tailormade paint claims to have a range of 12,000 colours in its databases, although only 980 are illustrated in its colour charts, including 140 shades of blue and 140 shades of violet. Here, the thirty-five 'rich blues' have seven names, each in five intensities: Blue Diamond, Hawaiian Blue, Azure Fusion, Celestial Blue, Venetian Crystal, Royal Regatta, Sapphire Springs. As with all paint colour charts, the names are pure invention, bearing no relation to names in common use. According to Jenny Balfour-Paul, in the eighteenth century, European dyers classified thirteen separate shades of indigo ranging from milk blue through midding blue to infernal or navy blue: only five of these names are now immediately recognizable as colour names: pale blue, sky blue, royal blue, deep blue and navy blue. Gage argues that among non-specialists, only about twelve colour names are now in common use.
17. A. Huxley (2004) *The Doors of Perception and Heaven and Hell* (London: Vintage) p. 13.
18. Huxley, *Heaven and Hell*, p. 57.
19. Huxley, *Doors of Perception*, p. 33.
20. Ibid., p. 32.
21. Ibid., p. 12.

22. Ibid., pp. 46–7. In Catholic theology, a gratuitous grace is one neither necessary nor sufficient to salvation.
23. Huxley, *Heaven and Hell*, p. 59.
24. Huxley, *Doors of Perception*, p. 18.
25. Cited in Ball, *Bright Earth*, p. 260.
26. P. Smith (1992) '"Parbleu": Pissarro and the Political Colour of an Original Vision', *Art History*, 15(2): 235.
27. Ibid., p. 240.
28. W. Kandinsky (1977) *Concerning the Spiritual in Art* (New York: Dover) [1911] p. 38.
29. Ibid., p. 39.
30. J. Golding (2000) *Paths to the Absolute* (London: Thames and Hudson) p. 74.
31. Gage, *Colour and Meaning*, p. 246.
32. Gage, *Colour and Culture*, p. 248ff.
33. W. Kandinsky and F. Marc (eds) (1974) *The Blaue Reiter Almanac* (London: Thames and Hudson) p. 17.
34. E. da Costa Meyer and F. Wasserman (eds) (2003) *Schoenberg, Kandinsky and the Blue Rider* (London, New York and Paris: The Jewish Museum, New York) p. 74.
35. Ibid., p. 68.
36. Kandinsky and Marc, *Blaue Reiter Almanac*, pp. 90, 102.
37. E. Bloch (1998) *Literary Essays* (Palo Alto: Stanford University Press) p. 507.
38. Ibid., p. 511.
39. Gage, *Colour and Meaning*, pp. 245–6.
40. Cited in Gage, *Colour and Culture*, p. 207. Although blue and yellow are often gendered, the gendering is more commonly the reverse of Marc's.
41. B. Haas (2006) 'Syntax', in H. Fischer and S. Rainbird (eds) *Kandinsky: The Path to Abstraction* (London: Tate Publishing).
42. Kandinsky, *Concerning the Spiritual in Art*, pp. 37–8.
43. Gage, *Colour and Meaning*, p. 191.
44. Cited in P. Vergo (2010) *The Music of Painting: Music, Modernism and the Visual Arts from the Romantics to John Cage* (London: Phaidon) p. 195.
45. M. Mayne (2008) *This Sunrise of Wonder* (London: Darton, Longman and Tod) p. 170.
46. Cited in F. Jameson (2005) *Archaeologies of the Future* (London: Verso) p. 401.
47. Cited in Ibid., p. 118.
48. http://www.tate.org.uk/ accessed 6 April 2011
49. Cited in Ball, *Bright Earth*, p. 260.
50. J. Miller (2001) *Seeing is Believing* (Truro: Dyllanson Truran) p. 49. See also J. Miller (2000) *Another Shade of Blue* (Truro: Dyllanson Truran). 'Another shade of blue' is also the title of several indifferent songs, a wonderful Lee Konitz CD, a book about depression in older Australians, and the website of the travel and underwater photographer Ty Sawyer. http://anothershadeofbluestore.com, accessed 10 January 2011.
51. Miller, *Seeing is Believing*, p. 114.
52. www.ask.com/wiki/John_Miller_(artist), accessed 10 January 2011.
53. D. Jarman (2000) *Chroma* (London: Vintage) pp. 108, 112, 115, 114. The chapter 'Into the Blue' is also the script of Jarman's film *Blue*.
54. www.danielthistlethwaite.com accessed 6 April 2011
55. F. Spalding (2009) *John Piper, Myfanwy Piper: Lives in Art* (Oxford: Oxford University Press) p. 486.

56. Ibid., p. 18.
57. Ibid., p. 38. *The Art of Spiritual Harmony* was the title of the first English translation, published in 1914 by Constable and Constable, of Kandinsky's *Concerning the Spiritual in Art*.
58. Spalding, *John Piper*, p. 71.
59. John Piper, cited in Ibid., p. 376.
60. John Piper, cited in Ibid., p. 376.
61. John Piper, cited in Ibid., p. 373.
62. Ibid., p. 379.
63. John Piper, cited in Ibid., p. 350.
64. Ibid., p. 422.
65. Bloch, *Philosophy of the Future*, p. 95.
66. P. D. Wedd (2008) *The Message of the Windows: What to Look for in the Chagall Windows at Tudeley*, Information Leaflet, Tudeley Church. See also P. Foster (ed.) (2002) *Chagall Glass at Chichester and Tudeley*, Otter Memorial Paper 14 (Chichester: University College Chichester).
67. Kandinsky, *Concerning the Spiritual in Art*, p. 41.
68. Gage, *Colour and Meaning*, p. 262.
69. Vergo, *Music of Painting*, p. 71.
70. Kandinsky, *Concerning the Spiritual in Art*, p. 3.
71. Vergo, *Music of Painting*, p. 61.
72. Čiurlionis is not well-known in the UK. His paintings are displayed in the M. K. Čiurlionis Art Museum in Kaunas and there are good images at http://ciurlionis.licejus.lt/, accessed 6 April 2011. Some of these fragile works were included in the exhibition *Eye-music* shown at Chichester and Norwich in 2007, which explored the relations between art, colour and music in the early twentieth century. See F. Guy, S. Shaw-Miller and M. Tucker (2007) *Eye-music: Kandinsky, Klee and All That Jazz* (Chichester: Pallant House Gallery).
73. Kandinsky, *Concerning the Spiritual in Art*, pp. 38, 40–1.
74. Gage, *Colour and Culture*, p. 244.
75. Vergo, *Music of Painting*, p. 105.
76. S. Shaw-Miller (2004) *Visible Deeds of Music: Art and Music from Wagner to Cage* (New Haven, CT: Yale University Press) p. 55.
77. T. Adorno (2009) 'Painting and Music Today', in *Night Music: Essays on Music 1928–1962* (London, New York, Calcutta: Seagull Books) p. 412.
78. Cited in Vergo, *Music of Painting*, p. 105.
79. Kandinsky and Marc, *Blaue Reiter Almanac*, pp. 129–30.
80. Kandinsky and Marc, *Blaue Reiter Almanac*; Shaw-Miller, *Visible Deeds of Music*.
81. http://en.wikipedia.org.wiki/Mysterium_(Scriabin), accessed 11 September 2012.
82. Schulz, 'Republic of Dreams', pp. 271–2.
83. M. Pastoureau (2002) *Blue: The History of a Colour* (Princeton, NJ: Princeton University Press); Gage, *Colour and Culture, Colour and Meaning*; Balfour-Paul, *Indigo*.
84. Balfour-Paul, *Indigo*, pp. 60ff., 181.
85. P. Auster (2005) *Oracle Night* (London: Faber and Faber) pp. 42–3.
86. Ibid., pp. 43–6.
87. E. Bloch (2000) *The Spirit of Utopia* (Stanford: Stanford California Press) p. 3.
88. Schulz, 'Republic of Dreams', pp. 270–2.

3 Echoes of Elsewhere

1. H. Carpenter (1998) *Dennis Potter: The Authorized Biography* (London: Faber and Faber) p. 350.
2. Ibid., p. 348.
3. L. Barton (2011) 'Hail, Hail, Rock 'n' Roll', *The Guardian, Film and Music section*, 26 May: 22.
4. E. Bloch (1986) *The Principle of Hope* (Oxford: Basil Blackwell) p. 1063. The best account of Bloch's musical philosophy is David Drew's introductory essay in E. Bloch (1985) *Essays on the Philosophy of Music* (Cambridge: Cambridge University Press).
5. F. Jameson (1974) *Marxism and Form: Twentieth-Century Dialectical Theories of Literature* (Princeton, NJ: Princeton University Press) p. 143.
6. Bloch, *Principle*, p. 1103.
7. Ibid., pp. 1069–70.
8. E. Bloch (1998) *Literary Essays* (Stanford: Stanford University Press) p. 58.
9. U. Le Guin (1975) 'The Ones Who Walk Away from Omelas', *The Wind's Twelve Quarters* (New York: Harper and Row); W. Nicholson (2001) *Slaves of the Mastery* (London: Egmont).
10. Bloch, *Principle*, p. 1097.
11. Ibid., p.1099.
12. Ibid., p.1098.
13. Ibid., pp. 1100, 1102.
14. Ibid., p. 1103.
15. Ibid., p. 1100.
16. Ibid., p. 1101.
17. Ibid., p. 1068.
18. Cited in Jacoby, *Picture Imperfect*, 107.
19. Bloch, *Essays on Music,* p. 78.
20. Ibid., p. 113.
21. Ibid., p. 79.
22. Ibid., p. 83.
23. D. Barenboim (2008) *Everything is Connected: The Power of Music* (London: Weidenfeld and Nicholson) p. 68.
24. T. De Nora (2000) *Music in Everyday Life* (Cambridge: Cambridge University Press) p. 28.
25. E. Bloch (1991) *Heritage of Our Times* (Cambridge: Polity Press) p. 230.
26. Barenboim uses the 'darkness to light' metaphor in rehearsing Beethoven's symphonies with WEDO. 'Barenboim on Beethoven', BBC2, 28 July 2012.
27. Cited in D. Kemp (2011) *Terry Frost: Lorca* (Rutland: Goldmark Art).
28. C. Caudwell (1937) *Illusion and Reality* (London: Macmillan).
29. G. Steiner (1989) *Real Presences: Is There Anything* in *What We Say?* (London: Faber and Faber) pp. 19, 218.
30. G. Steiner (1967) *Language and Silence* (Harmondsworth, Penguin) p. 151.
31. Steiner, *Real Presences*, p. 64.
32. Steiner, *Language and Silence*, p. 89.
33. B. M. Korstvedt (2010) *Listening for Utopia in Bloch's Musical Philosophy* (Cambridge: Cambridge University Press).
34. C. Lévi-Strauss (1969) *The Raw and the Cooked* (London: HarperCollins).

35. Steiner, *Real Presences*, p. 19; *Language and Silence*, p. 259.
36. A. Ross (2010) *Listen to This* (London: Fourth Estate) p. xi.
37. Ross, *Listen to This*, p. xi.
38. M. Solomon (1995) *Mozart: A Life* (London: Pimlico) p. 378.
39. Solomon, *Mozart*, p. 18.
40. Solomon, *Mozart*, p. 135.
41. Solomon, *Mozart*, p. 197.
42. Solomon, *Mozart*, p. 509.
43. Ross, *Listen to This*, pp. 71, 73, 80, 79.
44. T. W. Adorno (2009) *Night Music: Essays on Music 1928–1962* (London, New York, Calcutta: Seagull Books) p. 46.
45. Ross, *Listen to This*, pp. 137, 339.
46. Steiner, *Real Presences*, p. 226.
47. Ross, *Listen to This*, pp. 308–9.
48. Ibid., p. 304.
49. Ibid., pp. 300, 306.
50. Ibid., p. 302.
51. Ibid., p. 309.
52. Bloch, *Principle*, p.1059.
53. Bloch, *Essays on Music*, pp. 72, 73.
54. Ibid., p. 117.
55. Ibid., pp. 99, 100, 67.
56. Barenboim, *Everything*, p. 115.
57. J. Griffiths (2011)'The Power of Song', *The Guardian G2*, 15 March: 13.
58. J. Edwards (ed.) (2011) *Music Therapy and Parent-Infant Bonding* (Oxford: Oxford University Press); E. Dissanayake (2008) 'If Music Is the Food of Love, What about Survival and Reproductive Success?', *Musicae Scientiae* 169–95.
59. Bloch, *Essays on Music*, pp. 67–8.
60. Griffiths, 'Power of Song', p. 13.
61. Ross, *Listen to This*, pp. 291–2.
62. Cited in F. G. Lorca (1998) *In Search of Duende* (New York: New Directions Books) p. x.
63. Lorca, *Duende*, p. 58.
64. Ibid., p. 62.
65. Ross, *Listen to This*, pp. 25–6.
66. Lorca, *Duende*, p. 10.
67. Ibid., p. 14.
68. Cited in Ross, *Listen to This*, p. 231.
69. Ross, *Listen to This*, p. 51.
70. I. McEwan (2005) *Saturday* (London: Jonathan Cape) p. 28.
71. Solomon, *Mozart*, pp. 380–1.
72. Barenboim, *Everything*, p. 182.
73. Ibid., p.134.
74. Bloch, *Principle*, p. 1061.
75. Lorca, *Duende*, p. viii.
76. Cited in Steiner, *Real Presences*, p. 123.
77. Bloch, *Principle*, pp. 1090, 1092.
78. Ross, *Listen to This*, p. 32.
79. Cited in Ross, *Listen to This*, p. 291.

80. R. Hunter (2010) 'The Music of Change: Utopian Transformation in *Aufstieg und Fall der Stadt Mahagonny* and *Der Silbersee*', *Utopian Studies*, 21(2): 293–312.
81. Luis Gómez Romero (2010) 'Countess Almaviva and the Carceral Redemption: Introducing a Musical Utopia into the Prison Walls', *Utopian Studies*, 21(2): 274–92.
82. Ross, *Listen to This*, p. 288.
83. W. Nicholson (2000) *The Wind Singer* (London: Egmont) pp. 337–9.
84. P. Heyworth (1983) *Otto Klemperer: His Life and Times. Volume 1 1885–1933.* (Cambridge: Cambridge University Press) pp. 200–3.
85. Bloch, *Literary Essays*, p. 255.
86. Ibid., p. 251.
87. Ross, *Listen to This*, p. 155.
88. Yo Yo Ma, www.silkroadproject.org, accessed November 2010.
89. McEwan *Saturday*, p. 171.
90. McEwan, *Saturday*, pp. 171–2.
91. J. Gray (2007) 'What's It All about, Terry?' (Review of Terry Eagleton, *The Meaning of Life* (Oxford: Oxford University Press, 2007), *The Independent*, 2 March.
92. R. Holloway (2005) *Looking in the Distance: The Human Search for Meaning* (London: Canongate) pp. 132–3.
93. D. Barenboim and E. Said (2004) *Parallels and Paradoxes: Explorations in Music and Society* (London: Bloomsbury) p. 33.
94. R. Young (2010) *Electric Eden: Unearthing Britain's Visionary Music* (London: Faber and Faber).
95. John Harle (2008) in conversation with Robert Winston, University of Bristol Autumn Art Lectures, 10 November.
96. Barenboim and Said, *Parallels*, p. 156.
97. Rudolf Serkin, cited in Ross, *Listen to This*, p. 246.
98. L. Davidson (2010) 'A Quest for Harmony: The Role of Music in Robert Owen's New Lanark Community', *Utopian Studies*, 21(2): 232–51.
99. *Evaluation of Big Noise, Sistema Scotland*, March 2011, http://www.scotland.gov.uk/Publications/2011/03/16082812/0, accessed 4 April 2011.
100. Holloway, *Looking in the Distance*, p. 51.
101. http://www.musicmanifesto.co.uk/news/details/english-el-sistema-is-in-harmony/22353, accessed 17 January 2010.
102. http://www.musicmanifesto.co.uk/news/details/winning-in-harmony-bids-announced/22990, accessed 17 January 2010.
103. D. Henley (2011) *Music Education in England – A Review by Darren Henley for the Department for Education and the Department for Culture, Media and Sport* (London: Department for Education DFE-00011-2011) p. 21.
104. J. Galloway (2011) *All Made Up* (London: Granta).
105. D. Parkinson (2004) *Heimat: An Introduction* (Tartan Video) p. 68.
106. Barenboim, *Everything*, p. 182.
107. Barenboim and Said, *Parallels*, p. 173.
108. Barenboim, *Everything*, pp. 78–9, 68, 133, 134.
109. E. Lunn (1985) *Marxism and Modernism* (London: Verso) p. 274.
110. Bloch, *Principle*, p. 1070.
111. Ibid., p. 1070.
112. Ibid., p. 1080.

113. Ibid., p. 1080.
114. Ibid., p. 1085.
115. L. Cohen (2008) 'Anthem', in L. Cohen, *The Little Black Songbook* (London: Wise Publications) p. 14.
116. Bloch, *Principle*, p. 1096.
117. Ibid., p. 1088.
118. E. Bloch (2000) *The Spirit of Utopia* (Stanford, CA: Stanford Univerity Press) pp. 64–5. In all previous instances I have used the translation of 'The Philosophy of Music' in Bloch, *Essays on Music*. In this case, I have preferred Anthony Nassar's translation, which makes this point more clearly.
119. M. Solomon (1979) *Marxism and Art* (Sussex: Harvester) p. 577.
120. O. Golijov, www.silkroadproject.org, accessed November 2010.
121. Ross, *Listen to This*, p. xiii.
122. Steiner, *Real Presences*, p. 6.
123. Hunter, 'Music of Change', p. 308.
124. J. Boyes, *Jerusalem Revisited*, http://www.coopeboyesandsimpson.co.uk/jerusalem_revisited.htm.

4   Between Sociology and Utopia

1. H. G. Wells (1906) 'The So-called Science of Sociology', *Sociological Papers* 3: 367.
2. C. Wright Mills (1959) *The Sociological Imagination* (Oxford: Oxford University Press) pp. 6–7. Gregor McLennan reprises these questions in 2011: G. McLennan (2011) *Story of Sociology: A First Companion to Social Theory* (London: Bloomsbury).
3. Wells, 'So-called Science', p. 367.
4. L. L. Bernard and J. Bernard (1943) *Origins of American Sociology: The Social Science Movement in the United States* (New York: Thomas Y. Crowell and Co.).
5. R. Aron (1968) *Main Currents in Sociological Thought I* (Harmondsworth: Penguin) pp. 89, 96.
6. Ibid., p. 78.
7. Cited in V. Geoghegan (1987) *Utopianism and Marxism* (London: Methuen, 1987) p. 17.
8. E. Durkheim (1964) *The Division of Labor in Society* (New York: The Free Press) p. 353.
9. Ibid., pp. 5, 182.
10. Ibid., p. 375.
11. Ibid., p. 29, cf p. 384.
12. Ibid., p. 30.
13. Ibid., p. 389.
14. Ibid., p. 242.
15. Ibid., pp. 405–6.
16. Ibid., pp. 244, 250, 264.
17. Ibid., pp. 401–3.
18. T. Carlyle, *Past and Present*, Cited in S. Arata (2003) 'Introduction' to William Morris, *News from Nowhere* (Ontario: Broadview Press) p. 24.
19. Durkheim, *Division of Labor*, pp. 51–2.
20. Ibid., p. 240.

21. Ibid., p. 43.
22. Ibid., p. 33.
23. Ibid., p. 23 (Preface to second edition).
24. E. Durkheim (1962) *Socialism* (New York: Collier Books) p. 221.
25. Durkheim, *Division of Labor*, p. 408.
26. Ibid. p. 409.
27. See E. Durkheim (1964) *The Rules of Sociological Method* (New York: The Free Press) [1895]; T. Benton (1977) *Philosophical Foundations of the Three Sociologies* (London: Routledge and Kegan Paul).
28. Durkheim, *Division of Labor*, pp. 409, 31.
29. C. P. Gilman (1998) *Women and Economics* (New York: Dover) [1898] pp. 31–2.
30. Gilman, *Women*, pp. 37, 38.
31. Gilman, *Women*, p. 60.
32. Gilman, *Women*, p. 69.
33. D. Hayden (1982) *The Grand Domestic Revolution: A History of Feminist Designs for American Homes, Neighborhoods and Cities* (Cambridge, MA: MIT Press).
34. M. Beaumont (2005) *Utopia Ltd: Ideologies of Social Dreaming in England, 1870–1900* (Leiden: Brill).
35. K. Kumar (1978) *Prophecy and Progress: The Sociology of Industrial and Post-Industrial Society* (London: Allen Lane and Penguin).
36. M. Beaumont (2012) *The Spectre of Utopia: Utopian and Science Fictions at the Fin de Siècle* (Oxford and Bern: Peter Lang).
37. S. E. Bowman (1962) *Edward Bellamy Abroad: An American Prophet's Influence* (New York: Twayne).
38. W. Lepenies (1992) *Between Literature and Science: The Rise of Sociology* (Cambridge: Cambridge University Press) p. 139.
39. Lepenies, *Literature and Science*, p. 57. Tarde's novel was published in English as *Underground Man* in 1905 with a preface by Wells.
40. Cited in A. Macdonald (2003) 'Introduction' in Edward Bellamy (2003 [1888]) *Looking Backward 2000–1887* (Ontario: Broadbent) pp. 20–1.
41. *Review of Reviews* 2, 11. New York, November 1890, 457. Cited in Bellamy, *Looking Backward*, p. 265.
42. Bellamy, *Looking Backward*, p. 110.
43. Ibid., pp. 239, 179, 93, 234.
44. Ibid., pp. 233, 236, 228, 240.
45. Ibid., p. 72. The later *Equality* differs on this point. See E. Bellamy (1897) *Equality* (London: William Heinemann).
46. Bellamy, *Looking Backward*, pp. 75, 76, 185.
47. Ibid., p. 239.
48. Morris (1902) *News from Nowhere* (London: Longmans Green and Co.) [1891] p. 80.
49. N. Kelvin (ed.) (1987) *The Collected Letters of William Morris* (Princeton, NJ: Princeton University Press) Volume II, 1881–84, p. 45. The context of this remark was a letter to Frederic Harrison, President of the English Positivist Committee. Morris was declining an invitation to attend a lecture by the leader of the French Positivists, Pierre Lafitte, on the grounds that his French was not adequate to 'follow an intricate address'.
50. W. Morris (2003) 'Looking Backward', Appendix B to Bellamy, *Looking Backward*, [1889] p. 256.
51. Morris, *News from Nowhere*, p. 88.

52. See R. Levitas (2005) 'Beyond Bourgeois Right', *The European Legacy*, 9(5): 605–18.
53. Arata, 'Introduction', p. 25.
54. Morris, 'Looking Backward', p. 257.
55. Morris, *News from Nowhere*, p. 83.
56. H. G. Wells (1905) *A Modern Utopia* (London: Chapman & Hall) p. 2.
57. W. Lepenies (1992) *Between Literature and Science: The Rise of Sociology* (Cambridge: Cambridge University Press).
58. Wells, *Modern Utopia*, p. 7.
59. Ibid., p. 262.
60. Ibid., p. 123.
61. Ibid., p. 213.
62. Ibid., pp. 310, 172, 301, 289.
63. Ibid., p. 221.
64. Ibid., p. 282.
65. Ibid., pp. 171, 226, 172.
66. Ibid., pp. 363, 369–70.
67. R. Crossley (2011) 'The First Wellsians: A Modern Utopia and Its Early Disciples', *English Literature in Transition*, 54(4): 444–69.
68. C. Taylor (2007) *A Secular Age* (Cambridge, MA: Harvard University Press) pp. 161, 171, 172.

5 Utopia Denied

1. P. Abrams (1968) *The Origins of British Sociology: 1834–1914* (Chicago and London: University of Chicago Press) p. 3. See also R. Dahrendorf (1995) *LSE: A History of the London School of Economics and Political Science 1895–1995* (Oxford: Oxford University Press); A. H. Halsey (2004) *A History of Sociology in Britain* (Oxford: Oxford University Press); M. Studholme (2008) 'Patrick Geddes and the History of Environmental Sociology in Britain: A Cautionary Tale', *Journal of Classical Sociology*, 8(3): 367–9.
2. The earliest version of this article appeared as H. G. Wells (1905) 'The So-called Science of Sociology', *Independent Review*, pp. 21–37. A letter from Wells, also headed 'The So-called Science of Sociology', appeared in October 1905 in the *Fortnightly Review*, defending the earlier article against criticism. See H. G. Wells (1998) *Correspondence of H. G. Wells*, edited by D. C. Smith, 4 Vols (London: Pickering and Chatto) (2): 78–81. The article was published in revised form as H. G. Wells (1906) 'The So-called Science of Sociology', *Sociological Papers*, 3: 357–77 and again slightly revised for H. G. Wells (1914) *An Englishman Looks at the World: Being a Series of Unrestrained Remarks upon Contemporary Matters* (London, New York, Toronto and Melbourne: Cassell and Co.) pp. 192–206. Page references are to the 1906 version. A more detailed account of the context of Wells's intervention is given in Ruth Levitas (2010) 'Back to the Future: Wells, Sociology, Utopia and Method', *Sociological Review*, 58(4): 530–47.
3. The Co-Efficients were convened by Sidney Webb and were 'a group of men of diverse temperaments and varied talents, imbued with a common faith and a common purpose, and eager to work out, and severally to expound,

how each department of national life can be raised to its highest possible efficiency'. Quoted in N. Mackenzie and J. Mackenzie (1977) *The First Fabians* (London: Weidenfeld and Nicholson) p. 290; H. G. Wells (1984 [1934]) *Experiment in Autobiography* (London: Faber and Faber) p. 761; R. J. Harrison (2000) *The Life and Times of Sidney and Beatrice Webb 1858–1905: The Formative Years* (Basingstoke: Palgrave Macmillan) p. 326 ff.

4. Smith in Wells, *Correspondence*, 2: 26–7.
5. Wells, *Correspondence*, 2: 25.
6. Ibid., p. 43.
7. Ibid., p. 72.
8. Smith, in Wells, *Correspondence*, 2: 73.
9. S. Zizek (2005) 'Lenin Shot at Finland Station', *London Review of Books*, 27(16), August 18: 23.
10. Wells, *Autobiography*, p. 657.
11. Wells, 'So-called Science', p. 364.
12. Ibid., p. 365; Wells, *Autobiography*, p. 664.
13. Wells, 'So-called Science', p. 365.
14. Wells, *Autobiography*, p. 658.
15. Wells 'So-called Science', p. 368.
16. M. Weber (1949) *Methodology of the Social Sciences* (Glencoe: Free Press).
17. H. G. Wells (1905) *A Modern Utopia* (London: Chapman and Hall) pp. 318–9.
18. Wells, 'So-called Science', pp. 367–8.
19. Ibid., p. 367.
20. S. Collini (1979) *Liberalism and Sociology: L. T. Hobhouse and the Political Argument in England 1880–1914* (Cambridge: Cambridge University Press).
21. M. Studhome (1997) 'From Leonard Hobhouse to Tony Blair: A Sociological Connection?', *Sociology*, 31(3): 531–47; M. Studholme (2007) 'Patrick Geddes: Founder of Environmental Sociology', *Sociological Review*, 55(3): 441–59; M. Studholme (2008) 'Patrick Geddes and the History of Environmental Sociology in Britain: A Cautionary Tale', *Journal of Classical Sociology*, 8(3): 367–91.
22. V. Branford (2010 [1921]) *Whitherward? Hell or Eutopia* (General Books) p. 69.
23. See Branford, *Whitherward* and V. Branford and P. Geddes (2010 [1917]) *The Coming Polity: A Study in Reconstruction* (General Books). For recent discussion of the role of Branford and Geddes in British Sociology, see: L. Goldman (2007) 'Foundations of British Sociology 1880–1930: Contexts and Biographies', *The Sociological Review*, 55(3): 431–40; M. Savage (2007) '*The Sociological Review* and the History of British Sociology', *The Sociological Review*, 55(3): 429–30; J. Scott and C. T. Husbands (2007) 'Victor Branford and the Building of British Sociology', *The Sociological Review*, 55(3): 460–84; Studholme, 'Patrick Geddes: Founder of Environmental Sociology'; Studholme, 'Patrick Geddes and the History of Environmental Sociology'.
24. L. Mumford (2003) *The Story of Utopias: Ideal Commonwealths and Social Myths* (London: Harrap) p. 41.
25. Mumford, *Utopias*, p. 159.
26. Ibid., p. 189.
27. Ibid., pp. 203–5.

28. Ibid., p. 311.
29. Ibid., p. 268.
30. Ibid., p. 298.
31. Ibid., p. 272.
32. S. Bruce (1999) *Sociology: A Very Short Introduction* (Oxford: Oxford University Press) p. 83.
33. Halsey, *History*, p. 15.
34. Ibid., p. 7.
35. L. T. Hobhouse (1908) 'Editorial', *The Sociological Review*, 1(1): 4–5. See also L. T. Hobhouse (1908) 'The Roots of Modern Sociology', *Inauguration of the Martin White Professorships of Sociology* (17 December 1907) (London: John Murray and the University of London).
36. M. Nussbaum (2003) *Upheavals of Thought: The Intelligence of Emotions* (Cambridge: Cambridge University Press).
37. A. Sayer (2011) *Why Things Matter to People* (Cambridge: Cambridge University Press) pp. 4–5.
38. G. D. Mitchell (1970) *A Dictionary of Sociology* (London: Routledge) p. 217.
39. K. Mannheim (1979) *Ideology and Utopia* (London: Routledge and Kegan Paul) p. 173.
40. Ibid., p. 184. For a longer discussion of Mannheim, see R. Levitas (1990) *The Concept of Utopia* (London: Philip Allan) Chapter 3.
41. R. Dahrendorf (1958) 'Out of Utopia: Towards a Reorientation of Sociological Analysis', *American Journal of Sociology*, 64(2): 118, 117, 115. Wells's original says 'be not'.
42. R. Kilminster (1998) *The Sociological Revolution: From Enlightenment to the Global Age* (London: Routledge) p. 147.
43. A. Bammer (1991) *Partial Visions: Feminism and Utopianism in the 1970s* (London: Routledge).
44. H. Bradley (2013) *Gender* (Cambridge: Polity Press).
45. M. Phillips (2012) *The Moral Maze*, BBC Radio 4, 25 July.
46. F. Jameson (1991) *Postmodernism: Or, The Cultural Logic of Late Capitalism* (London: Verso).
47. See K. Kumar (1978) *Prophecy and Progress: The Sociology of Industrial and Post Industrial Society* (London: Allen Lane); K. Kumar (1995) *From Post-Industrial to Post-Modern Society* (Oxford: Basil Blackwell), Second Edition, Wiley-Blackwell 2004. For Kumar's more direct discussion of utopianism, see K. Kumar (1987) *Utopia and Anti-Utopia in Modern Times* (Oxford: Basil Blackwell).
48. Kumar, *Post-Industrial Society*, p. 135.
49. M. Horkheimer (1997) 'Traditional and Critical Social Theory' in M. Horkheimer (ed.) *Critical Theory: Selected Essays* (New York: Continuum Press) pp. 188–243.
50. A recent example is R. Skidelsky and E. Skidelsky (2012) *How Much is Enough?: The Love of Money and the Case for the Good Life* (London: Allen Lane). For a fuller discussion of Marcuse's utopianism, see Levitas, *Concept*, Chapter 6.
51. T. W. Adorno (2009) *Night Music: Essays on Music 1928–1962* (London: Seagull) p. 187.
52. L. Boltanski (2011) *On Critique: A Sociology of Emancipation* (Cambridge: Polity Press) p. 163.

53. Ibid., p. 7.
54. Ibid., p. 15.
55. Ibid., p. 107.
56. Ibid., p. 108.
57. Ibid., p. 115.
58. Sayer, *Why Things Matter*, p. 4.
59. Ibid., p. 57.
60. Boltanski, *Critique*, p. 115.
61. P. Hayden and C. el-Ojeili (eds) (2009) *Globalization and Utopia: Critical Essays* (Basingstoke: Palgrave Macmillan) p. 1.

6   Utopia Revised

1. T. Siebers (ed.) (1994) *Heterotopia: Postmodern Utopia and the Body Politic* (Ann Arbor: University of Michigan Press) pp. 2–3.
2. G. Deleuze and F. Guattari (1984) *Anti-Oedipus: Capitalism and Schizophrenia* (London: Athlone Press) [1972].
3. P. Goodchild (1996) *Deleuze and Guattari: An Introduction to the Politics of Desire* (London: Sage).
4. R. Williams (1980) *Problems in Materialism and Culture* (London: Verso) p. 200.
5. Siebers, *Heterotopia*, p. 152.
6. D. Harvey (2000) *Spaces of Hope* (Edinburgh: Edinburgh University Press).
7. T. Adorno (1974) *Minima Moralia* (London: NLB) p. 156.
8. J. Habermas (1979) *The New Conservatism* (Cambridge: Polity Press).
9. U. Beck (1992) *Risk Society* (London: Sage).
10. R. Wilkinson and K. Pickett (2009) *The Spirit Level* (London: Bloomsbury); O. Jones (2011) *Chavs: The Demonisation of the Working Class* (London: Verso).
11. As of 9 January 2012, Google Scholar gives only 178 citations for this work, compared with around 3604 for Bauman's (2000) *Liquid Modernity* (Cambridge: Polity Press) and over 1000 for each of his ten most-cited books.
12. Z. Bauman (2003) 'Utopia with No Topos', *History of the Human Sciences*, 16(1): 11.
13. Wells did get some things wrong in this piece: he also predicted also the decline of national loyalties, and failed to predict the contribution of aeroplane emissions to global warming. H. G. Wells (1914) 'Off the Chain', *An Englishman Looks at the World* (London: Cassell) pp. 15–21.
14. Bauman, 'Utopia', p. 11.
15. M. H. Jacobsen (2004) 'From Solid Modern Utopia to Liquid Modern Anti-Utopia? Tracing the Utopian Strand in the Sociology of Zygmunt Bauman', *Utopian Studies*, 15(1): 63–87; M. H. Jacobsen (2003) *Utopianism in the Work of Zygmunt Bauman: Towards a Sociology of Alternative Realities* (Aalborg: Aalborg Universitet).
16. E. Bloch (1986) *The Principle of Hope* (London: Basil Blackwell) p. 33.
17. Williams, *Problems*, p. 203.
18. See for example C. F. Kessler (ed.) (1984) *Daring to Dream: Utopian Stories by United States Women: 1836–1919* (Boston: Pandora); F. Bartkowski (1989) *Feminist Utopias* (Lincoln, New England: University of Nebraska Press);

and the invaluable bibliographical work by L. T. Sargent (1979) *British and American Utopian Literature, 1516–1975* (Boston: G. K. Hall); L. T. Sargent (1985) *British and American Utopian Literature, 1516–1985: An Annotated Chronological Bibliography* (New York and London: Garland) and A. Bammer (1991) *Partial Visions: Feminism and Utopianism in the 1970s* (London: Routledge).

19. Bammer, *Partial Visions*, p. 158.
20. Ibid., p. 7.
21. Ibid., p. 130.
22. Ibid., p. 18
23. L. Sargisson (1996) *Contemporary Feminist Utopianism* (London: Routledge).
24. Bammer, *Partial Vision*, p. 47.
25. T. Moylan (1986) *Demand the Impossible* (London: Methuen) p. 10.
26. Williams, *Problems*, p. 212.
27. P. Fitting (2003) 'Unmasking the Real? Critique and Utopia in Recent SF Films', in R. Baccolini and T. Moylan (eds) *Dark Horizons* (London: Routledge).
28. T. Moylan (2000) *Scraps of the Untainted Sky* (Oxford: Westview Press).
29. W. Morris (1902) *News from Nowhere* (London: Longmans Green and Co.) [1891] p. 95.
30. M. Piercy (1977) *Woman on the Edge of Time* (New York: Fawcett Crest) [1976] p. 153.
31. S. H. Elgin (1985) *Native Tongue* (London: Women's Press); C. Moore (1994) 'Natives', on *Christy Moore Live At the Point* (London: Grapevine); I. F. S. Cavalcanti (2000) 'Utopias of(f) Language in Contemporary Feminist Utopias', *Utopian Studies*, 11(2): 152–80.
32. A. S. Byatt (1996) *Babel Tower* (London: Chatto and Windus); P. Auster (2004) *The New York Trilogy* (London: Chatto and Windus).
33. W. Morris and E. Belfort Bax (1893) *Socialism: Its Growth and Outcome* (London: Swan Sonnenschein) p. 278.
34. Morris and Bax, *Socialism*, pp. 17–18.
35. W. Morris 'Looking Backward' in E. Bellamy, *Looking Backward*, p. 253, 257.
36. Cited in M. Abensour (1999) 'William Morris: The Politics of Romance' in Max Blechman (ed.) *Revolutionary Romanticism* (San Francisco: City Lights Books) p. 132.
37. Abensour, 'William Morris', pp. 133, 134.
38. Abensour, 'William Morris', p. 137. A simulacrum is an impressionistic or non-representational simulation that makes the real appear unreal.
39. Abensour, 'William Morris', p. 127.
40. D. Suvin (1979) *Metamorphoses of Science Fiction* (New Haven, CT: Yale University Press) p. 182.
41. Abensour, 'William Morris', p. 131.
42. M. Abensour (2008) 'Persistent Utopia', *Constellations*, 15(3): 406–21.
43. M. Abensour (2011) *Democracy Against the State* (Cambridge: Polity Press) p. xxviii. See also P. Mazzochi (2012) 'The Politics of Persistent Utopia: Miguel Abensour and the Opening of Insurgent Democracy', Society for Utopian Studies Annual Conference, Toronto.
44. Abensour, Democracy, p. xxxv.
45. Abensour, 'William Morris', p. 133.
46. Abensour, 'William Morris', p. 129.

47. Abensour, 'William Morris', pp. 128, 131.
48. R. Levitas (2005) *Morris, Hammersmith and Utopia* (London: William Morris Society) pp. 19–20.
49. R. P. Arnot (1934) *William Morris: A Vindication* (London: Martin Lawrence).
50. S. Zizek (2005) 'From Revolutionary to Catastrophic Utopia', in J. Rüsen, M. Fehr and T. W. Rieger (eds) *Thinking Utopia: Steps into Other Worlds* (New York: Berghan Books) p. 247 (glossing Merleau-Ponty).
51. Abensour, 'William Morris', p. 133. This is a sideswipe at Paul Meier. Abensour's later reference to the inadequacies of describing *News from Nowhere* as a scientific Utopia is directed at A. L. Morton. P. Meier (1978) *William Morris: The Marxist Dreamer* (Brighton: Harvester); A. L. Morton (1952) *The English Utopia* (London: Lawrence and Wishart); R. Levitas, *The Concept of Utopia*, Chapter 5.
52. Pers. comm., and see S. Coleman and P. O'Sullivan (eds) (1990) *William Morris and News from Nowhere: A Vision for Our Time* (Bideford: Green Books).
53. *Daily Herald*, 6 December 1948.
54. Williams, *Problems*, p. 202.
55. M. Beaumont (2012) *The Spectre of Utopia: Utopian and Science Fictions at the Fin de Siècle* (Bern: Peter Lang).
56. S. E. Bowman (1962) *Edward Bellamy Abroad: An American Prophet's Influence* (New York: Twayne) pp. 385–6. Bowman devotes a full chapter to 'The Theosophical Society: The Orient' (pp. 385–410). There is additional discussion of Theosophy in Beaumont, *Spectre of Utopia.*
57. 'The Religion of Solidarity' was written in 1874 but not published until 1940. There is an excerpt in E. Bellamy (2003) *Looking Backward 2000–1887* (Ontario: Broadview Press) [1888]. See also the discussion in Beaumont, *Spectre of Utopia.*
58. Cited in A. Macdonald (2003) 'Introduction' to Bellamy, *Looking Backward*, p. 24.
59. Wells, *Modern Utopia*, p. 262.
60. Ibid., p. 73–4.
61. Ibid., p. 247.
62. Ibid., p. 255.
63. Ibid., p. 257.
64. Ibid., p. 352.
65. Ibid., pp. 369–70.
66. Bellamy, *Looking Backward*, pp. 216–7.
67. F. Jameson (2005) *Archaeologies of the Future* (London: Verso) p. 416.
68. F. Jameson (1994) *The Seeds of Time* (New York: Columbia University Press) p. 90. On Jameson's use of the concept of utopia see P. Fitting (1998) 'The Concept of Utopia in the Work of Fredric Jameson', *Utopian Studies*, 9(2): 8–17.
69. Jameson, *Archaeologies*, p. 332.
70. Ibid., p. 211.
71. F. Jameson (1982) 'Progress versus Utopia: or, Can We Imagine the Future?', *Science-Fiction Studies*, 27(9): 147–58, 153. Jameson, *Archaeologies*, p. 289.
72. F. Jameson (1998) 'Comments', *Utopian Studies*, 9(2): 76.
73. Jameson, *Archaeologies of the Future*, p. 293.

74. Jameson, cited in Siebers, *Heterotopia*, p. 94.
75. T. J. Clark (1999) *Farewell to an Idea* (New Haven and London: Yale University Press) p. 164.
76. Ibid., p. 165.
77. Jameson, 'Comments', p. 75. The importance of perspective, of the 'vanishing point', and of 'horizon' is a common theme in Bloch, Jameson and Louis Marin.
78. Jameson uses the term 'reeducation of desire' in relation to Morris, defining it as the retraining of the population in terms of basic needs – quite the opposite of Abensour's meaning (Jameson, *Archaeologies*, pp. 149, 157). He also uses a quotation from *News from Nowhere* which is about the nineteenth century social realist novel to support a claim of 'Morris's outright antipathy to history', *Archaeologies*, p. 186.
79. Ibid., p. 188.
80. Ibid., p. 339.
81. Morris, *News from Nowhere*, p. 152.
82. J. Goode (1995) *Collected Essays of John Goode* (Keele: Keele University Press) p. 317.
83. Piercy, *Woman on the Edge of Time*, p. 141.
84. R. Sennett (1998) *The Corrosion of Character* (London: W. W. Norton).
85. Dostoyevsky, F. (1997) *The Double* (New York: Dover) [1846]; J. Hogg (1964) *The Private Memoirs and Confessions of a Justified Sinner* (London: Cresset Press) [1824]; R. L. Stevenson (1886) *The Strange Case of Dr. Jekyll and Mr. Hyde* (London: Longmans Green and Co.); D. Richardson (1979) *Pilgrimage* (London: Virago). 4 Vols [1915–35].
86. Jameson, *Archaeologies*, p. 293.
87. D. Harvey (2000) *Spaces of Hope* (Edinburgh: Edinburgh University Press) p. 180.
88. Ibid., p. 189.
89. Ibid., p. 188.
90. Ibid., p.159.
91. Ibid., p.155.
92. L. Sargisson (2012) *Fool's Gold? Utopianism in the Twenty-first Century* (London: Palgrave Macmillan).

7   The Return of the Repressed

1. M. D. Higgins (2011) *Renewing the Republic* (Dublin: Liberties Press) p. 95.
2. Higgins, *Renewing the Republic*, p. 61
3. See for example, C. el-Ojeili (2012) *Politics, Social Theory, Utopia and the World System* (London: Palgrave Macmillan); C. el-Ojeili (2003) *From Left Communism to Post-Modernism: Reconsidering Emancipatory Discourse* (Lanham, MD: University Press of America); J. C. Alexander (2001) 'Robust Utopias and Civil Repairs', *International Sociology*, 16: 579–91; M. H. Jacobsen and K. Tester (2012) *Utopia: Social Theory and the Future* (Farnham: Ashgate).
4. el-Ojeili, *Politics*, pp. 23, 194.
5. D. Harvey (2010) *The Enigma of Capital and the Crises of Capitalism* (London: Profile Books) p. 231.

6. I. Wallerstein (1999) *Utopistics*, (New York: The New Press) p.1.
7. J. Habermas (2010) 'The Concept of Human Dignity and the Realistic Utopia of Human Rights', *Metaphilosophy*, 41(4): 464–80; D. Barenboim (2008) 'Equal before Beethoven', *The Guardian*, Saturday 13 December. See also D. Singer (1999) *Whose Millennium? Theirs or Ours?* (New York: Monthly Review Press).
8. K. Mannheim (1979) *Ideology and Utopia* (London: Routledge and Kegan Paul) p. 175.
9. Mannheim, *Ideology and Utopia*, p. 177.
10. E. Bloch (1988) *The Utopian Function of Art and Literature* (Cambridge, MA: MIT Press) p. 7.
11. This anti-utopian process can be seen in the work of Anthony Giddens and in recent educational theory. S. Groarke (2004) 'Autonomy and Tradition: A Critique of the Sociological and Philosophical Foundations of Giddens's Utopian Realism', *Critical Review of International Social and Political Philosophy*, 7(3): 34–51; D. Webb (2009) 'Where's the Vision? The Concept of Utopia in Contemporary Educational Theory', *Oxford Review of Education*, 35(6): 743–60. See also D. Halpin (2009) 'Utopian Totalism versus Utopian Realism: A Reply to Darren Webb', *Oxford Review of Education*, 35(6): 761–64; D. Halpin (2003) *Hope and Education: The Role of the Utopian Imagination* (London: Routledge); R. Levitas (2004) 'Hope and Education', *Journal of Philosophy of Education*, 38(2): 269–73. Similar anti-utopian elements are present in the 'realistic utopia' by the American urban sociologist Herbert Gans (2008) *Imagining America in 2033: How the Country Put Itself Together after Bush* (Ann Arbor: University of Michigan Press).
12. Singer, *Whose Millennium?* pp. 259, 277, 279.
13. B. Adam and C. Groves (2007) *Future Matters: Action, Knowledge, Ethics* (Leiden: Brill) p. 200.
14. Ibid., p. 37.
15. Ibid., p. 172.
16. Ibid., p. 157.
17. Ibid., p. 158.
18. A. Bammer (1991) *Partial Visions: Feminism and Utopianism in the 1970s* (London: Routledge).
19. E. H. Carr (1995) *The Twenty Years Crisis: An Introduction to the Study of International Relation* (London, Macmillan) [1939] p. 85.
20. Ibid., p. 87.
21. J. Rawls (1999) *The Law of Peoples* (Cambridge, MA:Harvard University Press) p. 6.
22. p. 6.
23. Ibid., p. 12.
24. Ibid., p. 6.
25. Ibid., p. 12.
26. Ibid., p. 127.
27. E. Mendieta in R. Rorty (2006) *Take Care of Freedom and Truth will Take Care of Itself: Interviews with Richard Rorty* (Stanford: Stanford University Press), p. xii.
28. R. Rorty (1999) *Philosophy and Social Hope* (London: Penguin Books) pp. 234, 231.

29. Ibid., p. 208.
30. Ibid., pp. 214, 235, 277.
31. Ibid., p. 236.
32. Ibid., pp. 238–9.
33. Ibid., pp xiii–xiv.
34. Ibid., p. 203.
35. Ibid.
36. Ibid., pp. 233, 234.
37. Ibid., p. 231.
38. Ibid., p. 258.
39. Ibid., p. 257.
40. Ibid., p. 203.
41. R. Rorty (1997) *Achieving Our Country: Leftist Though in Twentieth Century America*, (Cambridge, MA: Harvard University Press) p. 8.
42. Ibid., pp. 18, 38.
43. Ibid., pp. 18–9.
44. Ibid., p. 23.
45. Rorty, *Interviews*, p. 95. Rorty's treatment of reality has been vigorously opposed: see for example, N. Geras (1995) *Solidarity in the Conversation of Humankind: Ungroundable Liberalism of Richard Rorty* (London: Verso).
46. Rorty, *Interviews*, p. 37.
47. Rorty, *Philosophy*, p. 234.
48. B. Obama (2008) acceptance speech November 2008, http://news.bbc.co.uk/1/hi/world/americas/us_elections_2008/7710038.stm, accessed 22 August 2012.
49. Martin Luther King, 'I Have a Dream', www.usconstitution.net/dream.html, accessed 17 February 2012.
50. L. Sargisson (2012) *Fool's Gold? Utopianism in the Twenty-First Century* (Basingtoke: Palgrave Macmillan) pp. 22–24.
51. Rorty, *Achieving Our Country*, p. 43.
52. Rorty, *Interviews*, p. 52. As on many points, Rorty also contradicts this elsewhere, claiming that 'to get caught up on Adorno and Marcuse one has to take Marx more seriously than he has ever been taken in America', *Interviews*, p. 39.
53. Rorty, *Achieving Our Country*, p. 43.
54. Rorty, *Interviews*, pp. 58–9.
55. Rorty, *Philosophy*, p. 211.
56. Rorty, *Interviews*, p. 40.
57. Rorty, *Philosophy*, p. 211.
58. Ibid., p. 204–5.
59. Ibid., p. 214. Rorty is quoting Leszek Kolakowski.
60. Rorty, *Interviews*, p. 85.
61. Ibid., pp. 53, 60.
62. Rorty, *Achieving Our Country*, p. 105.
63. R. Unger (1998) *Democracy Realised: The Progressive Alternative* (London: Verso) p. 3.
64. Ibid., p. 62.
65. Ibid., p. 20.
66. Ibid.

67. Ibid., p. 16.
68. Ibid., p. 19.
69. Ibid., p. 59.
70. R.Unger (2007) *The Self Awakened: Pragmatism Unbound* (Cambridge, MA: Harvard University Press) p. 23.
71. Unger, *Self*, pp. 49, 51.
72. Unger, *Democracy*, pp. 165–6.
73. Ibid., p. 29.
74. Ibid., p. 17.
75. Ibid., p. 18.
76. Ibid., p. 29
77. Ibid., p. 12
78. Ibid., pp. 20, 15; *Self*, p. 113.
79. Unger, *Democracy*, pp. 111–2.
80. J. Goode (1971) 'William Morris and the Dream of Revolution', in C. Swann (ed.) (1995) *Collected Essays of John Goode* (Keele: Keele University Press) p. 312.
81. Unger, *Democracy*, p. 12.
82. Ibid., p. 231.
83. Ibid., p. 74.
84. Ibid., p. 92.
85. Unger, *Self*, p. 41.
86. Ibid., p. 86.
87. Unger, *Democracy*, p. 237.
88. Unger, *Self*, p. 2.
89. Unger, *Democracy*, p. 237.
90. E. O. Wright (2010) *Envisioning Real Utopias* (London: Verso) p. xiii.
91. Wright, *Real Utopias*, p. 10.
92. Bammer, *Partial Visions*, p. 7.
93. P. Friere (1972) *Cultural Action for Freedom* (Harmondsworth: Penguin Books) p. 14.
94. Wright, *Real Utopias*, p. 21.
95. Ibid., p. 11.
96. Ibid., p. 121
97. Ibid., p. x.
98. Ibid., pp.5–6.
99. Ibid., p. 6.
100. Ibid.
101. Ibid.
102. Ibid.
103. Ibid., pp. 124, 260.
104. W. Hudson (2003) *The Reform of Utopia* (Aldershot: Ashgate).
105. D. Cooper (2013) *Everyday Utopias: The Conceptual Life of Promising Spaces* (Durham: Duke University Press).
106. L. Sargisson (1999) *Utopian Bodies and the Politics of Transgression* (London: Routledge); L. Sargisson and L. Sargent (1999) *Living in Utopia: New Zealand's Intentional Communities* (Aldershot: Ashgate).
107. D. Hancox (2012) *Utopia and the Valley of Tears: A Journey through the Spanish Crisis* (Amazon Kindle) Hancox, l. 890–7. (Kindle editions have location

numbers, not page references, to indicate position in the text. There is no print edition of this title.)

108. Ibid., l. 897.
109. Gordillo, cited in Hancox, *Utopia*, l. 691.
110. Hancox, *Utopia*, l. 1127.
111. Gordillo, cited in Hancox, *Utopia*, l. 902.
112. Hancox, *Utopia*, l. 1454.
113. Gordillo, cited in Hancox, l. 922.
114. Wright, *Real Utopias*, p. 10.
115. Ibid., p. 25.
116. Ibid., p. 27.
117. Ibid., p. 28.
118. Ibid., pp. 260–1.
119. J. Urry (2011) *Climate Change and Society* (Cambridge: Polity) p. 139.

8　Utopia as Archaeology

1. I. McEwan (2005) *Saturday* (London: Jonathan Cape) p. 172.
2. W. Bell and J. A. Mau (eds) (1971) *The Sociology of the Future* (New York: Russell Sage Foundation) p. xii.
3. D. Harvey (2000) *Spaces of Hope* (Edinburgh: Edinburgh University Press) p. 159.
4. R. Levitas (ed.) (1986) *The Ideology of the New Right* (Cambridge: Polity); R. Levitas (1998) *The Inclusive Society? Social Exclusion and New Labour* (Basingstoke: Macmillan).
5. M. Young (1994) 'Meritocracy Revisited', *Society*, 31(6): 87.
6. M. Young (1958) *The Rise of the Meritocracy* (London: Thames and Hudson) p. 74.
7. K. Davis and W. E. Moore (1945) 'Some Principles of Stratification', *American Sociological Review*, 10(2): 243.
8. See for example M. M. Tumin (1953) 'Some Principles of Stratification: A Critical Analysis', *American Sociological Review*, 18(4): 393. See also Ralf Dahrendorf's (1958) 'Out of Utopia: Towards a Reorientation of Sociological Analysis', *American Journal of Sociology*, 64(2): 115–27. Dahrendorf criticizes functionalist sociology for collapsing representations of the real into utopia. His presentation of utopia is unequivocally and conventionally negative.
9. P. Townsend (1959) 'The Truce on Inequality', *New Statesman*, 26 September, p. 381.
10. A. H. Halsey (2004) *A History of Sociology in Britain* (Oxford: Oxford University Press) pp. 110–11.
11. M. Young (2001) 'Down with Meritocracy', *The Guardian*, 29 June.
12. Young, *Rise*, p. 11.
13. Ibid., p. 103.
14. Ibid., p. 43.
15. Ibid., p. 147.
16. Ibid., p. 86.
17. Ibid., p. 135.

18. Ibid., p. 136.
19. Ibid., p. 139.
20. W. Hutton (2010) *Them and Us: Changing Britain – Why We Need a Fair Society* (London: Little, Brown) pp. 315, 239.
21. Ibid., pp. 33, 57.
22. Ibid., p. 272.
23. Ibid., p. 40.
24. W. Shakespeare, *Hamlet*, Act II, Scene 2.
25. Hutton, *Them and Us*, pp. 26, 78.
26. Ibid., p. 80.
27. Ibid., p. 40.
28. Ibid., p. 61.
29. S. Lansley (2012) *The Cost of Inequality* (London: Gibson Square) p. 213; See also, S. Lansley (2006) *Rich Britain* (London: Politico's).
30. E. Lawlor, H. Kersley and S. Steed (2009) *A Bit Rich* (New Economics Foundation), http://www.neweconomics.org/publications/bit-rich, accessed 28 August 2012.
31. Hutton, *Them and Us*, p. 78.
32. Ibid., p. 38.
33. Ibid., p. 27.
34. Ibid., p. 70.
35. Ibid., pp. 78–9.
36. Ibid., pp. 79–80.
37. Cabinet Office (2011) *Opening Doors, Breaking Barriers: A Strategy for Social Mobility* (London: HMSO) p.11.
38. Ibid., pp. 3, 11. See also Department for Work and Pensions (2012) *Social Justice: Transforming Lives* (London: HMSO) p. 12.
39. Lansley, *Cost*, pp. 65–67, 70–72.
40. R. Wilkinson and K. Pickett (2009) *The Spirit Level: Why Equality Is Better for Everyone* (London: Penguin).
41. W. B. Michaels (2007) *The Trouble with Diversity: How We Learned to Love Identity and Ignore Inequality* (Boston: Holt McDougal).
42. Vince Cable cited in Lansley, *Cost*, p. 243.
43. Hutton, *Them and Us*, pp. 342, 281–3.
44. Ibid., pp. 82, 24–5.
45. C. el-Ojeili (2012) *Politics, Social Theory, Utopia and the World-System* (Basingstoke: Palgrave Macmillan) pp. 26–7.
46. M. Abensour (2011) *Democracy Against the State* (Cambridge: Polity Press) p. xxxvi.
47. See my discussion of Etzioni and the difference between his position and that of John Macmurray in Levitas, *The Inclusive Society?* Chapter 5.
48. See Chapter 5 above.
49. P. Blond (2010) *Red Tory* (London: Faber and Faber) p. 285.
50. el-Ojeili, *Politics*, p. 27.
51. K. Malik (2009) *From Fatwa to Jihad: The Rushdie affair and Its Legacy* (London: Atlantic Books).
52. Lansley, *Cost*, p. 94.
53. http://www.investopedia.com/terms/s/sustainablegrowthrate.asp#axzz1o5 dEorXg, accessed 3 March 2012.

54. http://www.allbusiness.com/glossaries/sustainable-growth/4947519–1. html, accessed 3 March 2012.
55. N. Stern (2009) *A Blueprint for a Safer Planet: How to Manage Climate Change and Create a New Era of Progress and Prosperity* (London: Bodley Head) p. 34.
56. Ibid., p. 10.
57. Ibid., p. 41.
58. Ibid., p. 52.
59. Ibid., p. 162.
60. Ibid., p. 155.
61. Ibid., p. 191.
62. Ibid., p. 179.
63. Ibid., p. 107.
64. G. Monbiot (2009) 'Stop Blaming the Poor. It's the Wally Yachters Who Are Burning the Planet', *The Guardian*, 28 September.
65. W. Morris (1894) *How I Became a Socialist*, http://www.marxists.org/archive/ morris/works/1894/hibs/index.htm. accessed 28 August 2012.
66. J. E. Stiglitz, A. Sen and J.-P. Fitoussi (2009) *Report by the Commission on the Measurement of Economic Performance and Social Progress*, http://www.stiglitz-sen-fitoussi.fr/documents/rapport_anglais.pdf, accessed 28 August 2012.
67. New Economics Foundation (2009) *The Happy Planet Index 2: Why Good Lives Don't Have to Cost the Earth*, p. 10, http://www.neweconomics.org/sites/ neweconomics.org/files/The_Happy_Planet_Index_2.0_1.pdf, accessed 28 August 2012.

9 Utopia as Ontology

1. C Wright Mills (1959) *The Sociological Imagination* (Oxford: Oxford University Press) p. 7.
2. M. Harris (1980) 'Sociobiology and Biological Reductionism', in A. Montagu (ed.) *Sociobiology Examined* (Oxford: Oxford University Press) p. 18.
3. N. Geras (1983) *Marx's Theory of Human Nature: Refutation of a Legend* (London: Verso).
4. J. Carey (ed.) (1999) *The Faber Book of Utopias* (London: Faber and Faber) p. xii.
5. Ibid., pp. xiii–xiv.
6. J. Thomas (1998) 'Max Weber's Estate: Reflections on Wilhelm Hennis's *Max Webers Wissenschaft vom Menschen*', *History of the Human Sciences*, 11(2): 124.
7. A. Lincoln (2007) 'Down Here Below', *Abbey Sings Abbey*, Universal Classics.
8. S. Cain (2012) 'Why the World Needs Introverts', *The Guardian*, Tuesday 13 March; B. Ehrenreich (2009) *Smile or Die* (London: Granta).
9. W. Leiss (1978) *The Limits to Satisfaction* (London: Marion Boyars) p. 75.
10. A. Sayer (2011) *Why Things Matter to People: Social Science, Values and Ethical Life,* (Cambridge: Cambridge University Press) p. 245.
11. Ibid., front matter.
12. Ibid., p. 112.
13. Ibid., p. 9.

14. Ibid., p. 140.
15. Ibid., p. 145.
16. E. Bloch (1986) *The Principle of Hope* (Oxford: Basil Blackwell) p. 1.
17. Sayer, *Why Things Matter*, pp. 114, 110.
18. Ibid., p. 110.
19. Ibid., p. 113.
20. Ibid., p. 42.
21. Ibid., p. 57.
22. S. Gerhardt (2004) *Why Love Matters: How Affection Shapes a Baby's Brain* (London: Routledge).
23. Sayer, *Why Things Matter*, p. 127.
24. Ibid., p. 5.
25. Ibid., pp. 111, 112.
26. Ibid., p. 203.
27. Ibid., p. 133.
28. Ibid., p. 215.
29. Ibid., p. 227.
30. Ibid.
31. Ibid., pp. 249, 214.
32. R. M. Unger (1998) *Democracy Realised: The Progressive Alternative* (London: Verso) p. 15.
33. R. M. Unger (2007) *The Self Awakened: Pragmatism Unbound* (Cambridge, MA: Harvard University Press) pp. 2, 85.
34. Ibid., pp. 26–7. The reference to awakening to our true nature – and thus the idea of the self awakened itself – appears to be a reference to the Buddhist Metta Prayer 'may all beings awaken to their true nature'.
35. Ibid., p. 209.
36. Ibid., pp. 40–1.
37. Ibid., p. 38.
38. Ibid., p. 217.
39. Ibid., p. 13; R. M. Unger (1984) *Passion: An Essay on Personality* (New York: Free Press) pp. 95, 97, 123.
40. Unger, *Passion*, p. vii.
41. Ibid., p. 95.
42. Ibid., p. 107.
43. Bloch, *Principle of Hope*, p. 927.
44. Unger, *Passion*, p. 123.
45. Ibid., p. 109.
46. Ibid., p. 110.
47. Ibid., pp. 105–6.
48. Ibid., p. 269.
49. Ibid.
50. J. Macmurray (1935) *Creative Society: A Study of the Relation of Christianity to Communism* (London: SCM Press) p. 159.
51. W. Morris (1907) *A Dream of John Ball and A King's Lesson* (London: Longmans Green and Co.) [1883] pp. 33–4.
52. M. Buber (2000) *I and Thou* (London: Simon and Schuster).
53. C. Davis (2004) *Levinas* (Cambridge: Polity Press) pp. 31, 46.
54. Ibid., p. 32.

55. Ibid., p. 141.
56. Unger, *Passion*, p. 210.
57. A. Phillips and B. Taylor (2009) *On Kindness* (London: Hamish Hamilton).
58. Unger, *Passion*, p. 237.
59. Ibid., p. 99.
60. Ibid., p. 239.
61. Ibid., p. 245.
62. Unger, *Self*, p. 150.
63. Unger, *Passion*, p. 247.
64. Unger, *Democracy*, p. 168.
65. Unger, *Self*, p. 165.
66. Unger, *Democracy*, p. 181.
67. P. Pullman (2005) 'Against Identity', in Lisa Appignesi (ed.) *Free Expression is no Offence* (London: Penguin).
68. D. Barenboim and E. Said (2004) *Parallels and Paradoxes: Explorations in Music and Society* (London: Bloomsbury) p. 5.
69. B. Adam and C. Groves (2007) *Future Matters: Action, Knowledge, Ethics* (Leiden: Brill), p. 151.
70. V. Geoghegan (1997) 'Remembering the Future', in Jamie Owen Daniel and Tom Moylan (eds) *Not Yet: Reconsidering Ernst Bloch* (London: Verso) p. 22.
71. N. Thompson (ed.) (2012) *Living as Form: Socially Engaged Art from 1991–2011* (New York: Creative Time Press).
72. P. Friere (1972) *Pedagogy of the Oppressed* (Harmondsworth: Penguin) pp. 20–1.
73. P. Friere (1972) *Cultural Action for Freedom* (Harmondsworth: Penguin), p. 52.
74. R. Shaull, in Friere, *Pedagogy of the Oppressed*, p. 12.
75. E. Bloch (2009) *Atheism in Christianity* (London: Verso) [1972] p. 50.
76. Bloch, *Atheism*, pp. 55, 57.
77. Unger, *Self*, pp. 28–9, 181, 217.
78. Bloch, *Atheism*, p. 247.
79. Ibid., p. 224.
80. Unger, *Self*, p. 123.
81. C. Hitchens (2007) *God is Not Great: How Religion Poisons Everything* (London: Atlantic Books) p. 283.
82. Ibid., p. 286.
83. Sayer, *Why Things Matter*, p. 207.
84. P. Bennett (2009) *The Last Romances and the Kelmscott Press* (London: William Morris Society) p. 13.

10   Utopia as Architecture

1. 'The Land of Cokaygne', in A. L. Morton (ed.) (1952) *The English Utopia* (London: Lawrence and Wishart) p. 280.
2. M. D. Higgins (2011) *Renewing the Republic* (Dublin: Liberties Press) pp. 95–6.
3. Ibid., p. 96.
4. Ibid., p. 61.
5. UNICEF (2007) *Child Poverty in Perspective: An Overview of Child Well-being in Rich Countries*, Report Card 7 (Florence: UNICEF Innocenti Research Centre) p. 10.

6. W. Morris (1887) *What Socialists Want* http://www.marxists.org/archive/morris/works/1887/want.htm, accessed 6 April 2012.
7. W. Morris (1884) *Useless Work Versus Useless Toil*, http://www.marxists.org/archive/morris/works/1884/useful, accessed 6 April 2012.
8. K. Marx and F. Engels (1848) 'The Manifesto of the Communist Party', in K. Marx and F. Engels (1968) *Selected Works* (London: Lawrence and Wishart) p. 53.
9. Cited in J. Beecher and R. Bienvenu (eds) (1983) *The Utopian Vision of Charles Fourier: Selected Texts on Work, Love and Passionate Attraction* (Columbia: University of Missouri Press) p. 30.
10. George Osborne, UK Chancellor of the Exchequer, Andrew Marr Show, BBC1, 2 September 2012.
11. A. Bammer (1991) *Partial Visions* (London: Routledge) p. 126.
12. B. Russell (1932) *In Praise of Idleness*, http://www.zpub.com/notes/idle.html, accessed 11 September 2012.
13. D. Harvey (2010) *The Enigma of Capital* (London: Profile) p. 225.
14. For an overview of this project visit, http://nowhereisland.org/ accessed 9 September 2012.
15. http://www.bankofideas.org.uk/welcome/, accessed 6 April 2012.
16. https://occupywiki.org.uk/wiki/Free_University, accessed 6 April 2012.
17. Morris, *Useless Work.*
18. A. Gorz (1999) *Reclaiming Work* (Cambridge: Polity) p. 54.
19. Ibid.
20. R. Sennett (2008) *The Craftsman* (London: Penguin).
21. Morris, *Useless Work.*
22. A. Sayer (2011) *Why Things Matter to People: Social Science, Values and Ethical Life* (Cambridge: Cambridge University Press) p. 214.
23. M. Glucksmann (1995) 'Why "Work"? Gender and the "Total Social Organization of Labour"', *Gender Work and Organization*, 2(2): 63–75.
24. P. Seeger (1958) 'Oh, Had I a Golden Thread', http://www.peteseeger.net/goldthred.htm, accessed 9 September 2012.
25. A. Meyer (2000) *Contraction and Convergence: The Global Solution to Climate Change* (Totnes: Green Books) p. 12.
26. http://www.schumacherinstitute.org.uk/converge, accessed 10 April 2012.
27. Ibid.
28. Harvey, *Enigma*, p. 256.
29. UNDP (United Nations Development Programme) (1999) *Human Development Report 1999*, (New York: United Nations), p. 36; UNDP (2009) *Human Development Report* (New York: United Nations) p. 35.
30. P. Townsend (1993) 'Closing Remarks at a Celebration to Mark a Retirement from the University of Bristol', Excerpted in *Peter Townsend 1928–2009* (Bristol: The Policy Press) 2009, p. 16.
31. Townsend, *Closing Remarks*, p. 16.
32. P. Townsend (2002) 'Poverty, Social Exclusion and Social Polarisation: The Need to Construct an International Welfare State', in Peter Townsend and David Gordon (eds) *World Poverty: New Policies to Defeat an Old Enemy* (Bristol: The Policy Press) pp. 3–24.
33. I am indebted to Nathaniel Coleman for this observation.
34. N. Coleman (2005) *Utopias and Architecture* (London: Routledge).

35. R. Unger (2007) *The Self Awakened: Pragmatism Unbound* (Cambridge, MA: Harvard University Press) p. 117.
36. See n. 28.
37. W. Morris (1894) *How I Became a Socialist*, http://www.marxists.org/archive/morris/works/1894/hibs/index.htm, accessed 9 September 2012.
38. Morris, *How I Became a Socialist*.
39. F. Jameson (1988) *Brecht on Method* (London: Verso 1998).
40. http://occupylsx.org/, accessed 6 April 2012.
41. Harvey, *Enigma*, p. 227.
42. Ibid.
43. W. Morris (1907) *A Dream of John Ball and A King's Lesson* (London: Longmans, Green and Co.) [1886] p. 36.
44. E. Bloch (2000) *The Spirit of Utopia* (Stanford: Stanford California Press) p. 3.

Select Bibliography

Abensour, M. (1999) 'William Morris: The Politics of Romance', in Max Blechman (ed.) *Revolutionary Romanticism* (San Francisco: City Lights Books).

Abensour, M. (2008) 'Persistent Utopia', *Constellations*, 15(3): 406–21.

Abensour, M. (2011) *Democracy Against the State* (Cambridge, Polity Press).

Abrams, P. (1968) *The Origins of British Sociology: 1834–1914* (Chicago and London: University of Chicago Press).

Adam, B. and Groves, C. (2007) *Future Matters: Action, Knowledge, Ethics* (Leiden: Brill).

Adorno, T. (1974) *Minima Moralia* (London: NLB).

Adorno, T. (2009) *Night Music: Essays on Music 1928–1962* (London, New York, Calcutta: Seagull Books).

Alexander, J. C. (2001) 'Robust Utopias and Civil Repairs', *International Sociology*, 16: 579–591.

Arendt, H. (1951) *The Origins of Totalitarianism* (New York: Harcourt, Brace and Co.).

Armstrong, K. (2009) *The Case for God: What Religion Really Means* (London: Bodley Head).

Arnot, R. P. (1934) *William Morris: A Vindication* (London: Martin Lawrence).

Aron, R. (1968) *Main Currents in Sociological Thought I* (Harmondsworth: Penguin).

Auster, P. (2004) *The New York Trilogy* (London: Chatto and Windus).

Auster, P. (2005) *Oracle Night* (London: Faber and Faber).

Baccolini, R. and Moylan, T. (2003) *Dark Horizons* (London: Routledge).

Balfour-Paul, J. (2006) *Indigo: More than a Colour* (London: Archetype Publications).

Ball, P. (2001) *Bright Earth: The Invention of Colour* (London: Viking).

Bammer, A. (1991) *Partial Visions: Feminism and Utopianism in the 1970s* (London: Routledge).

Barenboim, D. (2008) *Everything is Connected: The Power of Music* (London: Weidenfeld and Nicholson).

Barenboim, D. and Said, E. (2004) *Parallels and Paradoxes: Explorations in Music and Society* (London: Bloomsbury).

Bartkowski, F. (1989) *Feminist Utopias* (Lincoln, New England: University of Nebraska Press).

Bauman, Z. (2003) 'Utopia with no Topos', *History of the Human Sciences*, 16(1): 11–25.

Beaumont, M. (2005) *Utopia Ltd: Ideologies of Social Dreaming in England, 1870–1900* (Leiden: Brill).

Beaumont, M. (2012) *The Spectre of Utopia: Utopian and Science Fictions at the* Fin de Siècle (Oxford and Bern: Peter Lang).

Beck, U. (1992) *Risk Society* (London: Sage).

Beecher, J. and Bienvenu, R. (eds) (1983) *The Utopian Vision of Charles Fourier: Selected Texts on Work, Love and Passionate Attraction* (Columbia: University of Missouri Press).

Bell, W. and Mau, J. A. (eds) (1971) *The Sociology of the Future* (New York: Russell Sage Foundation).

Bellamy, E. (1897) *Equality* (London: William Heinemann).

Bellamy, E. (2003 [1888]) *Looking Backward 2000–1887* (Ontario: Broadbent).

Benton, T. (1977) *Philosophical Foundations of the Three Sociologies* (London: Routledge and Kegan Paul).

Berlin, I. (1990) *The Crooked Timber of Humanity* (London: John Murray).

Bernard, L. L. and Bernard, J. (1943) *Origins of American Sociology: The Social Science Movement in the United States* (New York: Thomas Y. Crowell and Co.).

Bloch, E. (1970) *A Philosophy of the Future* (New York: Herder and Herder).

Bloch, E. (1985) *Essays in the Philosophy of Music* (Cambridge: Cambridge University Press).

Bloch, E. (1986) *The Principle of Hope* (London: Basil Blackwell), 3 vols.

Bloch, E. (1988) *The Utopian Function of Art and Literature* (Cambridge Massachusetts: MIT Press).

Bloch, E. (1991) *Heritage of Our Times* (Cambridge: Polity Press).

Bloch, E. (1998) *Literary Essays* (Palo Alto: Stanford University Press).

Bloch, E. (2000) *The Spirit of Utopia* (Stanford: Stanford Univerity Press) [1923].

Bloch, E. (2009) *Atheism in Christianity* (London: Verso) [1972] p. 50.

Blond, P. (2010) *Red Tory* (London: Faber and Faber).

Boltanski, L. (2011) *On Critique: A Sociology of Emancipation* (Cambridge: Polity Press).

Bowman, S. E. (1962) *Edward Bellamy Abroad: An American Prophet's Influence* (New York: Twayne).

Bradley, H. (2013) *Gender* (Cambridge: Polity Press).

Branford, V. (2010 [1921]) *Whitherward? Hell or Eutopia* (General Books).

Branford, V. and Geddes, P. (2010 [1917]) *The Coming Polity: A Study in Reconstruction* (General Books).

Bruce, S. (1999) *Sociology: A Very Short Introduction* (Oxford: Oxford University Press).

Buber, M. (1949) *Paths in Utopia* (London: Routledge and Kegan Paul).

Buber, M. (2000) *I and Thou* (London: Simon and Schuster).

Byatt, A. S. (1996) *Babel Tower* (London: Chatto and Windus).

Campanella, T. (1981) *The City of the Sun: A Poetical Dialogue* (Berkeley, Ca.: University of California Press) [1623].

Carey, J. (ed.) (1999) *The Faber Book of Utopias* (London: Faber and Faber).

Carpenter, H. (1998) *Dennis Potter: the Authorized Biography* (London: Faber and Faber) pp. 350–1.

Carr, E. H. (1995) *The Twenty Years Crisis: An Introduction to the Study of International Relation* (London: Macmillan) [1939].

Cavalcanti, I. F. S. (2000) 'Utopias of(f) Language in Contemporary Feminist Utopias', *Utopian Studies,* 11(2): 152–80.

Claeys, G. (2011) *Searching for Utopia: The History of an Idea* (London: Thames and Hudson).

Clark, T. J. (1999) *Farewell to an Idea* (New Haven and London: Yale University Press).

Coleman, N. (2005) *Utopias and Architecture* (London: Routledge).

Coleman, S. and O'Sullivan, P. (eds) (1990) *William Morris and News from Nowhere: A Vision for our Time* (Bideford: Green Books).

Collini, S. (1979) *Liberalism and Sociology: L. T. Hobhouse and the Political Argument in England, 1880–1914* (Cambridge: Cambridge University Press).

Cooper, D. (2013) *Everyday Utopias: The Conceptual Life of Promising Spaces* (Durham: Duke University Press).

Crossley, R. (2011) 'The First Wellsians: A Modern Utopia and Its Early Disciples', *English Literature in Transition*, 54(4): 444–69.

Da Costa Meyer, E. and Wasserman, F. (eds) (2003) *Schoenberg, Kandinsky and the Blue Rider* (London, New York and Paris: The Jewish Museum, New York).

Dahrendorf, R. (1958) 'Out of Utopia: Towards a Reorientation of Sociological Analysis', *American Journal of Sociology*, 64(2): 115–27.

Dahrendorf, R. (1995) *LSE: A History of the London School of Economics and Political Science 1895–1995* (Oxford: Oxford University Press).

Daniel, J. O and Moylan, T. (eds) (1997) *Not Yet: Reconsidering Ernst Bloch* (London: Verso).

Davidson. L. (2010) 'A Quest for Harmony: The Role of Music in Robert Owen's New Lanark Community', *Utopian Studies*, 21(2): 232–51.

Davis, C. (2004) *Levinas* (Cambridge: Polity Press) pp. 31, 46.

Davis, J. C. (1981) *Utopia and the Ideal Society* (Cambridge: Cambridge University Press).

Davis, K. and Moore, W. E. (1945) 'Some Principles of Stratification', *American Sociological Review*, 10(2): 242–9.

De Nora, T. (2000) *Music in Everyday Life* (Cambridge: Cambridge University Press).

Deleuze, G. and Guattari, F. (1984) *Anti-Oedipus: Capitalism and Schizophrenia* (London: Athlone Press) [1972].

Deller, J. (2010) *Procession* (London: Cornerhouse).

Dissanayake, E. (2008) 'If Music is the Food of Love, What About Survival and Reproductive Success?' *Musicae Scientiae*, 169–95.

Durkheim, E. (1962) *Socialism* (New York: Collier Books).

Durkheim, E. (1964) *The Rules of Sociological Method* (New York: The Free Press) [1895].

Durkheim, E. (1964) *The Division of Labor in Society* (New York: The Free Press).

Arata, S. (2003) 'Introduction' to William Morris, *News from Nowhere* (Ontario: Broadview Press).

Edwards, J. (ed.) (2011) *Music Therapy and Parent-Infant Bonding* (Oxford: Oxford University Press).

Ehrenreich, B. (2009) *Smile or Die* (London: Granta).

Elgin, S. H. (1985) *Native Tongue* (London: Women's Press).

Eliot, T. S. (2001) *Four Quartets* (London: Faber and Faber) [1936–42].

el-Ojeili, C. (2003) *From Left Communism to Post-Modernism: Reconsidering Emancipatory Discourse* (Lanham, Maryland: University Press of America).

el-Ojeili, C. (2012) *Politics, Social Theory, Utopia and the World System* (London: Palgrave Macmillan).

Engels, F. (2010) *The Origins of the Family, Private Property and the State* (London: Penguin) [1895].

Fischer, H. and Rainbird, S. (eds) *Kandinsky: The Path to Abstraction* (London: Tate Publishing).

Fitting, P. (1998) 'The Concept of Utopia in the Work of Fredric Jameson', *Utopian Studies*, 9(2): 8–17.

Fitting, P. (2003) 'Unmasking the Real? Critique and Utopia in Recent SF Films', in Baccolini, R. and Moylan, T. (eds) *Dark Horizons* (London: Routledge) pp. 155–66.

Forrester, V. (1999) *The Economic Horror* (Cambridge: Polity Press).

Forster, M. (1989) *Have the Men had Enough?* (London: Chatto and Windus).

Friere, P. (1972) *Cultural Action for Freedom* (Harmondsworth: Penguin Books).

Friere, P. (1972) *Pedagogy of the Oppressed* (Harmondsworth: Penguin Books).

Gage, J. (1993) *Colour and Culture* (London: Thames and Hudson).

Gage, J. (2000) *Colour and Meaning* (London: Thames and Hudson).

Galloway, J. (2011) *All Made Up* (London: Granta).

Gans, H. (2008) *Imagining America in 2033: How the Country Put Itself Together after Bush* (Ann Arbor: University of Michigan Press).

Geoghegan, V. (1987) *Utopianism and Marxism* (London: Methuen).

Geoghegan, V. (1996) *Ernst Bloch* (London: Routledge).

Geoghegan, V. (1997) 'Remembering the Future', in Jamie Owen Daniel and Tom Moylan (eds) *Not Yet: Reconsidering Ernst Bloch* (London: Verso).

Geras, N. (1983) *Marx's Theory of Human Nature: Refutation of a Legend* (London: Verso).

Geras, N. (1995) *Solidarity in the Conversation of Humankind: Ungroundable Liberalism of Richard Rorty* (London: Verso).

Gerhardt, S. (2004) *Why Love Matters: How Affection Shapes a Baby's Brain* (London: Routledge).

Gilman, C. P. (1914) *The Man-Made World, or, Our Androcentric Culture* (New York: Charlton) [1911].

Gilman, C. P. (1924) *His Religion and Hers: A Study of the Faith of our Fathers and the Work of our Mothers* (London: Fisher Unwin) [1923].

Gilman, C. P. (1972) *The Home: Its Work and Influence* (Chicago: University of Illinois Press) [1903].

Gilman, C. P. (1979) *Herland* (London: The Women's Press) [1915].

Gilman, C. P. (1998) *Women and Economics* (New York: Dover) [1898].

Glucksmann, M. (1995) 'Why "Work"? Gender and the "Total Social Organization of Labour"', *Gender Work and Organization*, 2(2): 63–75.

Golding, J. (2000) *Paths to the Absolute* (London: Thames and Hudson).

Goldman, L. (2007) 'Foundations of British Sociology 1880–1930: Contexts and Biographies', *The Sociological Review*, 55(3): 431–40.

Goodchild, P. (1996) *Deleuze and Guattari: An Introduction to the Politics of Desire* (London: Sage).

Goode, J. (1995) *Collected Essays of John Goode* (Keele: Keele University Press).

Gorz, A. (1999) *Reclaiming Work* (Cambridge: Polity).

Gorz, A. (1999) *Reclaiming Work: Beyond the Wage-Based Society* (Cambridge: Polity Press).

Gray, J. (2007) *Black Mass: Apocalyptic Religion and the Death of Utopia* (London: Allen Lane).

Griffin, M. J., and Moylan, T. (eds) (2007) *Exploring the Utopian Impulse* (Bern: Peter Lang).

Griffiths, J. (2011) 'The Power of Song', *The Guardian G2*, 15 March.

Guy, F., Shaw-Miller, S. and Tucker, M. (2007) *Eye-music: Kandinsky, Klee and All that Jazz* (Chichester: Pallant House Gallery).

Habermas, J. (1979) *The New Conservatism* (Cambridge: Polity Press).

Habermas, J. (2010) 'The Concept of Human Dignity and the Realistic Utopia of Human Rights', *Metaphilosophy*, 41(4): 464–80.

Halpin, D. (2003) *Hope and Education: The Role of the Utopian Imagination* (London: Routledge).

Halpin, D. (2009) 'Utopian Totalism Versus Utopian Realism: A Reply to Darren Webb', *Oxford Review of Education*, 35(6): 761–64.

Halsey, A. H. (2004) *A History of Sociology in Britain* (Oxford: Oxford University Press).

Hancox, D. (2012) *Utopia and the Valley of Tears: A Journey through the Spanish Crisis* (Amazon: Kindle).

Harris, M. (1980) 'Sociobiology and Biological Reductionism', in A. Montagu (ed.) *Sociobiology Examined* (Oxford: Oxford University Press).

Harrison, R. J. (2000) *The Life and Times of Sidney and Beatrice Webb 1858–1905: The Formative Years* (Basingstoke: Palgrave Macmillan).

Harvey, D. (2000) *Spaces of Hope* (Edinburgh: Edinburgh University Press).

Harvey, D. (2010) *The Enigma of Capital and the Crises of Capitalism* (London: Profile Books) p. 231.

Hayden, D. (1982) *The Grand Domestic Revolution: A History of Feminist Designs for American Homes, Neighborhoods and Cities* (Cambridge, Mass.: MIT Press).

Hayden, P. and el-Ojeili, C. (eds) (2009) *Globalization and Utopia: Critical Essays* (Basingstoke: Palgrave Macmillan).

Hayek, F. von (1946) *The Road to Serfdom* (London: Routledge and Kegan Paul).

Henley, D. (2011) *Music Education in England – A Review by Darren Henley for the Department for Education and the Department for Culture, Media and Sport*, (London: Department for Education DFE-00011-2011).

Heyworth, P. (1983) *Otto Klemperer: His Life and Times. Volume 1 1885–1933.* (Cambridge: Cambridge University Press).

Higgins, M. D. (2011) *Renewing the Republic* (Dublin: Liberties Press).

Hitchens, C. (2007) *God is Not Great: How Religion Poisons Everything* (London: Atlantic Books) p. 283.

Hobhouse, L. T. (1908) 'Editorial', *The Sociological Review*, 1(1): 4–5.

Hobhouse, L. T. (1908) 'The Roots of Modern Sociology', *Inauguration of the Martin White Professorships of Sociology 17 December 1907* (London: John Murray and the University of London).

Holloway, R. (2005) *Looking in the Distance: The Human Search for Meaning* (London: Canongate).

Holloway, R. (2009) *Between the Monster and the Saint: The Divided Spirit of Humanity* (London: Canongate).

Horkheimer, M. (1997) *Critical Theory: Selected Essays* (New York: Continuum Press).

Hudson, W. (2003) *The Reform of Utopia* (Aldershot: Ashgate).

Hunter, R. (2010) 'The Music of Change: Utopian Transformation in *Aufstieg und Fall der Stadt Mahagonny* and *Der Silbersee*', *Utopian Studies*, 21(2): 293–312.

Hutton, W. (2010) *Them and Us: Changing Britain – Why We Need a Fair Society* (London: Little, Brown).

Huxley, A. (1932) *Brave New World* (London: Chatto and Windus).

Huxley, A. (1962) *Island* (London: Chatto and Windus).

Huxley, A. (2004) *The Doors of Perception and Heaven and Hell* (London: Vintage).

Huxley, A. (2009) *The Perennial Philosophy* (New York: HarperCollins) [1945].

Jackson, T. (2011) *Prosperity without Growth: Economics for a Finite Planet* (London: Earthscan).

Jacobsen, M. H. (2003) *Utopianism in the Work of Zygmunt Bauman: Towards a Sociology of Alternative Realities* (Aalborg: Aalborg Universitet).

Jacobsen, M. H. (2004) 'From Solid Modern Utopia to Liquid Modern Anti-Utopia? Tracing the Utopian Strand in the Sociology of Zygmunt Bauman', *Utopian Studies*, 15(1): 63–87.

Jacobsen, M. H. and Tester, K. (2012) *Utopia: Social Theory and the Future* (Farnham: Ashgate).

Jacoby, R. (1999) *The End of Utopia: Politics and Culture in an Age of Apathy* (New York: Basic Books).

Jacoby, R. (2005) *Picture Imperfect: Utopian Thought for an Anti-utopian Age* (New York: Columbia University Press).

Jameson, F. (1994) *The Seeds of Time* (Columbia University Press).

Jameson, F. (1974) *Marxism and Form: Twentieth-Century Dialectical Theories of Literature* (Princeton, New Jersey: Princeton University Press).

Jameson, F. (1982) 'Progress Versus Utopia: Or, Can We Imagine the Future?' *Science-Fiction Studies*, 27(9): 147–58.

Jameson, F. (1988) *Brecht on Method* (London: Verso 1998).

Jameson, F. (1991) *Postmodernism: Or, The Cultural Logic of Late Capitalism* (London: Verso).

Jameson, F. (2005) *Archaeologies of the Future* (London: Verso).

Jarman, D. (2000) *Chroma* (London: Vintage).

Jones, O. (2011) *Chavs: The Demonisation of the Working Class* (London: Verso).

Kandinsky, W. and Marc, F. (eds) (1974) *The Blaue Reiter Almanac* (London: Thames and Hudson) [1912].

Kandinsky, W. (1977) *Concerning the Spiritual in Art* (New York: Dover) [1911].

Kateb, G. (1963) *Utopia and Its Enemies* (Illinois: Free Press of Glencoe).

Kateb, G. (1967) 'Utopia and the Good Life', in F. E. Manuel (ed.) *Utopias and Utopian Thought* (Boston: Beacon Press).

Kaufmann, M. (1879) *Utopias* (London: Kegan Paul).

Kelvin, N. (ed.) (1984–96) *The Collected Letters of William Morris* (New Jersey: Princeton University Press), 5 Vols.

Kessler, C. F. (ed.) (1984) *Daring to Dream: Utopian Stories by United States Women 1836–1919* (Boston: Pandora).

Kilminster, R. (1998) *The Sociological Revolution: From Enlightenment to the Global Age* (London: Routledge).

Korstvedt, B. M. (2010) *Listening for Utopia in Bloch's Musical Philosophy* (Cambridge: Cambridge University Press).

Kumar, K. (1978) *Prophecy and Progress: The Sociology of Industrial and Post-Industrial Society* (London: Allen Lane).

Kumar, K. (1987) *Utopia and Anti-Utopia in Modern Times* (Oxford: Basil Blackwell).

Kumar, K. (1995) *From Post-Industrial to Post-Modern Society* (Oxford: Basil Blackwell), Second Edition, Wiley-Blackwell 2004.

Lansley, S. (2006) *Rich Britain* (London: Politico's).

Lansley, S. (2012) *The Cost of Inequality* (London: Gibson Square).

Lawlor, E., Kersley, H. and Steed, S. (2009) *A Bit Rich* (London: New Economics Foundation).

Le Guin, U. (1974) *The Dispossessed: An Ambiguous Utopia* (New York: Harper and Row).

Le Guin, U. (1975) 'The Ones Who Walk Away from Omelas', *The Wind's Twelve Quarters* (New York: Harper and Row).

Le Guin, U. (1986) *Always Coming Home* (London: Victor Gollancz).

Leiss, W. (1978) *The Limits to Satisfaction* (London: Marion Boyars).

Lepenies, W. (1992) *Between Literature and Science: The Rise of Sociology* (Cambridge: Cambridge University Press).

Levitas, R. (1990) *The Concept of Utopia* (Hemel Hempstead: Philip Allan), reissued 2010, 2011 (Bern: Peter Lang).

Levitas, R. (1997) 'Educated Hope: Ernst Bloch on Abstract and Concrete Utopia', in Jamie Owen Daniel and Tom Moylan (eds) (1997) *Not Yet: Reconsidering Ernst Bloch* (London: Verso).

Levitas, R. (1998) *The Inclusive Society? Social Exclusion and New Labour* (Basingstoke: Macmillan), Second Edition, 2006.

Levitas, R. (2001) 'Against Work: A Utopian Incursion into Social Policy', *Critical Social Policy*, 21(4): 449–65.

Levitas, R. (2004) 'Hope and Education', *Journal of Philosophy of Education*, 38(2): 269–73.

Levitas, R. (2005) 'After the Fall: Reflections on Culture, Freedom and Utopia after 11 September', in *Anglo-Saxonica: Revista do centro de Estudos Anglisticos da Universidade de Lisboa*, Serie II, 23: 299–317.

Levitas, R. (2005) 'Beyond Bourgeois Right', *The European Legacy*, 9(5): 605–18.

Levitas, R. (2005) *Morris, Hammersmith and Utopia* (London: William Morris Society).

Levitas, R. (2007) 'Looking for the Blue: The Necessity of Utopia', *Journal of Political Ideologies*, 12(3): 289–306.

Levitas, R. (2010) 'Back to the Future: Wells, Sociology, Utopia and Method', *Sociological Review*, 58(4): 530–47.

Levitas, R. (ed.) (1986) *The Ideology of the New Right* (Cambridge: Polity).

Lorca, F. G. (1998) *In Search of Duende* (New York: New Directions Books).

Löwy, M. (1988) *Redemption and Utopia: Jewish Libertarain Thought in Central Europe* (Stanford: Stanford University Press).

Lunn, E. (1985) *Marxism and Modernism* (London: Verso).

Mackenzie, N and Mackenzie, J. (1977) *The First Fabians* (London: Weidenfeld and Nicholson).

Malik, K. (2009) *From Fatwa to Jihad: The Rushdie Affair and Its Legacy* (London: Atlantic Books).

Mannheim, K. (1979) *Ideology and Utopia* (London: Routledge and Kegan Paul).

Manuel, F. E. and Manuels, F. P. (1979) *Utopian Thought in the Western World* (London: Souvenir Press).

Marcuse, H. (1979) *The Aesthetic Dimension* (London: Macmillan).

Marx, K. and Engels, F. (1848) 'The Manifesto of the Communist Party', in K. Marx and F. Engels (1968) *Selected Works* (London: Lawrence and Wishart).

Mayne, M. (2008) *This Sunrise of Wonder* (London: Darton, Longman and Tod).

Jameson, F. (2005) *Archaeologies of the Future* (London: Verso).

Mazzochi, P. (2012) 'The Politics of Persistent Utopia: Miguel Abensour and the Opening of Insurgent Democracy', Society for Utopian Studies Annual Conference, Toronto.

McEwan, I. (2005) *Saturday* (London: Jonathan Cape).

McLennan, G. (2011) *Story of Sociology: A First Companion to Social Theory* (London: Bloomsbury).

Meier, P. (1978) *William Morris: The Marxist Dreamer* (Brighton: Harvester).

Meyer, A. (2000) *Contraction and Convergence: The Global Solution to Climate Change,*(Totnes: Green Books).

Miller, J. (2001) *Seeing is Believing* (Truro: Dyllanson Truran).

Miller, J. (2000) *Another Shade of Blue* (Truro: Dyllanson Truran).

Mills, C. W. (1959) *The Sociological Imagination* (Oxford: Oxford University Press).

Monbiot, G. (2009) 'Stop Blaming the Poor: It's the Wally Yachters Who are Burning the Planet', *The Guardian*, 28 September.

Morris, W. (1887) *What Socialists Want,* http://www.marxists.org/archive/morris/works/1887/want.htm, accessed 6 April 2012.

Morris, W. (1894) *How I Became a Socialist,* http://www.marxists.org/archive/morris/works/1894/hibs/index.htm.

Morris, W. (1907) *A Dream of John Ball and A King's Lesson* (London: Longmans Green and Co.) [1883].

Morris, W. and Bax, E. B. (1893) *Socialism: Its Growth and Outcome* (London: Swan Sonnenschein).

Morris, W. (1884) *Useless Work versus Useless Toil,* http://www.marxists.org/archive/morris/works/1884/useful, accessed 6 April 2012.

Morris, W. (1902 [1891]) *News from Nowhere* (London: Longmans Green and Co.).

Morris, W. (2003 [1889]), 'Looking Backward', Appendix B to Bellamy, *Looking Backward 2000–1887* (Ontario: Broadbent).

Morton, A. L. (1952) *The English Utopia* (London: Lawrence and Wishart).

Moylan, T. (1986) *Demand the Impossible* (London: Methuen).

Moylan, T. (2000) *Scraps of the Untainted Sky* (Oxford: Westview Press).

Moylan, T. and Baccolini, R. (eds) (2007) *Utopia, Method, Vision: The Use Value of Social Dreaming* (Bern: Peter Lang).

Mumford, L. (2003) *The Story of Utopias: Ideal Commonwealths and Social Myths* (London: Harrap).

New Economics Foundation (2009) *The Happy Planet Index 2: Why good lives don't have to cost the earth,* http://www.neweconomics.org/sites/neweconomics.org/files/The_Happy_Planet_Index_2.0_1.pdf, accessed 28 August 2012.

Nicholson, W. (2000) *The Wind Singer* (London: Egmont).

Nicholson, W. (2001) *Slaves of the Mastery* (London: Egmont).

Nussbaum, M. (2003) *Upheavals of Thought: The Intelligence of Emotions* (Cambridge: Cambridge University Press).

Bennett, P. (2009) *The Last Romances and the Kelmscott Press* (London: William Morris Society).

Pastoureau, M. (2002) *Blue: The History of a Colour* (Princeton: Princeton University Press)

Phillips, A. and Taylor, B. (2009) *On Kindness* (London: Hamish Hamilton).

Piercy, M. (1976) *Woman on the Edge of Time* (New York: Alfred A Knopf).

Piercy, M. (1977) *Woman on the Edge of Time* (New York: Fawcett Crest) [1976].

Popper, K. (1945) *The Open Society and Its Enemies* (London: Routledge and Kegan Paul).

Popper, K. (1986) 'Utopia and Violence', *World Affairs*, 149(1): 3–9.

Pullman, P. (2005) 'Against Identity', in Lisa Appignesi (ed.) *Free Expression is no Offence* (London: Penguin).

Pullman, P. (2011) *His Dark Materials* (London: Everyman), 3 Vols.

Rawls, J. (1971) *A Theory of Justice* (Cambridge, Mass.:Harvard University Press).

Rawls, J. (1999) *The Law of Peoples* (Cambridge, Mass.:Harvard University Press).

Richardson, D. (1979) *Pilgrimage* (London: Virago), 4 Vols.

Ricoeur, P. (1986) *Lectures on Ideology and Utopia* (New York: Columbia University Press).

Robinson, M. (2010) *Absence of Mind: The Dispelling of Inwardness from the Modern Myth of the Self* (New Haven: Yale University Press).

Rogers, R. and Gumuchdjian, P. (1997) *Cities for a Small Planet* (London: Faber and Faber).

Romero, L. G. (2010) 'Countess Almaviva and the Carceral Redemption: Introducing a Musical Utopia into the Prison Walls', *Utopian Studies*, 21(2): 274–92.

Rorty, R. (1997) *Achieving Our Country: Leftist Thought in Twentieth Century America* (Cambridge, Mass.: Harvard University Press).

Rorty, R. (1999) *Philosophy and Social Hope* (London: Penguin Books).

Rorty, R. (2006) *Take Care of Freedom and Truth will Take Care of Itself: Interviews with Richard Rorty* (Stanford: Stanford University Press).

Ross, A. (2010) *Listen to This* (London: Fourth Estate).

Rowling, J. K. (1997) *Harry Potter and the Philosopher's Stone* (London: Bloomsbury).

Russ, J. (1975) *The Female Man* (New York: Bantam Books).

Russell, B. (1932) *In praise of idleness*, http://www.zpub.com/notes/idle.html, accessed 11 September 2012.

Sargent, L. T. (1979) *British and American Utopian Literature, 1516–1975* (Boston: G. K. Hall).

Sargent, L. T. (1985) *British and American Utopian Literature, 1516–1985: An Annotated Chronological Bibliography* (New York and London: Garland).

Sargent, L. T. (2011) *Utopianism: A Very Short Introduction* (Oxford: Oxford University Press).

Sargisson, L. (1996) *Contemporary Feminist Utopianism* (London: Routledge).

Sargisson, L. (1999) *Utopian Bodies and the Politics of Transgression* (London: Routledge).

Sargisson, L. (2012) *Fool's Gold? Utopianism in the Twenty-first Century* (London: Palgrave Macmillan).

Sargisson, L. and Sargent, L. T. (1999) *Living in Utopia: New Zealand's Intentional Communities* (Aldershot: Ashgate).

Savage, M. (2007) '*The Sociological Review* and the History of British Sociology', *The Sociological Review*, 55(3): 429–30.

Sayer, A. (2005) *The Moral Significance of Class* (Cambridge: Cambridge University Press).

Sayer, A. (2011) *Why Things Matter to People: Social Science, Values and Ethical Life* (Cambridge: Cambridge University Press).

Schulz, B. (1998) 'The Republic of Dreams', B. Schulz, *The Collected Works of Bruno Schultz* ed. J. Ficowski (London: Picador) pp. 266–72.

Scott, J. and Husbands, C. T. (2007) 'Victor Branford and the Building of British Sociology', *The Sociological Review*, 55(3): 460–84.

Sennett, R. (1998) *The Corrosion of Character* (London: W. W. Norton).

Sennett, R. (2008) *The Craftsman* (London: Penguin).

Sennett, R. (2012) *Together* (London: Allen Lane).

Sennett, R. and Cobb, R. (1977) *The Hidden Injuries of Class* (Cambridge: Cambridge University Press) [1972].

Shaw-Miller, S. (2004) *Visible Deeds of Music: Art and Music from Wagner to Cage* (New Haven: Yale University Press).

Siebers, T. (ed.) (1994) *Heterotopia: Postmodern Utopia and the Body Politic* (Ann Arbor: University of Michigan Press).

Singer, D. (1999) *Whose Millennium? Theirs or Ours?* (New York: Monthly Review Press).

Smith, P. (1992) '"Parbleu": Pissarro and the Political Colour of an Original Vision', *Art History*, 15(2): 223–47.

Solomon, M. (1979) *Marxism and Art* (Sussex: Harvester).

Solomon, M. (1995) *Mozart: A Life* (London: Pimlico). Sontag, S. (2004) Regarding the Pain of Others (London: Penguin)

Sontag, S. (2004) *Regarding the Pain of Others* (London: Penguin)

Spalding, F. (2009) *John Piper, Myfanwy Piper: Lives in Art* (Oxford: Oxford University Press).

Steiner, G. (1967) *Language and Silence* (Harmondsworth: Penguin).

Steiner, G. (1989) *Real Presences: Is there anything in what we say?* (London: Faber and Faber).

Stern, N. (2009) *A Blueprint for a Safer Planet: How to Manage Climate Change and Create a New Era of Progress and Prosperity* (London: Bodley Head).

Stiglitz, J. E., Sen, A. and Fitoussi, J.-P. (2009) *Report by the Commission on the Measurement of Economic Performance and Social Progress*, http://www.stiglitz-sen-fitoussi.fr/documents/rapport_anglais.pdf, accessed 28 August 2012.

Streeck, W. (2011) 'Markets Versus Voters?' *New Left Review*, 71, September/October: 5–30.

Studholme, M. (1997) 'From Leonard Hobhouse to Tony Blair: A Sociological Connection?' *Sociology*, 31(3): 531–47.

Studholme, M. (2007) 'Patrick Geddes: Founder of Environmental Sociology', *Sociological Review*, 55(3): 441–59.

Studholme, M. (2008) 'Patrick Geddes and the History of Environmental Sociology in Britain: A Cautionary Tale', *Journal of Classical Sociology*, 8(3): 367–9.

Suvin, D. (1979) *Metamorphoses of Science Fiction* (New Haven: Yale University Press).

Swift, Katherine (2008) *The Morville Hours* (London: Bloomsbury).

Talmon, J. (1970 [1951]) *The Origins of Totalitarian Democracy* (London: Sphere Books).

Taylor, C. (2007) *A Secular Age* (Cambridge, Mass.:Harvard University Press).

Taylor, K. and Goodwin, B. (2009) *The Politics of Utopia: A Study in Theory and Practice* (Bern: Peter Lang).

Thomas, J. (1998) 'Max Weber's Estate: Reflections on Wilhelm Hennis's *Max Webers Wissenschaft vom Menschen*', *History of the Human Sciences*, 11(2): 121–8.

Thompson, E. P. (1977) *William Morris: Romantic to Revolutionary* (London: Merlin Press).

Thompson, N. (ed.) (2012) *Living as Form: Socially Engaged Art from 1991–2011,* (New York: Creative Time Press).

Tillich, P. (1949) *The Shaking of the Foundations* (Harmondsworth: Penguin).

Tillich, P. (1964) *Theology of Culture* (Oxford: Oxford University Press).

Tillich, P. (1973) 'Critique and Justification of Utopia', in Frank E. Manuel (ed.) *Utopias and Utopian Thought* (London: Souvenir Press).

Tillich, P. (1980) *The Courage To Be* (New Haven, CT: Yale University Press) [1952].

Townsend, P. (1959) 'The Truce on Inequality', *New Statesman,* 26 September, p. 381.

Townsend, P. (2002) 'Poverty, Social Exclusion and Social Polarisation: The Need to Construct an International Welfare State', in Peter Townsend and David Gordon (eds) *World Poverty: New Policies to Defeat an Old Enemy* (Bristol: The Policy Press) pp. 3–24.

Tumin, M. M. (1953) 'Some Principles of Stratification: A Critical Analysis', *American Sociological Review,* 18(4): 387–94.

Unger, R. M. (1998) *Democracy Realised: The Progressive Alternative* (London: Verso).

Unger, R. M. (2007) *The Self Awakened: Pragmatism Unbound* (Cambridge, Mass.: Harvard University Press).

Unger, R. M. (1984) *Passion: An Essay on Personality* (New York: Free Press). Macmurray, J. (1935) *Creative Society: A Study of the Relation of Christianity to Communism* (London: SCM Press).

Urry, J. (2011) *Climate Change and Society* (Cambridge: Polity).

Utopian Studies 1998 9 (2) Special issue on the work of Fredric Jameson.

Vergo, P. (2010) *The Music of Painting: Music, Modernism and the Visual Arts from the Romantics to John Cage* (London: Phaidon).

Wallerstein, I. (1999) *Utopistics* (New York: The New Press).

Webb, D. (2009) 'Where's the Vision? The Concept of Utopia in Contemporary Educational Theory', *Oxford Review of Education,* 35(6): 743–60.

Weber, M. (1949) *Methodology of the Social Sciences* (Glencoe: Free Press).

Wells, H. G. (1905) *A Modern Utopia* (London: Chapman & Hall).

Wells, H. G. (1906) 'The So-called Science of Sociology', *Sociological Papers,* I: 357–77.

Wells, H. G. (1914) *An Englishman Looks at the World: Being a Series of Unrestrained Remarks upon Contemporary Matters* (London, New York, Toronto and Melbourne: Cassell and Co.).

Wells, H. G. (1984 [1934]) *Experiment in Autobiography* (London: Faber and Faber).

Wells, H. G. (1998) *Correspondence of H. G. Wells,* edited by D. C. Smith (London: Pickering and Chatto), 4 Vols.

Wells, H. G. (1999) *Anticipations of the Reaction of Mechanical and Scientific Progress upon Human Life* (New York: Dover) [1902].

Wilkinson, R. and Pickett, K. (2009) *The Spirit Level* (London: Bloomsbury).

Williams, R. (1973) *The Country and the City* (London: Chatto and Windus).

Williams, R. (1980) *Problems in Materialism and Culture* (London: Verso).

Wright, E. O. (2010) *Envisioning Real Utopias* (London: Verso).

Wright, P. (1985) *On Living in an Old Country* (London: Verso)

Young, M. (1958) *The Rise of the Meritocracy* (London: Thames and Hudson).

Young, M. (1994) 'Meritocracy Revisited', *Society,* 31(6): 87–9.

Young, M. (2001) 'Down with Meritocracy', *The Guardian*, 29 June.

Young, R. (2010) *Electric Eden: Unearthing Britain's Visionary Music* (London: Faber and Faber).

Zizek, S. (2005) 'From Revolutionary to Catastrophic Utopia', in J. Rüsen, M. Fehr and T. W. Rieger (eds) *Thinking Utopia: Steps into Other Worlds* (New York: Berghan Books).

Zizek, S. (2005) 'Lenin Shot at Finland Station', *London Review of Books*, 27(16), 18 August: 23.

Index

Printed and bound by
CPI Group (UK) Ltd, Croydon, CR0 4YY